*Realizing Equality in Policy*

# Realizing Equality in Policy

EDITED BY ALEXANDER KAUFMAN

UNIVERSITY OF MICHIGAN PRESS

ANN ARBOR

Published in the United States of America by the
University of Michigan Press
First published July 2025

A CIP catalog record for this book is available from the British Library.

Library of Congress Control Number: 2024060628
LC record available at https://lccn.loc.gov/2024060628

ISBN 978-0-472-07742-7 (hardcover : alk. paper)
ISBN 978-0-472-05742-9 (paper : alk. paper)
ISBN 978-0-472-22221-6 (e-book)

Cover image: *Old Scholar in a Vaulted Chamber ("St. Anastasius")*, Rembrandt van Rijn (oil on wood, 1631). Photograph courtesy Linn Ahlgren / Nationalmuseum.

Authorized Representative: Easy Access System Europe, Mustamäe tee 50,
10621 Tallinn, Estonia, gpsr.requests@easproject.com

*To John Rawls, Ronald Dworkin, and G. A. Cohen—*
*all of whose contributions deeply enriched the discipline.*

# Acknowledgments

Earlier versions of three chapters were previously published. A version of chapter 1 was published in *Philosophy and Public Issues* 10, no. 1 (2020): 383–424. A version of chapter 2 was published in *Oxford Studies in Political Philosophy* 9 (2023): 153–82. Section two of chapter 3 contains revised versions of portions of chapters 6 and 7 of *Rawls's Egalitarianism* (Cambridge University Press, 2018).

# Contents

Digital materials related to this title can be found on the Fulcrum platform via the following citable URL: https://doi.org/10.3998/mpub.14387750

# Introduction

Alexander Kaufman

Economic and social inequality have emerged as the defining features of the world economy in the late 20th and early 21st centuries. As Thomas Piketty summarizes current data, "the process by which wealth is accumulated and distributed [in the United States and Western Europe] contains powerful forces pushing toward . . . an extremely high level of inequality."[1]

Increased inequality has been particularly pronounced in the United States. In 2018, members of the wealthiest 20% of households received 52% of total income, while the top 5% received 23.1% of total income.[2] The poorest 20% of households, in contrast, received 3.1% of income. Extreme as the income inequality reflected in that Census data might seem, an updated study of income data by economists Emmanuel Saez and Thomas Piketty indicates that the Census data seriously *understates* income inequality in the United States. Saez and Piketty found that the top *1*% of earners received 23.5% of income, while the top 10% received over 50% of income.[3] This unequal distribution, moreover, is the product of a continuous and ongoing pattern of income redistribution from the lower quintiles to the wealthiest earners. According to Census data, the share of total income received by the top 5% of earners increased from 15.6% in 1969 to 23.1% in 2018, while the income share of the lowest quintile declined steadily from 5.6% of income in 1969 to its current level of 3.1%.[4] Between 1973 and 2003, the average real income of the bottom 90% of earners fell by 7%, while the income of the top 1% increased by 148%.[5] During this period, Census Bureau data indicate that the income share of the top 1% increased from 7.74% to 19.34%.[6]

The distribution of *wealth* in the United States is even more asymmetrical. The members of the top quintile of households in 2005 possessed 84.4% of wealth. The top 1% alone possessed 33% of wealth, while the bottom 40% possessed 0.7%.[7] Moreover, wealth inequality has increased dramatically in recent decades. In 1983, the richest 1% possessed on average 1,500 times the wealth of those in the bottom 40% of households. In 2001, the wealth of the richest 1% was almost 4,400 times the wealth of the bottom 40%.[8]

Such dramatic and steadily increasing inequality might conceivably be justifiable if permitting such inequality were to the benefit of the less advantaged. Yet the available evidence does not support such a claim. As the share of the highest quintile increased from 40.6% to 52% of income between 1969 and 2018, the share of the lowest quintile fell from 5.6% to 3.1%. In fact, the share of the lowest three quintiles fell from 35.7% to 25.5% between 1969 and 2018—the lowest 60% of the distribution, that is, lost 28.2% of its income share during this period. Moreover, as noted above, the average real income of the bottom 90% of earners fell by 7% between 1973 and 2003. The percentage of Americans living in poverty during this period remained consistently between 12% and 13% until 2010, when the percentage rose to 15%.[9] The available evidence, then, shows no sign that permitting inequalities in favor of the more fortunate during this period generated benefits for the less advantaged.

The inequality in income distribution parallels inequality in access to secondary education, higher education, and employment. The quality gap between the secondary educational opportunity available to less and to more advantaged students not only failed to decrease, rather, it has increased significantly. A recent study based on data compiled by the Department of Education examined the academic achievement gap between children from high- and low-income families and found that the gap between the academic achievement of children from families with incomes at the 90th percentile of family and those from families at the 10th percentile increased by 75% between the early 1940s and 2001.[10] Indeed, the study notes that "[t]he relationship between family socioeconomic status characteristics and student achievement is one of the most robust patterns in educational scholarship."[11]

Opportunity in higher education is characterized by similar inequality. Students from families with higher incomes were more likely to enter college and were even more likely to complete college than children from families with lower incomes: the probability of college entry for children in the top quartile in 1982 was 80%, while the probability for children in the bottom quartile was 29%. The contrast in completion rates was even more extreme: 54% of children from the top quartile completed college, while the completion rate for children from the lowest quartile was 9%.[12] Children of higher income families are thus more than twice as likely to enter college and six times as likely to complete college as children of lower income families.

Inequality in the opportunity to attend highly selective colleges is even more acute. Of students attending highly selective colleges, 74% are from families in the top quartile, while 3% are from the lowest quartile.[13]

Moreover, contrary to conventional wisdom, social mobility in the United States is limited. A recent study found that about 60% of persons in the bottom quintile of the population remained in that quintile nine years later.[14] Studies of social mobility report "high levels of [intergenerational income] persistence in the United States."[15] Indeed, the Economic Mobility Project reports that "there is a stronger link between parental education and children's economic, educational, and socio-economic outcomes" in the United States than in any of the other countries investigated (e.g., Australia, Canada, Denmark, Finland, France, Germany, Italy, Sweden, and the UK).[16]

While most Western European states intervene more aggressively than the United States to reduce inequality, Piketty identifies a similar phenomenon of increasing inequality of incomes and wealth in the economies of major Western European states. Wealth and income inequality in France, Germany, and Great Britain, for example, is rapidly approaching late 19th century levels: "[w]e . . . observe a steady rise [in private wealth] from 1950 on, a rise so sharp that private fortunes in the early twenty-first century seem to be on the verge of returning to [an aggregate equal to] five or six years of national income in both Britain and France."[17] The aggregate distribution of income and wealth in the international arena strongly reflects the trend of increasing inequality. In 1960, the aggregate income of the wealthiest quintile of countries was 30 times greater than the aggregate income of the lowest quintile of countries; by 1997, that ratio had increased to 74:1.[18]

These increases in income inequality raise fundamental questions of egalitarian justice. This volume explores the potential of current theoretical work on egalitarian justice to address some of these questions and to provide insights relevant to the resolution of policy quandaries inspired by rising inequality.

The subject of egalitarian justice has inspired an extensive literature—including major contributions by John Rawls, Richard Arneson, G. A. Cohen, Ronald Dworkin, Martha Nussbaum, and Amartya Sen—and continues to inspire important work by a large number of theorists and philosophers. While early contributions to this literature focused on controversies regarding the question of what egalitarians should aim to equalize (e.g., welfare, resources, capabilities, access to advantage, opportunity for welfare), more recent work has focused on questions of responsibility for disadvantage, the status of freedom as an egalitarian concern, and whether the investigation of moral questions regarding equality must be located within and oriented by a broader ideal of distributive justice.

Currently, egalitarian theorists disagree primarily about the character of egalitarianism itself: Is egalitarianism essentially an allocative theory—a theory whose purpose is to allocate stocks of goods over persons? Or is it essentially a relational theory—a theory, that is, whose purpose is to establish just social relations within which persons may coexist as equals? Advocates of the allocative view of egalitarianism argue that egalitarians should aim primarily to compensate persons for undeserved bad luck. The approach is therefore referred to as *luck egalitarianism*. Luck egalitarians have focused primarily on identifying a criterion for separating well-being deficits for which it is appropriate to hold the person responsible (because those deficits are the product of genuine choice) from those for which persons should not be held responsible (because they are the product of bad brute luck). If a well-being deficit results from genuine choice, luck egalitarians argue, the person is responsible for their misfortune, and egalitarians have no duty to assist. If a well-being deficit is the product of bad brute luck, however, the person's misfortune is undeserved, and egalitarians should aim to compensate the person for their disadvantage. Luck egalitarianism thus faces the challenge of defining a plausible criterion of "genuine" choice (and resolving the associated issues relating to the free will question).

Advocates of the relational view of egalitarianism argue that it is inappropriate for egalitarians to ground egalitarian obligation in judgments regarding responsibility for disadvantage. Such assignments of responsibility, they argue, reflect disrespect for the affected individuals, and in any case misunderstand the point and character of egalitarian justice. A moral concern for equality, they argue, is best understood as the view that a just society should show equal concern and respect for the interests of each person—and society shows this kind of concern by creating institutions within which persons can live together as equals.

Both views argue for a substantial social investment in education, healthcare, and policies relating to employment (including both job training and job creation). These egalitarian theories differ, however, regarding the kind and extent of assistance to be offered, the duration of that assistance, the persons who should be eligible for assistance, and the kinds of considerations that justify assistance. A comparative assessment of the approaches to policy recommended by these two perspectives may generate new insights regarding the justification and proper nature and extent of policies relating to social and economic equality.

In this volume, leading scholars address central questions of egalitarian justice. Rather than focusing on the subtle distinctions that divide egalitarian views, this volume works from the assumption that both the luck-egalitarian and the relational views can offer important insights regarding politics and policy. The essays in this volume therefore include contributions of leading luck-egalitarian and relational-egalitarian scholars elaborating the practical policy implications of their views in relation to rising inequality as it affects policy in education, healthcare, antipoverty efforts, employment, and economic policy.

Chapters in part I reexamine a number of basic issues regarding social and economic policy from an egalitarian perspective. These chapters focus on three themes. First, what is the fundamental nature of the injustice associated with inequality? Second, what standard of reasoning and justification must policies designed to address that injustice satisfy? Third, to what extent are egalitarian concerns relating to these issues connected to elements of the background moral and intellectual tradition? Vrousalis's chapter focuses on the first theme. He argues that one of the most fundamental injustices associated with inequality is economic domination that deprives workers of the ability to employ their productive abilities freely. The chapters by Gheaus, Kaufman, and Segall address the second theme. Gheaus assesses the degree to which policies to address inequalities deriving from gendered norms can be justified in the context of a politically liberal society that aspires to political neutrality. Kaufman examines the form of reasoning employed in a leading theory of egalitarian justice—Rawls's justice as fairness—to justify the design of just institutions. Segall defends the employment of the second-person standpoint to justify claims regarding the requirements of justice. Garthoff's chapter addresses the third theme, discussing the grounding of egalitarian claims in the two leading traditions of leftist political thought, socialism and left-liberalism.

Chapters in part II focus on practical policy implications of egalitarian intuitions. Arneson's chapter argues that basic elements of egalitarian thought provide strong support for Nordic social welfare institutions. Gerver's chapter tests the scope of egalitarian justifications for policy interventions. Suppose that a persuasive argument that a person has not received fair compensation is sufficient to justify a claim for compensation if presented by a disadvantaged claimant; could the same argument justify a claim for compensation by a rich claimant? Leßmann's chapter focuses on determining the appropriate method for specifying a metric of well-being for one of the leading egalitarian theories—the capabilities approach. Reidy's chapter focuses on international justice and argues that liberal democratic peoples have compelling reasons to recognize, respect, and include societies with traditionalist conservative or fundamentalist political cultures as free equals in international political and law-making activity—and that these reasons parallel the reasons that doctrinally Kantian or Millian citizens in a liberal democracy have to recognize, respect, and include traditionalist conservative religious compatriots as free equals in their domestic political and law-making activity. Wall's chapter argues that egalitarian concerns about the welfare of individuals can justify legal paternalism.

## Part I: Basic Ideas

Jon Garthoff's chapter examines the relation of the two leading traditions of leftist political thought, socialism and left-liberalism. Although these traditions are neither exhaustive of leftism nor exclusive of each other, they operate with considerable independence from—and often, antagonism to—one another. This is true both in academic contexts and in broader sites of conversation and activism. In this chapter, Garthoff argues that in present conditions the broad aims of these two traditions are consonant and complementary; in addition, he suggests that each is strengthened and enriched by engagement with the other. The essay thus works toward remedying the separation and opposition of these traditions by articulating commitments common to both and characteristic of leftism as such. The essay also helps to explain why some political orientations and policy proposals—notably including meritocracy and universal basic income—cannot form the basis for pan-left solidarity.

This chapter articulates a pan-left position comprising three core positive commitments and three core critical commitments. It does so with special emphasis on anticapitalist features of Rawlsianism, for these mutually support themes more prominent in the socialist tradition. The aim is not to assess the relative significance of the two traditions, but rather to emphasize their consonance, notwithstanding their disagreements on some important matters. Articulating this consonance is intended to encourage sympathy and solidarity between those attracted to these respective traditions. It is intended also to enhance the appeal of each by incorporating themes more fully developed in the other.

Anca Gheaus's chapter focuses on the gendered division of labor. Feminists have long identified the gendered division of labor as a cornerstone of gender injustice. This is partly because of the ways in which the gendered division of labor is bad for women. But essential to feminists' complaint is also the fact that gender norms give people incentives to take on different social and economic roles according to their sex; even if gender roles were equally rewarded, the function of gender norms in preference formation would remain problematic. For many decades, feminists have sought to dismantle the gendered division of labor and advocated various policies meant to achieve this goal. And yet there is an ongoing, unresolved debate about the kinds of justification that can support such state policies. Liberal states are supposed to refrain from justifying their policies by appeal to controversial (even if reasonable) conceptions of how individuals should lead their private lives; call this "the neutrality constraint." Gender norms in general, and norms mandating a gendered division of labor in particular, are part of conceptions of the good life held by numerous individuals.

Gheaus formulates a version of each of these arguments that respects the neutrality constraint and defends the following conclusion: political liberals may be right that states ought not try to dissuade adults from leading lives informed by gender norms. Yet, they must acknowledge two aims of justice concerning gender norms. The first aim is forward-looking and requires that children be protected from undue influence in forming their ambitions and values; in particular, children have a right to be free from adults' attempts to foist gender norms on them. The second aim is backward-looking and requires that individuals who have been wronged by a failure to implement the first aim are owed reparation; in particular, policies that offset the disadvantage that certain women (or men) incur as a result of gender norms are legitimate even if the women (or men) in question have internalized, and thereby endorse, gender norms.

Alexander Kaufman's chapter focuses on insights from John Rawls regarding a defensible approach to reasoning about the justice of institutions. Rawls describes a society whose institutions are effectively regulated by the principles of its public conception of justice as *a well-ordered society*. The institutions of a well-ordered society must, in Rawls's theory, satisfy a set of demanding requirements. These requirements operate *jointly* and together define the substance of Rawls's conception of social justice (*justice as fairness*). Since these requirements apply collectively "as a unit" (TJ[19] 73, JAF,[20] 46n10[21]), no single criterion determines the nature of just social institutions. Rather, just institutions are the product of a complex process of reasoning. The set of institutions generated through this process realizes the principles of *democratic equality* and—Rawls argues—generates social conditions that are well designed to realize a social ideal of reciprocity. Such a social arrangement ensures to each person real freedom to choose what form of life to lead, but also requires that each person be responsible for generating his or her own just share of social goods. The form of reasoning that is to govern the process of designing institutions for a well-ordered society under justice as fairness remains incompletely understood. This chapter examines this process of reasoning and the nature of institutional arrangements that satisfy its requirements.

Shlomi Segall's chapter addresses a number of objections to the account of luck equality that he developed in *Why Inequality Matters*. In that work, Segall attempted to marry two related but often distinct literatures. He referred to debates about luck egalitarianism as a competitor to Rawlsian justice, and the more axiological literature on the value of equality. Segall's analysis sought to determine whether equality is valuable, or more accurately, what makes inequality bad. He argued, predictably, that the answer lies in the luck-egalitarian mantra. The unfairness of being worse off than another through no fault of one's own is the source of evil that makes inequality bad. Part of what drew criticism was the fact that to bolster that answer, Segall alluded to complaints that worse-off individuals might have against better-off individuals, and the corresponding duties that the latter might have to answer those complaints. Segall addresses two types of complaints regarding this employment of the second-person standpoint. Some critics have raised concerns about the *content* of that complaint, whereas others have raised concerns about the overall legitimacy of alluding to the second-person standpoint for the type of project Segall was pursuing.

Nicholas Vrousalis's chapter criticizes a leading interpretation of Kant's political philosophy in order to develop and support his view that economic injustice is a form of domination. According to an influential "Toronto" interpretation of Kant's political philosophy, the Kantian objection to economic dependence is fundamentally about poverty. Eliminate poverty—read: propertylessness—and you have eliminated economic dependence. According to this view, Kant's political economy of independence *just is* the dialectic of property and propertylessness under the modern state. Vrousalis argues that crucial passages in the *Doctrine of Right* presuppose an account of Kantian economic dependence broader than mere propertylessness. Economic independence, for Kant, is coextensive with self-standing (*selbstständig*) production for a competitive market—that is, independent commodity production. Kant's political economy of independence is therefore not about property and propertylessness, as the Toronto interpretation holds, but about the independent exercise of productive purposiveness by free and equal people. Under legitimate public power, each commonwealth member exercises her share of the productive powers unsubjected to alien control. For Kant, the normative disempowerment of the poor—their inability to legislate universally because an alien will have *de facto* control over the conditions of their agency—also afflicts the worker subject to a capitalist boss, *whether the worker is poor or not.*

## Part II: Policy

Richard Arneson's chapter evaluates the egalitarian justification of Nordic social democracy (NSD) as exhibited in the Scandinavian countries of Sweden, Denmark, Finland, and Norway. NSD combines (1) political democracy, (2) generous welfare state policies that work to compress both pre-tax-and-transfer and post-tax-and-transfer inequality of incomes, (3) forms of taxation and public spending and regulation that foster economic efficiency and growth and thereby avoid equity versus efficiency conflict, and (4) policies that promote women's employment and child welfare and thereby promote equality of life prospects between men and women and fair treatment of people in successive generations.

NSD attracts plausible criticisms. One is the right-wing objection that NSD excessively restricts people's freedom to live as they choose without suffering unfair takings of their legitimate property holdings, instead imposing "cradle to grave socialism." A second is the left-wing objection, advanced by John Rawls, that NSD fails to achieve genuine political democracy by virtue of failure to implement equal opportunity for political influence. A third is the global justice objection that NSD, instituted in rich countries such as Sweden, Denmark, Finland, and Norway, at best only implements egalitarian redistribution among people all of whom qualify as rich by global standards, and does nothing to fulfill the higher-priority justice requirement to improve the condition of the global poor. A sharpened version of this last objection holds that sustaining NSD conflicts with the desideratum that rich countries open their borders to wide immigration from poor countries, which is in current circumstances a global justice requirement.

Arneson's chapter examines these three criticisms from the standpoint of a welfarist egalitarianism that holds that the just society maximizes an appropriate balance of the goals of greater total well-being summed across persons and more fair (equal) distribution of well-being across persons.

Mollie Gerver's chapter considers whether the wealthy can assert a right to compensation for gender-based discrimination. In 2013 the millionaire Ellen Pao attempted to sue her employer for gender-based discrimination. The chapter considers whether Pao had a right to assets lost from wrongful discrimination she faced. One reason we might suppose she had no right to these assets is because, more generally, the wealthy do not have a right to additional wealth beyond the wealth they already possess. If Pao had no right to assets beyond those she possessed, she had no right to assets lost from discrimination, and these assets should have been redistributed to those in greater need instead. Yet such distribution might seem unfair to Pao, who had a right to pay equal to men, and who could not easily obtain this equal pay without full compensation. This chapter first considers whether classic arguments in support of compensation can justify wealthy individuals obtaining compensation for discrimination. It demonstrates that they cannot. It then presents two novel and more promising arguments.

Ortrud Leßmann's chapter examines issues relating to the specification of metrics of justice in the capabilities theories developed by Amartya Sen and Martha Nussbaum. She argues that differing responses to issues relating to the incommensurability of values are at the heart of differences between these two approaches. In particular, she argues that the differences between Sen and Nussbaum can be seen as paradigmatic of the difficulties faced by egalitarian approaches that require a pluralistic metric of justice: Nussbaum initially focused the debate on issues relating to selecting and listing dimensions, thereby distracting attention from another problem of pluralistic metrics, namely how plural values relate to each other. Sen deals with this problem by representing the metric as a multidimensional mathematical space in analogy to the commodity space in economics. Nussbaum mainly warns against trading off values; Leßmann argues that even a political conception of justice such as Nussbaum's must distinguish between aggregative evaluation and trading off values and therefore must say more about the structure of the metric.

Rawls argues that *The Law of Peoples* extends *Political Liberalism* and thus articulates a, perhaps the only, realistic reasonable basis for free equals (polities, in the case of *Peoples*) to engage in and sustain political and law-making activity (international, in the case of *Peoples*) capable of being stable in the right way. Focusing on Rawls's discussion of the fictional "Kazanistan," David Reidy's chapter argues that as free equals liberal democratic peoples have compelling reasons to recognize, respect, and include "Kazanistan" as also a free equal in international political and law-making activity, and that these reasons parallel the reasons that as free equals doctrinally Kantian or Millian citizens in a liberal democracy have to recognize, respect, and include traditionalist conservative religious compatriots as free equals in their domestic political and law-making activity. In both cases, while recognition, respect, and inclusion cannot guarantee the full liberalization or democratization of those to whom it is extended, their free moral development and so enduring liberalization or democratization is not possible without it. Further, by withholding recognition, respect, and inclusion, whether from "Kazanistan" in the international case or traditionalist conservative religious compatriots in the domestic case, those who withhold it put at risk the capacity of their own political and law-making activity to endure as stable for the right reasons. Thus, those who seek as free equals to undertake and sustain political and law-making activities stable in the right way will have compelling reasons to admit to those activities some participants who will, perhaps forever, understand themselves and their participation in the relevant activity on rather different terms. This constitutes no abdication of egalitarianism.

Steven Wall's chapter considers the distributive ideal of equality and its relation to legal paternalism. In particular, Wall critically examines the egalitarian distributive argument for paternalism. In analyzing this argument, Wall assumes that equal concern is best understood in terms of welfare. If governments care equally about the fate of those they govern, then they must care equally about how they fare. This will yield a provisional result about the desirability of legal paternalism from the standpoint of egalitarian justice. With this provisional result in hand, Wall then considers several key concerns pressed by Dworkin that emanate from equality of respect, asking whether they force a retreat, and if so how much of a retreat, from the provisional result. In this way, the conclusions reached about the distributive argument for paternalism make contact with, and are sensitive to, both of Dworkin's reigning principles.

## NOTES

1. Piketty (2014), 27.
2. U.S. Census Bureau (2018), table 2, p. 10.
3. Saez (Winter 2008; updated 9/13).
4. U.S. Census Bureau (2012), table 2, p. 10.
5. Bouchey and Weller (2005), 31.
6. The World Top Income Database, Paris School of Economics, available at http://topincomes.parisschoolofeconomics.eu/#Database
7. Bouchey and Weller (2005), 38–39.
8. Bouchey and Weller (2005), 38–39.
9. U.S. Census Bureau (2012), 52, table B-1.
10. Reardon (2011), 95.
11. Reardon (2011), 92.
12. Bailey and Dynarski (2011), 120–21.
13. A total of 9% of students attending highly selective colleges are from the bottom half of the distribution. Research by Anthony P. Carnevale and Stephen J. Rose, cited in Stiglitz (2012), 308n83.
14. Gottschalk and Spolaore (2002).
15. Jantti (2009), 196.
16. "Does America Promote Mobility as Well as Other Nations?," Economic Mobility Project of the Pew Charitable Trusts (November 2011), 2, available at http://economicmobility.org/assets/pdfs/CRITA_FINAL.pdf, cited in Stiglitz (2012), 106n73. See Huggett and Yaron (2011).
17. Piketty (2014), 25.
18. De Vita (2007), 103.
19. Rawls ([1971] 1999). This work is cited in the text in parentheses and preceded by TJ.
20. Rawls (2001). This work is cited in the text in parentheses and preceded by JAF.
21. The two principles are intended to apply in tandem and to work as a unit (JAF 46n10).

## REFERENCES

Bailey, M. J., and S. M. Dynarski. 2011. "Inequality in Post-Secondary Education." In *Whither Opportunity*, ed. Duncan and Murnane, 117–32.

Bouchey, H., and C. E. Weller. 2005. "What the Numbers Tell Us." In *Inequality Matters*, ed. Lardner and Smith, 27–40.

Cancian, M., and S. Danziger, eds. 2009. *Changing Poverty, Changing Policies.* New York: Russell Sage.

De Vita, A. 2007. "Inequality and Poverty in a Global Perspective." In *Freedom from Poverty as a Human Right*, ed. Pogge, 103–32.

Duncan, G. J., and R. J. Murnane, eds. 2011. *Whither Opportunity: Rising Inequality, Schools, and Children's Life Chances.* New York: Russell Sage.

Gottschalk, P., and E. Spolaore. 2002. "On the Evaluation of Economic Mobility." *Quarterly Journal of Economics* 69: 191–208.

Huggett, M., G. Ventura, and A. Yaron. 2011. "Sources of Life-time Inequality." *American Economic Review* 101, no. 7: 2923–54.

Jantti, M. 2009. "Mobility in the United States in Comparative Perspective." In *Changing Poverty, Changing Policies*, ed. Cancian and Danziger, 180–200.

Lardner, J., and D. A. Smith, eds. 2005. *Inequality Matters.* New York: New Press.

Piketty, T. 2014. *Capital in the Twenty-First Century.* Cambridge, MA: Harvard University Press.

Pogge, T. 2007. *Freedom from Poverty as a Human Right.* Oxford: Oxford University Press.

Rawls, J. 1999 (1971). *A Theory of Justice.* Cambridge, MA: Harvard University Press.

Rawls, J. 2001. *Justice as Fairness: A Restatement.* Cambridge, MA: Harvard University Press.

Reardon, S. F. 2011. "The Widening Academic Achievement Gap Between the Rich and the Poor: New Evidence and Possible Explanations." In *Whither Opportunity*, ed. Duncan and Murnane, 91–116.

Saez, E. 2008. "Striking It Richer: The Evolution of Top Incomes in the United States." *Pathways Magazine.* Winter; updated 9/13.

Stiglitz, J. E. 2012. *The Price of Inequality.* New York: Norton.

U.S. Census Bureau. 2012. *Current Population Report: Income, Poverty, and Health Insurance Coverage in the United States.* Washington, DC: U.S. Department of Commerce.

U.S. Census Bureau. 2018. *Current Population Report: Income, Poverty, and Health Insurance Coverage in the United States.* Washington, DC: U.S. Department of Commerce.

# PART I

# Basic Ideas

CHAPTER I

# Rawlsian Anticapitalism and Left Solidarity

Jon Garthoff

## 1. Introduction

Two prominent traditions of leftist political thought are socialism and left-liberalism. Though these traditions are neither exhaustive of leftism nor exclusive of each other, they operate with considerable independence from—and often, antagonism to—one another. This is true both in academic contexts and in broader sites of conversation and activism.[1] In this essay I provide a summary explanation of how in present political conditions the broad aims of these two traditions are consonant and complementary, and also of how each is strengthened and enriched by engagement with the other.[2] The essay thus works toward remedying the separation and opposition of these traditions by articulating commitments common to both and characteristic of the type of leftism needed today. It also helps explain why some political orientations and policy proposals, notably including meritocracy and universal basic income, are poor bases for left solidarity.

The principal intellectual figure of the socialist tradition is of course Karl Marx, while in our context the principal intellectual figure of the liberal tradition is John Rawls. In emphasizing the potential for solidarity among (some) socialists and (some) liberals, the essay also emphasizes the consonance of themes between these two great political theorists. I focus attention especially on Rawls's anticapitalism, which—notwithstanding the important contributions of Samuel Freeman and William Edmundson—has not received due consideration.[3]

One important aspect of Rawls's anticapitalism, rightly emphasized by Freeman, is his strong association between capitalism and utilitarianism. Neither entails the other, but capitalist economic systems and utilitarian philosophy share an instrumental understanding of rationality, an emphasis on putative measures of welfare, the use of aggregation as the measure of group welfare, and the aim to grow welfare thus putatively measured and aggregated. These features leave utilitarians poorly situated to diagnose and criticize capitalism's most fundamental failings: that capitalist elections are exercises in consumer choice and that capitalist markets treat human labor as a mere commodity. I discuss affinities between capitalism and utilitarianism in section 3C below.[4]

Rawls's anticapitalism is not limited to his opposition to utilitarianism, however, and my discussion does not focus on affinities between these positions. In what follows I articulate a left position comprising three core positive commitments and three core critical commitments. I do so with special emphasis on anticapitalist features of Rawls's view, since these mutually support themes that are more prominent within the socialist tradition. The aim is not to assess the relative significance of the two traditions, but rather to emphasize their consonance, despite disagreement on some important matters. Articulating this consonance is intended to help encourage sympathy and solidarity between those attracted to these respective traditions. It is intended also to enhance the appeal of each by incorporating themes more fully developed in the other.[5]

My aim in this essay thus also differs from that of Edmundson, who argues that a Rawlsian conception of justice requires a socialist economic macrostructure.[6] In my judgment Edmundson argues effectively that a socialist economic system more securely satisfies the requirements of justice as Rawls understands them, provided this socialist economic system can gain purchase in a society's public political culture. Edmundson does not discuss at length, however, what I take to be both the greatest challenge to his primary conclusion and the most likely reason Rawls did not elaborate a socialist position: that the ideas needed to sustain socialism—even a liberal socialism of the sort Rawls views as compatible with justice—might be sufficiently alien from a society's public political culture that a socialist socioeconomic system might be less stable within that political culture, notwithstanding the greater relative stability of such a system within a different culture.[7] This concern is perhaps most pressing in Rawls's home country of the United States, where the socialist tradition has been marginalized.

In my view, which I conjecture accords with Rawls's views of these matters, we do not now know whether socialism is in that way alien to the political cultures of the United States or other developed economies. Accordingly my recommendation is to advocate neither for nor against socialism, but instead to advocate for major institutional reforms to realize what Rawls (unfortunately, given the term's distinct use by Margaret Thatcher) labels a "property-owning democracy."[8] We should do so, not with confidence that such a socioeconomic system is most just, however, but instead with the more open-ended attitude that future generations will be better positioned to judge whether to pursue additional major institutional reforms realizing socialism.[9]

Thus the position I articulate here is not opposed to Edmundson's most important claims, but it refrains from endorsing his claim that Rawlsian justice requires socialism. Nevertheless it agrees with much of the spirit of Edmundson's book, including in particular his claim that much of the power of Rawls's work remains latent, despite its enormous influence and the voluminous literature of commentaries it has inspired.[10] The position I articulate here also agrees with both Freeman and Edmundson that, regardless of what we make of socialism as an ultimate political ambition, it is crucial in the current political environment to advance a politics that is full-throated in its critique of capitalism.

## 2. The Three Positive Commitments

In this section I describe what I take to be the core positive commitments of any adequate leftism today. I do this relatively briefly, since the most interesting and controversial features of these commitments are best explored in the context of their negative implications. The point of this section is not to fully elaborate, still less to fully defend, the broad leftist position I endorse. It is instead to provide fundamental orientation that helps explain the more controversial negative claims that follow in section 3.

Many people think they hold leftist political views when in fact they do not, so there can be value in policing the boundaries of leftism. Such policing is not, however, my main ambition. The claims I articulate here are not primarily descriptive; I am interested less in defining leftism as such, and more in enunciating a broad but substantive account of what makes a leftism today worthy of the name. The main conclusion is a prescription about how to approach questions of large-scale socioeconomic structure within today's politics. I also think it important at present to advocate for left solidarity transnationally, but my focus here is on how leftism is best articulated within domestic politics.

### *2A. Social Egalitarianism*

The first and most important positive commitment of leftism is to be democratic, where this involves commitment not only to voting procedures with a broad franchise but also more strongly to creating and sustaining a public political culture that realizes a fundamental *social equality* of all persons.

Such social egalitarianism suffuses the work of both Marx and Rawls. The *Manifesto of the Communist Party* famously declares the ambition to "raise the proletariat to the position of the ruling class to win the battle for democracy."[11] To the extent that Marx and Engels had reservations about democracy, this was because they thought that some societies lack adequate institutions to support democratic reform (so a violent revolution establishing communism might be justified) or because they thought the state itself might eventually "wither away" and become unnecessary.[12]

Regardless of the prospects for improving nondemocratic societies using (internally) violent means, the former reservation is moot in the contemporary context. No socialist should advocate for large-scale violence in contemporary politics, and no one of any political orientation should think widespread violence is likely to produce anything other than a powerful and anti-progressive reaction.[13]

The latter reservation is not best understood as an importantly antidemocratic strand in Marxian thought, since it is predicated on achievement of democracy's fundamental goal—the equal social standing of all people—through nonstate means. I tend (with Rawls) to doubt that this goal is achievable in that way. I also think future people will be better positioned to judge the issue, however, and furthermore that it is important to maintain solidarity with leftist anarchists within the current political environment. The view I articulate here is thus noncommittal about both the feasibility and the desirability of a stateless society in the distant future. I help myself to the assumption that in the medium term, however, even anarchists should not advocate abolishing the state.

Rawls's commitment to democracy, in the full-throated sense of social equality of all persons, is absolute bedrock in his view.[14] It is deeper even than his commitment to liberalism, since he justifies core liberal commitments in terms of their necessity to maintain the social equality of genuine democracy, rather than the other way around.[15] The extreme depth of Rawls's commitment to democracy and social equality can be missed in a cursory reading of his work, for he does not attempt to defend democracy directly; indeed he does not even articulate at length the virtues of democratic societies with respect to other political systems. Rawls refrains from such positive defenses of democracy, however, only because he takes a commitment to social equality to be definitional of his enterprise. More specifically, it is only in the context of a public political culture aspiring to democratic equality that Rawls claims his account of justice has purchase.[16]

This section should not be taken to imply that Marx and Rawls agreed about what an ideal society would look like. Rawls explicitly rejects the aim of creating a communist society within which the "circumstances of justice" no longer hold.[17] In Rawls's view, reasonable disagreement about what makes life fulfilling will persist in an ideally just society, for example, and human benevolence will always remain limited in its motivational efficacy.[18]

### *2B. Structural Emphasis*

The second positive commitment of any leftism worthy of the name is to a *structural* understanding of political and economic systems. One mark of an emphasis on structure is focus on the social milieu against which political action takes place, a milieu that is itself dynamically recreated by that same action.

In Marxian thought there is special emphasis on power structures, including in particular economic power structures. From the beginning, however, Marx and his followers displayed cognizance of the complex interplay between economic power and cultural understandings. Thus Engels famously introduces the term "false consciousness" to denote the internalization by the working classes of cultural understandings inimical to their social empowerment.[19] Later theorists would provide far more detailed accounts of this interplay, while retaining the original emphasis on structures of power that guide and sustain the evolution of a political culture.[20]

In Rawls, commitment to structural analysis manifests in his idea of the "basic structure of society," the large-scale institutional framework that constitutes cooperation among citizens at the societal level.[21] This structure is responsible for securing "background justice," which is justice in the ground rules against which important social transactions like elections and labor markets take place.[22] It is to this basic structure that a conception of justice, in Rawls's understanding, in the first instance applies.

Rawls's emphasis on the basic structure of society contrasts with a focus on the pedigree of the status quo. Rawls associates focus on pedigree with Lockean, commonly right-libertarian, political thought.[23] Rawls's emphasis on the basic structure also contrasts with emphasis on the outcomes produced by actions or policies as such, as is prominent in both utilitarian and luck-egalitarian political thought.[24]

Emphasis on the basic structure of society also contrasts with focus on the attitudes and choices of individuals. In Rawls's approach, critiques of social injustice should focus neither on the consumer choices of individuals, for example, nor on the investment decisions or rent-seeking behavior of specific businesses. Instead, the focus is on the background system of rules and understandings that permits and encourages these decisions and behaviors to undermine social equality.

These respective structural emphases are, in my view, importantly complementary. They share a focus on how society is presently constituted, rather than on how it came to be that way. The Marxian emphasis is on the power structures of institutions, and on how these dynamically recreate themselves in an ongoing way. This helps bring out the importance of widespread and effective economic agency, of workers not being vulnerable to exploitation by capitalists. It also helps bring out the importance of energetic agonism in the face of such exploitation, of the need to defeat the interests of would-be exploiters. The Rawlsian emphasis is instead on the fairness of institutions that underlie major social transactions. Rawls also emphasizes the ideas that publicly regulate these institutions, and how these ideas dynamically recreate themselves. While Marx and Rawls are of course not in agreement about all important matters, for the most part the emphasis each provides does not compete with that provided by the other.[25] Theorists may disagree on the relative importance of the structural emphases found in Marx and Rawls, but those favoring one should acknowledge that the other provides a helpful accounting of important aspects of political dynamics not as fully developed by the other.

### *2C. Transformational Change*

The third positive commitment is to a *transformational* understanding of what is needed in the present political circumstances. Unlike the first two commitments, this third commitment is not characteristic of the leftism needed in all historical conditions. At present, however, any left political position should regard society as in need of an overhaul in both its broad socioeconomic institutions and its broadly animating political ideas.

It perhaps goes without saying that not only Marx in particular but the entire socialist tradition endorses transformational changes to contemporary politics and economics. The core socialist claim is that ownership of the largest-scale means of production, and accordingly the capacity to make society-defining investment decisions, must lie in the hands of the public rather than the hands of any private individual or association.[26] In socialist systems the public must control the "commanding heights" of the economy.[27] To achieve this goal would require a radical change from the status quo. At present these means of production are held, and these investment decisions are made, by large corporations.

Talk of "transformational" change opposes incremental approaches to politics and public policy. It also deliberately shoots the gap between leftists who regard themselves as reformers and those who regard themselves as revolutionaries. Reform is necessary but not sufficient, since major changes to existing power structures are needed to ensure that positive reforms are not undone. A revolution in how we think about politics and economics is needed, but not a violent revolution that overthrows the government. Transformation is change not just in extent but also in kind, and the transformation leftists should advocate is toward a noncapitalist economic order; but this talk of transformation need not suggest violence.

Rawls lacks the radical style of many Marxians. In part for this reason, he is sometimes accused—in my view mistakenly—of an insufficiently radical or progressive agenda.[28] In my view this accusation is blunted by the fact that Rawls explicitly rejects not only laissez-faire but also welfare-state capitalism, and also by his contention that we must develop and specify a noncapitalist social system distinct from these.

Rawls regards laissez-faire capitalism as a complete nonstarter, since it does not even purport to bind the citizenry together into a cooperative unity.[29] Its ideology is instead one of competitiveness, extolling rather than lamenting the fact that capitalist economies inevitably produce winners and losers, permitting rather than mitigating the fact that unregulated capitalist economies generate terrible life circumstances for a large number of citizens. Laissez-faire economies also involve minimal investment in public goods, exacerbating the plight of those within them who fare worst.

Laissez-faire economic systems furthermore characteristically subject large portions of the population to the tyranny of "private government."[30] People are largely dependent on private enterprises for the goods essential to survival, and so are subject to extreme forms of domination in their workplaces. Both the monopolistic tendency of capitalist economies and the strong tendency of monopolies to capture and control the government proceed unchecked within a laissez-faire capitalist regime.

Welfare-state capitalism is a vast improvement over laissez-faire capitalism. Guaranteed retirement income, unemployment insurance, and health insurance greatly improve the prospects of working people in welfare-state systems. Free public education and massive infrastructure projects greatly enhance the opportunities open to citizens in general. Public campaign finance, aggressive antitrust enforcement, and extensive government regulation both to enhance market competition and to protect public goods like clean air and water prevent the worst tyrannies of capitalism's private governments.[31]

Notwithstanding the world-historical improvements that the welfare state–establishing structural transformations constituted, and notwithstanding the need to defend existing welfare state institutions in a time of re-ascendant monopolism and corporate capture of government, Rawls flatly rejects the welfare state as a potentially just economic system.[32] It is crucial to the primary purposes of this paper to consider in some detail his reasons for rejecting welfare-state capitalism, and to expand on these with an eye toward unifying them with socialist grounds for rejecting capitalism. I undertake that task in the following section, using three central negative commitments of the "synthesized" leftism I recommend as an organizational structure.[33]

## 3. The Three Negative Commitments

I begin this section by briefly articulating features of the socioeconomic system Rawls favorably juxtaposes with welfare-state capitalism, property-owning democracy.[34] In so doing I elaborate the first negative commitment of this essay's synthesized leftism, its commitment to antiauthoritarianism. This involves opposition not only to totalitarian or antidemocratic politics, but to totalitarian and antidemocratic economics.

I then turn to a more controversial negative commitment of this left position, namely its antimeritocracy. Rawls is explicit about his antimeritocratic commitments, and these are crucial to his case for rejecting welfare-state capitalism. Especially important is the connection between antimeritocracy and reciprocity. A welfare state does not constitute or express the worth of all citizens by emphasizing the need for each citizen to contribute to political and economic life. It instead emphasizes that citizens are fitting recipients of society's concern.[35]

The third and most controversial negative commitment is to antiwelfarism. Rawls is explicitly antiwelfarist, but his discussion of the issue focuses mainly on problems of publicity, the difficulty of identifying both when an adequate provision of welfare has occurred and where above that threshold it is permissible to tolerate inequalities for the sake of expanding the total quantity of welfare produced.[36] In what follows I go beyond this discussion while remaining in a Rawlsian spirit, emphasizing (like Freeman) the affinities between capitalism and utilitarianism. These affinities are present not only in laissez-faire but also in welfare-state capitalism. They are not limited to total and average utilitarianism, moreover, but extend also to restricted versions of utilitarianism. (Restricted utilitarianism rules out as unacceptable, prior to any application of the principle of utility, social arrangements involving either the extreme deprivation of failing to meet basic needs or the extreme domination of slavery or caste-based subordination.[37]) As I explain below, capitalism and utilitarianism each lack an adequate understanding of the human person as a locus of respect, and so each is unable stably to sustain fully satisfactory social relationships.

### *3A. Antiauthoritarianism*

The first and perhaps least controversial critical commitment is to be *antiauthoritarian*. This commitment flows directly from the social equality of left politics. This is of course a mark of liberal thought in general, and Rawls is no exception, including especially his placement of political liberties above other goods in his conception of justice.[38] As a tradition, socialism is more mixed in its attitude toward political liberties, and is also more mixed in its tolerance of strongly centralized economic authorities. With Rawls I assume that for contemporary societies with fully developed economies strongly centralized economic planning is not recommended.[39] Thus the only forms of socialism we should seriously consider are ones that are liberal in that they rule out such centralized authority in their socioeconomic arrangements.

Liberalism in this broad sense is relatively uncontroversial, but the antiauthoritarianism of synthesized leftism extends beyond this. This position opposes authoritarian political regimes, to be sure; but it also opposes authoritarianism inside the economic sphere, and further supports increased democratization of the workplace. At a minimum this includes protection of workers' rights to unionize, aggressive antitrust enforcement, and extensive mandatory representation of workers on the boards of large corporations.[40]

All these are important features of property-owning democracy. They distinguish it from welfare-state capitalism by empowering workers and by aggressively resisting monopolies. A property-owning democracy must also have other features not present in welfare-state capitalism, however, if it is to be a candidate for a just economic system. It must include policies of taxation and transfer, for example, beyond what is needed to secure a "social safety net" or "suitable social minimum" for all citizens.[41] The defining feature of property-owning democracy is its broad dispersal of productive assets; the tendency of markets to consolidate economic power requires robust policies of tax and transfer to maintain that dispersal over time.[42]

Property-owning democracy does not, however, entail mandatory worker ownership of at least a substantial part of large private productive enterprises. Such a requirement would suffice for a socialist regime by any reasonable definition; socialism does not entail that all property be owned by the government. Since property-owning democracy is by definition not a socialist economic system, it does not mandate this.

As was indicated in the introductory section, the synthesized left position I articulate here is—like Rawls's conception of justice—noncommittal regarding whether worker ownership (or management, in the case of public enterprises) of large private productive enterprises is required by justice. Since this requirement is a main tenet of socialism, it may seem to prevent the view from serving as a basis for a left solidarity encompassing socialists. But this is not correct, for in contemporary societies the best route to worker ownership of large private productive enterprises is plausibly to first achieve property-owning democracy. If this is right, then in present conditions socialists too should advocate for institutions of a property-owning democracy in the medium term, even if they do so in the belief that their achievement must be followed by additional efforts to realize socialism.[43]

The point of remaining noncommittal about socialism in the present context, moreover, is not merely the political goal of enabling a broad coalition that includes both socialists and nonsocialists. It is also the epistemic claim, which I think all on the left should accept, that citizens in a property-owning democracy would be much better positioned to know whether socialism is a requirement of justice. The question of socialism is not a matter of mere speculation, but it is one about which we all should recognize our fallibility.

Before leaving the topic of antiauthoritarianism, I must mention the feature of property-owning democracy and liberal democratic socialism that Rawls most emphasizes when arguing for the superiority of these systems to welfare-state capitalism: that they are compatible with realizing the "fair value" of the political liberties. This idea is sometimes glossed as the thought that political liberties must be guaranteed not only in form but in substance, and also as the thought that citizens must not only have liberties but be in a position to exercise them meaningfully.

These glosses are helpful, but they do not capture the full idea of the fair value of the political liberties. It may help, in explaining why, to compare the political liberties under laissez-faire capitalism with the political liberties under welfare-state capitalism.[44] Under laissez-faire capitalism there is a legal right to think, speak, publish, assemble, and associate politically. For many citizens, however, this right cannot be meaningfully exercised. The system permits extreme deprivations, such that finding food or shelter may dominate the lives of many who live under the regime. In such circumstances it is an understatement to characterize possession of political liberties as hollow. Indeed under such circumstances the political liberties themselves become a major vehicle of social inequality, since those who can meaningfully exercise them wield far greater political influence than those who cannot.

In welfare-state capitalism all citizens can, in at least some important sense, meaningfully exercise the political liberties. No one is forced by lack of luck or talent to live in a condition of utter deprivation, so some opportunities are present for the voices of all citizens to be heard. All citizens are, we might say, recognized as fully empowered to participate in political discourse.[45] There is accordingly substance, and not merely form, to political liberties in a welfare-state capitalist regime.

But this is still a far cry from realizing the fair value of the political liberties. This occurs not when all citizens are in this minimal sense meaningfully able to exercise substantial liberties, but rather when all citizens can influence political decisions on an equal footing.[46] The great disparities of wealth and income permitted by welfare-state capitalism prevent this sort of equality.[47] All citizens are recognized in political discourse, but they are not all respected as co-determiners of the policies and actions to be implemented or undertaken.[48]

Synthesized leftism agrees with Rawls in insisting on achieving the fair value of political liberties for all citizens, and also in his view that capitalism is incompatible with realizing this goal. In this way synthesized leftism incorporates both the liberal's sensitivity to the erosion of individual liberty through the consolidation of political power (whether by the government or large private interests) and the socialist's sensitivity to the authoritarian control characteristic of concentrated economic power.[49]

### *3B. Antimeritocracy*

The second—and perhaps more surprising—critical commitment of the leftism advocated here is to be *antimeritocratic*. There are multiple reasons this commitment may surprise. One is that a genuine meritocracy would be far more just than present social arrangements. In the case of the United States, the lack of a meaningful estate tax is enough to condemn the society as failing to enable fairness in the background of its social transactions. Even more damaging is the differential quality of available education and healthcare, with class, race, and location unfairly determining both quality and access. The fact that meritocracy would be a great improvement over the status quo does not, however, establish that meritocracy is compatible with justice. Full realization of the welfare state, including especially high-quality healthcare and education for all, would be a great improvement; but it would not suffice for justice as a leftist in contemporary circumstances should understand it.

A second and related reason is that many who regard themselves as on the political left also regard themselves as advocates for meritocracy. Again the fact that the welfare state is not fully realized helps explain how this is possible. Our outrageous inequalities appropriately focus the attention of the left on the unfair and antimeritocratic advantages of the wealthy, which entails that justice could be enhanced by moving toward meritocracy.[50] The view that a genuine meritocracy would be more just than the status quo again does not entail a meritocratic system is compatible with the ideals of justice most appropriate to our circumstances.

Rawls clearly opposes meritocracy. Regardless of whether merit is understood in terms of ethical virtue or economic productivity, it is in Rawls's view insufficiently publicly assessable to form the basis for shared cooperative activity.[51] Public assessability is crucial to Rawls because it enables broad cognizance of when institutions and citizens live up to the demands of justice as they understand them, which in turn mutually assures citizens of good faith and thereby stabilizes the system of cooperation.[52]

Though not emphasized in the same way by Rawls, a related concern is that meritocratic understandings of justice are highly vulnerable to being coopted by the already powerful. People are reluctant to believe that the social positions of others are mostly due to luck. Those who are relatively successful are reluctant to believe their relative success is mostly due to luck, moreover, even the luck of one's circumstances of birth. Thus those who occupy positions of greater power due to luck (or worse) are commonly able to encourage widespread belief that talent, effort, or virtue played a much larger role than in fact it did in determining their position in society.[53]

These are telling objections to meritocracy, arguably decisive against the view. But more profound is the fact that meritocratic political understandings are incompatible with fundamental social equality, since they apportion social power in accord with features not shared equally by citizens. Broadly speaking, social power correlates strongly with economic power. This does not mean that social equality entails economic equality, but it does entail that economic inequalities must be carefully regulated and given special justification. Rawls asserts his difference principle to regulate permissible inequalities, and the justification for this principle is that the inequalities it permits redound to the advantage of the least advantaged, thereby expressing deep reciprocity and minimizing the "strains of commitment" of belonging to the least advantaged group.[54] This justification has nothing to do with talent or virtue, so Rawls can comfortably claim natural talents are a "common asset."[55] This expresses the idea that talents are to be marshaled for the common good, rather than the idea that those with talents are to be rewarded for having and using them by being accorded greater social power.

I have focused this section on Rawls's anticapitalism, spending relatively little space discussing socialism. This is mainly because Marx's antimeritocracy is obvious. It is most baldly witnessed by his adoption of the famous socialist dictum "from each according to his ability, to each according to his needs" as the fundamental distributive principle of a communist society.[56]

It should be noted that earlier in the same work Marx observes that the principle "to each according to his contribution," which was also popular within the socialist tradition of his day, is appropriate to a society in transition from capitalism to communism.[57] This principle can be read in a meritocratic way, and G. A. Cohen's Marxian luck-egalitarianism is similar in this respect.[58] Still, since both Marx and Marxians like Cohen overwhelmingly emphasize social egalitarianism, there is strong pressure to understand their commitment to principles that are open to meritocratic interpretations as subordinated to a more fundamental antimeritocratic position.[59] And regardless of how Marx or Cohen thinks socialism is best understood, meritocratic socialist views—no less than meritocratic liberal views—should be rejected for the reasons articulated previously within this subsection.

### 3C. Antiwelfarism

The third—perhaps most surprising—critical commitment is to be *antiwelfarist*. As has already been observed, this commitment partly consists in rejecting the welfare state as the model for an ideal socioeconomic system. Welfare state provisions such as guaranteed retirement income, unemployment insurance, healthcare, and education are of course great improvements over laissez-faire policies and are to be defended against those who would reduce or eliminate them in the name of fiscal responsibility. But left politics must articulate a conception of society differing not only in extent but also in kind from the welfare state. And in so doing, it must also articulate a conception of broad socioeconomic activity differing in kind from capitalism.

One major problem with the welfare state is specifying the level of welfare provision in a way that is satisfying to the public. This is in part a problem of disagreement, since what constitutes the "suitable social minimum" of welfare is sensitive to context and may vary among reasonable citizens. It is also in part a problem of publicity, since even if we stipulate unanimity about the level of welfare to be provided, welfare is notoriously inscrutable. It will be difficult to discern, even at the level of broad socioeconomic groups, when that level has been reached, and so other political values may be invoked to shape the production and distribution of resources.[60]

But as occurred in the last section with meritocracy, there is a problem with welfarism more profound and fundamental than its inscrutability. In this case the objection is that welfare state institutions fail to constitute the citizenry as reciprocal producers of social goods. Instead they are characteristically experienced as redistributing, in a pejorative sense, fruits of productive activity. These institutions thereby encourage a reactionary conception of economic activity as comprising "makers" and "takers."[61]

Any proposal to replace existing welfare state programs with universal basic income reinforces these reactionary social understandings, and is for that reason alone to be resisted. The fact that universal basic income is not means-tested, and so is not narrowly tailored to address problems of need, does not preclude a social understanding according to which that is its primary purpose and justification. (Compare the fact that the mortgage interest tax deduction in the United States benefits the wealthy, for example, yet is understood to be justified by its promotion of home ownership by the middle class.) I expect this sort of putative justification for universal basic income to become far more prevalent, as this policy proposal is increasingly conjoined with the worry that mechanization and automatization of the economy will fail to generate enough jobs.[62] Wherever possible, the means-testing of aid programs is to be avoided for similar reasons.

Proposals to augment existing programs with a universal basic income are more difficult to assess, as these could form part of the basis of a new socioeconomic system. But even these proposals are fraught, since they discourage conceiving of economic production as reciprocally cooperative.[63] Accordingly, I think universal basic income should be supported only as part of a broader package of progressive policies, notably including large increases for the wealthy in capital gains, income, and estate taxes.[64]

Furthermore, left opposition to welfarism should extend beyond this, in denying the adequacy of the welfare state as a model for socioeconomic cooperation. It should reject welfare itself as the metric by which social institutions are most fundamentally assessed, and not only because of its inscrutability. As Rawls emphasizes, the social provision of welfare without deeper reciprocity engenders political alienation and apathy.[65] As Marxians emphasize, the social provision of welfare without meaningful ways to exercise economic agency engenders social alienation.[66] These characteristic byproducts of reactionary economic conceptions are not only dispiriting, they corrode social bonds and thereby threaten stability. They are also vulnerable to exploitation by demagogues and xenophobes who would correlate the supposed classes of makers and takers with membership in religions, ethnic groups, and political parties.

One way to capture what all these concerns have in common is to say that welfare-state capitalist societies fail to live up to their understandings of citizens as sharing in human dignity. Like utilitarianism understood as a moral doctrine, a politics that aims most fundamentally at welfare or desire-satisfaction cannot capture what is most important in our social lives as human beings. Welfare is at best an appropriate focus of human social relations with lower animals.

This is inadequate even as account of our relations with higher animals.[67] These animals have capacities for comprehension and for reasons-response. Accordingly, we can relate to them with mutual recognition, acknowledging not only that their welfare is a matter of genuine worth rather than indifference, but that their appreciation of their own treatment matters in its own right. This enables not just mutual intelligibility but also mutual accountability. In a welfare state we at least achieve this level of mutual esteem in social relations with others, provided that the welfare state includes equal (if not fair) political liberty.

More than this is required for fully adequate social relations with other human persons. Not only must we not be indifferent to one another, and not only must we not be unintelligible or unaccountable to them, we must also relate to them in terms of mutual consent, as reasonable social equals.[68] This equality must include, as socialists often emphasize and as Rawls does too with the notion of the fair value of political liberties, roughly equal social power when deciding matters of societal importance.

Yet even roughly equal social power does not fully capture what is needed for a fully adequate political and socioeconomic system. This rough equality of social power must flow from a social understanding of each of us as respectworthy beings and must be grounded in a political culture that dynamically recreates that social understanding across new circumstances and across generations.[69] Only a society like that reliably and stably elicits engagement and affiliation that secures just social cooperation indefinitely. If the reflections of this essay are on the right track, capitalism is incompatible with such a society. I do not think any of us knows with certainty whether socialism is the best framework for understanding what such a society looks like. But regardless of the answer to that question, we must fill out Rawls's sketch of property-owning democracy (perhaps eschewing the label), since if we are to progress transformatively then that socioeconomic system will probably be at least an important stage in the progression.

As left-liberals sometimes remind us, economic goods are not the be-all and end-all of justice. Political liberties are at least as important, provided we bear in mind not just that merely formal liberties can be useless, but also that there are multiple gradations of meaningful exercise of political liberties. Not only are we not mere tools for promoting welfare, as both capitalism and utilitarianism too often suggest, but our welfare is not the most important thing about how we relate to others politically.[70] Nor is mutual responsibility, as crucial as it is for us to be both intelligible and accountable in our social relations with others. Mutual consent and equality are the only social relations worthy of our social and political nature.

As socialists sometimes remind us, these social understandings are only successful, and are only sustainable, when backed by matching power relations. All the indispensable notions for characterizing successful human social relations—including justice, fairness, consent, equality, freedom, accountability, and welfare—can be coopted and be replaced with simulacra. Unlike Marx in his more critical moments, I think it would be an error to jettison or radically reunderstand these crucial notions.[71] But as we preserve and develop these notions to help guide and animate our political life, we must guard against their being used, knowingly or otherwise, for reactionary purposes. Furthermore—as Marx and Rawls were careful to note—even good versions of these ideas are not sufficient. We need a leftism where these ideas and the social power relations that ensure their positive deployment are mutually reinforcing. To succeed, this leftism must draw on both the left-liberal and socialist traditions. My hope is that this dynamic synthesis engenders and deepens respect and solidarity across what is arguably the most prominent fissure in left politics.

## 4. Conclusion

The leftism emerging from these reflections is broad and substantive, encapsulating major themes of both the left-liberal and socialist traditions. It criticizes the institutions of contemporary welfare-state capitalism while making progress toward articulating a superior socioeconomic model. It is noncommittal, however, on the important question of whether private ownership of most wealth is compatible with this new model. Accordingly, it leaves open whether the ultimate goal is property-owning democracy, liberal democratic socialism, or even a form of antiauthoritarian communism (if such is possible).[72]

As has been emphasized above, however, the failure of leftism to articulate a consensus ambition at that level need not constitute an obstacle to leftists unifying around it. All leftists should oppose both Soviet-style command economies and the violent overthrow of the current political regimes, since each would engender a worse authoritarianism than presently obtains. What is needed now is a common vision to channel righteous outrage about today's injustices into a feedback loop of democratic advance rather than into a feedback loop of authoritarian retreat. This vision is no mere modus vivendi; it is a major step along a common path.

Accordingly I think advocates both for and against socialism should adopt a more relaxed attitude toward their dispute. Both sides are fallible. Neither side needs to know who is correct to make common cause for both immediate and medium-term goals.[73] An opportunity is presented by the passage of political power to generations more removed from the Cold War and more open to ideas drawn from the socialist tradition. With the global climate worsening and transnational right-authoritarianism rising, the opportunity is one we cannot afford to miss.[74]

ACKNOWLEDGMENT

I thank Georgi Gardiner, Douglas Garthoff, and especially Yannig Luthra for extremely valuable comments on an earlier draft of this essay. I also thank two anonymous reviewers for *Philosophy and Public Issues*; their thoughtful, constructive feedback also prompted important and necessary improvements to the essay.

NOTES

1. There are of course many exceptions here, including David Schweickart (1993) and John Roemer (1994).

2. On this broad point it may help to compare and contrast this essay with Simone Chambers (2012).

3. See Freeman (2011, 2013) and Edmundson (2017).

4. While I will not pursue the issue here, I think this relation is important not only for understanding leading intellectual justifications for capitalism, but also for understanding the persistent influence of utilitarianism. In my view the doctrine has been multiply refuted in both ethical theory and political philosophy, and yet it lives on as a "zombie doctrine." For classical refutations see Rawls (1971), Bernard Williams (1973), and Samuel Scheffler (1982).

5. For early discussions of the relationship between Rawls and Marx, see Richard Miller (1974) and Arthur DiQuattro (1983); for a more recent discussion see Daniel Brudney (2013).

6. See Edmundson (2017), especially chapter 10.

7. Rawls distinguishes liberal from "command" socialism in Rawls (2001), especially sections 41–42. As he presents these two socioeconomics systems, both involve societal ownership of the means of production. In a liberal socialist society, Rawls writes, "economic power is dispersed among firms . . . [that] carry out their activities within a system of free and workably competitive markets"; he writes further that within a liberal socialism "[f]ree choice of occupation is also assured." See Rawls (2001), 138.

8. Rawls provides his fullest account of the socioeconomic system he calls "property-owning democracy" in Rawls (2001), especially sections 41–42. For further exposition see Martin O'Neill (2009, 2012) and Alan Thomas (2016). See also note 34 below, and more generally section 3. I do not weigh in here on the details of what property-owning democracy consists in, except insofar as is necessary to differentiate it from other socioeconomic types. A relatively generic understanding of the idea suffices for the broad aim of this essay.

9. I do endorse, however, Waheed Hussain's claim that justice requires "democratic corporatism": workers and other societal stakeholders must have representa-

tives within economic structures that empower them to shape major decisions. For development of this idea see Hussain (2012).

10. See Edmundson (2017), especially chapter 3.

11. Marx and Engels (1848), 26; see also Engels (1847). For fuller discussion of the complex role of democracy in Marxian thought, see Richard Wolff (2000).

12. See chapter 2 of Engels (1878) and chapter IX of Engels (1884); see also Marx (1872, 1891).

13. I say "widespread" violence so as to remain neutral about whether smaller-scale acts of violence might be justified, and perhaps even constructive, when performed by members of especially harshly oppressed groups in response to ongoing structures of oppression. The main points of this essay do not rely on any particular view about that question.

14. See, for example, Rawls (2001), 33–35. For further comment and elaboration on Rawls's egalitarianism, see O'Neill (2008), Andrew Mason (2015), and Christian Schemmel (2015a).

15. One place where this order of argument is explicit is Rawls (2001), 197. The priority of equal political liberty over economic considerations is a paradigm liberal commitment, and Rawls argues for this claim in part on the ground that it conduces to a better-functioning and more stable democracy; see lecture VII of Rawls (1993) and section 30 of Rawls (2001). For discussion see Joshua Cohen (2003).

16. See, for example, Rawls (2001), 18–38.

17. Rawls's clearest summary account of the circumstances of justice is found in section 24 of Rawls (2001). See also section 22 of Rawls (1971), and for the idea's source see book III of David Hume (1739).

18. I thank an anonymous reviewer for suggesting that these differences between Marx and Rawls be highlighted.

19. See Engels (1893).

20. Antonio Gramsci (1971) merits special mention; also important is Louis Althusser (1970).

21. See section 2 of Rawls (1971), lecture VII of Rawls (1993), and section 4 of Rawls (2001).

22. See section 14 of Rawls (1971) and sections 14–16 of Rawls (2001). As Brudney (2013) notes, Rawls thus (like Marx) focuses on the production of goods in his account of distributive justice.

23. See section 15 of Rawls (2001). Rawls names Robert Nozick (1974) as an exemplar of this approach; see John Locke (1689) for the historical inspiration.

24. For defenses of luck-egalitarianism see Richard Arneson (2000) and Kok-Chor Tan (2008); for criticisms see Elizabeth Anderson (1999) and Susan Hurley (2001). For an interesting juxtaposition of this piece by Anderson with Edmundson's book, see Kristina Meshelski (2019).

25. Rawls criticizes Marx most explicitly in section 52 of Rawls (2001).

26. For an account of socialism in the context of Rawlsian political thought, again see Edmundson (2017).

27. See sections 41–42 of Rawls (2001) for Rawls's notion of "command," and for further discussion of the idea of "commanding heights" of the economy see Edmundson (2017), especially chapter 2.

28. See, for example, Charles Mills (2005). For avowedly radical Rawlsianism, see Anthony Laden (2001).

29. Rawls discusses laissez-faire capitalism in section 41 of Rawls (2001). In Edmundson's apt paraphrase of Rawls's critique, "what does not at least aim to realize the two principles will not succeed in doing so"; see Edmundson (2017), 77.

30. For much more on this idea see Anderson (2017).

31. As this list attests, in the United States construction of the welfare state was never completed. Neither the New Deal nor its extensions in the postwar era achieved public healthcare or campaign finance; indeed the specific reformist route pursued on these matters served only to enhance the influence of large corporations on the lives of the citizenry at large.

32. See sections 41–42 of Rawls (2001), where Rawls emphasizes the failure of the welfare state to engender reciprocity among citizens. Like publicity, reciprocity figures in Rawls's thought both as a consideration in its own right and as a constituent of stability. On Rawls's conception of stability, see Jon Garthoff (2016).

33. I use the label "synthesized" because the broad view outlined in this paper synthesizes prominent features of socialism with prominent features of left-liberalism.

34. For more on property-owning democracy, again see sections 41–42 of Rawls (2001) as well as Freeman (2007), 219–36, Freeman (2013), and chapter 2 of Edmundson (2017). See also note 8 above.

35. Brudney (2013) includes illuminating discussion of the distinction between concern and respect in the context of the work of both Marx and Rawls.

36. See section 38 of Rawls (2001).

37. Rawls defines the "principle of restricted utility" in section 34 of Rawls (2001), and in the following four sections he argues that his favored conception of justice, justice as fairness, is superior to this principle.

38. See chapter IV of Rawls (1971), especially section 39.

39. Rawls briefly discusses command economies, and then dismisses them, in section 41 of Rawls (2001).

40. See Hussain (2012).

41. Rawls discusses the "suitable social minimum" in section 34 of Rawls (2001).

42. Edmundson labels this tendency the "fact of domination"; see Edmundson (2017), especially chapter 3. He also notes the interesting fact that Rawls introduces a notion of "periodicity" with the idea of property-owning democracy, since there must be some interval after which the fact of domination is remedied in a nonsocialist system, to maintain broad dispersal of wealth. Edmundson plausibly sees this as an important vulnerability of a property-owning democracy, one that generates publicity and reciprocity issues broadly analogous to those generated by welfare-state capitalism's need to specify a suitable social minimum. See Edmundson (2017), especially chapter 10.

43. It may help to bear in mind here that, as Nien-hê Hseih emphasizes, it is not sufficient to realize property-owning democracy that there be widespread dispersal of wealth. Available work must also be meaningful, and workers must have significant say about the conditions of their work. For further development of these points see Hseih (2012), and see also Hussain (2012).

44. Rawls discusses liberties at length in chapter IV of Rawls (1971), and he later revises his account in light of criticism due to H. L. A. Hart (1973). Rawls compares the role of liberties in these two capitalist systems in sections 45–46 of Rawls (2001).

45. This is arguably not true in the present United States, another mark of the fact that in the United States construction of the welfare state was never completed.

46. Rawls discusses the fair value of political liberties in sections 45–46 of Rawls (2001); this discussion was prompted in part by Norman Daniels (1975). See also Daniels (2003).

47. For a different way of situating the fair value of political liberties with respect to the comparison between property-owning democracy and welfare-state capitalism, see O'Neill (2012), especially 81–84.

48. Thus I endorse the contention advanced by Stuart White (2012) that Rawls is appropriately understood as a republican theorist; see also, in this connection, Thomas (2012). White's contention dovetails with a view defended in Hussain (2012), namely that we should expect greater political involvement by workers with a greater say over their working conditions.

49. Socialists are also more sensitive, and appropriately so, to the tendency of capitalist economic systems to devolve into fascist regimes. It is unfortunate that Rawls does not include a right-totalitarian system among the socioeconomic paradigms he discusses in sections 41–42 of Rawls (2001).

50. Rawls in particular is often mistaken for a meritocrat by non-experts, in part because his style is that of a professional academic rather than that of an agitating activist. These misunderstandings also stem from the fact that many actual liberals endorse meritocracies incompatible with Rawls's conception of justice.

51. In Rawls's taxonomy, meritocracy is a type of perfectionism, which he considers and rejects in section 50 of Rawls (1971). Meritocracy also runs directly afoul of the Rawlsian conviction that inequalities must redound to the benefit of the least advantaged.

52. Rawls discusses the problem of assurance in section 42 of Rawls (1971).

53. Meritocracy is thus appropriately associated with elitism, which is a major political drawback of the idea in a democracy.

54. In section 39 of Rawls (2001), he argues that the difference principle is to be preferred to the principle of restricted utility on the ground that it involves fewer "strains of commitment." Alexander Kaufman (2018) rightly emphasizes the importance of this ground in Rawls's case for the difference principle.

55. Rawls refers to natural talents as a common asset in section 17 and section 29 of Rawls (1971). Indeed, he says this idea encapsulates the spirit of both the difference principle and justice as fairness as a whole.

56. See part I of Marx (1891). Regardless of whether socialism is correct, I (like Rawls) do not endorse this as a principle of distributive justice.

57. See part I of Marx (1891). Here again I would join Rawls in rejecting this as a principle of distributive justice for societies at any stage of development.

58. See Cohen (1989) for the germ of his luck-egalitarianism.

59. I thank an anonymous reviewer for encouraging acknowledgment of the movements of socialist thought that can be heard in a meritocratic key.

60. See section 38 of Rawls (2001). It is characteristic of Rawls to emphasize publicity considerations of this sort at every turn. He deploys such considerations to oppose utilitarian invocations of welfare, happiness, or desire-satisfaction as a currency of justice. He also uses them to oppose Amartya Sen's proposed currency of justice: if capabilities are functions from resources to welfare, happiness, or desire-satisfaction, then they are also problematically inscrutable. See Sen (1987, 1992), and section 51 of Rawls (2001).

61. There is a strong tendency in capitalist economic systems to lionize leading capitalists; consider the near-cult status of billionaires Steve Jobs, Bill Gates, Warren Buffett, and Elon Musk. This fuses a meritocratic rationale for capitalist institutions with these institutions' understanding of productive activity as primarily individualistic rather than reciprocal. Thus, these figures are not only to be rewarded for their supposedly greater talent, virtue, or productivity with a greater share of social power; those who are not rewarded are meant to admire them and to be grateful to them for their use of their talent, virtue, or productivity. These complexes of ideas are to be rejected utterly.

62. Thus this concern would also apply to what Schemmel terms a "universal welfare state"; see Schemmel (2015b). This is of course different from a rationale for a universal basic income that emphasizes its potential to enable all citizens to participate fully in democratic politics.

63. Rawls was mindful of the potential of such proposals to undermine reciprocity in social cooperation, hence his (somewhat notorious) remark: "Surfers must somehow support themselves." See section 53 of Rawls (2001).

64. For a more promising set of policy proposals, see Thad Williamson (2012a, 2012b).

65. Rawls articulates this sentiment in section 39 of Rawls (2001).

66. Marx's fullest account of alienation (*Entfremdung*) is found in Marx (1932).

67. Accordingly, laissez-faire is not an adequate account of human social relations with conscious animals in general, even if it is appropriate to leave most wild animals alone.

68. Though the distinctions are not identical, there is a parallel between the distinction I draw here between responsibility and reasonableness and that drawn in Rawls (1999). There is furthermore a parallel between both of these distinctions and the distinction between the second and third levels of Lawrence Kohlberg's scheme of moral cognitive development. See chapter VIII of Rawls (1971), Kohlberg (1973), and see also David Reidy (2017). I hope to investigate these parallels in future work.

69. Rawls discusses self-respect in section 67 of Rawls (1971).

70. For further discussion see Freeman (2011) and Brudney (2013). I think these considerations are serious enough to entail not only that the principle of restricted utility is inferior to justice as fairness, but also that it cannot join with justice as fairness as part of a shared family of reasonable conceptions of the good. For the idea of such a family of conceptions of justice, see Rawls (1997).

71. See Marx (1844, 1891). For discussion see Allen Wood (1981), section 52 of Rawls (2001), and Rawls (2007), 335–53.

72. For further discussion of varieties of socialist reform and their historical roots, see Axel Honneth (2017).

73. Thomas Piketty (2013) makes important observations about the atypical character of the postwar period that enabled it to combine economic growth with reduced inequality. This could be interpreted as evidence against the stability of property-owning democracy, since it suggests that private ownership of society's means of investment is not normally compatible with leftward progress. This could also be interpreted, however, as evidence that the historical record is idiosyncratic and so a limited guide to what is possible both inside and outside of socialist economic structures.

74. At the time of this writing, moreover, the COVID-19 global pandemic is raging.

## REFERENCES

Althusser, Louis. 1970. *On the Reproduction of Capitalism: Ideology and Ideological State Apparatuses*, trans. G. M. Goshgarian, ed. Jacques Bidet. New York: Verso.

Anderson, Elizabeth. 1999. "What Is the Point of Equality?" *Ethics* 109 (2): 287–337.

Anderson, Elizabeth. 2017. *Private Government: How Employers Rule Our Lies (and Why We Don't Talk about It)*. Princeton: Princeton University Press.

Arneson, Richard. 2000. "Luck Egalitarianism Interpreted and Defended." *Philosophical Topics* 32 (1/2): 1–20.

Brudney, Daniel. 2013. "The Young Marx and the Middle-Aged Rawls." In *A Companion to Rawls*, ed. Jon Mandle and David Reidy. Hoboken, NJ: Wiley-Blackwell.

Chambers, Simone. 2012. "Justice or Legitimacy, Barricades or Public Reason? The Politics of Property-Owning Democracy." In *Property-Owning Democracy: Rawls and Beyond*, ed. Martin O'Neill and Thad Williamson. Chichester: Blackwell.

Cohen, G. A. 1989. "On the Currency of Egalitarian Justice." *Ethics* 99 (4): 906–44.

Cohen, Joshua. 2003. "For a Democratic Society." In *A Cambridge Companion to Rawls*, ed. Samuel Freeman. Cambridge: Cambridge University Press.

Daniels, Norman. 1975. "Equal Liberty and Unequal Worth of Liberty." In *Reading Rawls*, ed. Norman Daniels. New York: Basic Books.

Daniels, Norman. 2003. "Democratic Equality: Rawls's Complex Egalitarianism." In *A Cambridge Companion to Rawls*, ed. Samuel Freeman. Cambridge: Cambridge University Press.

DiQuattro, Arthur. 1983. "Rawls and Left Criticism." *Political Theory* 11 (1): 53–78.

Edmundson, William. 2017. *John Rawls: Reticent Socialist*. Cambridge: Cambridge University Press.

Engels, Friedrich. 1847. *Principles of Communism*. Open source material at https://marxists.architexturez.net/history/usa/pubs/lrlibrary/03-LRL-princip-of-comm.pdf

Engels, Friedrich. 1878. *Anti-Dühring*. Open source material at https://www.marxists.org/archive/marx/works/1877/anti-duhring/

Engels, Friedrich. 1884. *Origin of the Family, Private Property, and the State*. Open source material at https://www.marxists.org/archive/marx/works/download/pdf/origin_family.pdf

Engels, Friedrich. 1893. "Letter to Franz Mehring." Open source material at https://www.marxists.org/archive/mehring/1893/histmat/app.htm
Freeman, Samuel. 2007. *Rawls*. New York: Routledge.
Freeman, Samuel. 2011. "Capitalism in the Classical and High Liberal Traditions." *Social Philosophy and Policy* 28 (2): 19–55.
Freeman, Samuel. 2013. "Property-Owning Democracy and the Difference Principle." *Analyse & Kritik* 35 (1): 9–36.
Garthoff, Jon. 2016. "Rawlsian Stability." *Res Publica* 22 (3): 285–99.
Gramsci, Antonio. 1971. *Selections from the Prison Notebooks*, trans. and ed. Quintin Hoare and Geoffrey Nowell Smith. New York: International Publishers. [Written from 1929 to 1935.]
Hart, H. L. A. 1973. "Rawls on Liberty and Its Priority." *University of Chicago Law Review* 40 (3): 534–55.
Honneth, Axel. 2017. *The Idea of Socialism*. Cambridge: Polity Press.
Hseih, Nein-hê. 2012. "Work, Ownership, and Productive Enfranchisement." In *Property-Owning Democracy: Rawls and Beyond*, ed. Martin O'Neill and Thad Williamson. Chichester: Blackwell.
Hume, David. 1739. *A Treatise of Human Nature*. Open source material at https://www.gutenberg.org/files/4705/4705-h/4705-h.htm
Hurley, Susan. 2001. "Luck and Equality." *Proceedings of the Aristotelian Society* Supplemental 75 (1): 51–72.
Hussain, Waheed. 2012. "Nurturing the Sense of Justice: The Rawlsian Argument for Democratic Corporatism." In *Property-Owning Democracy: Rawls and Beyond*, ed. O'Neill and Williamson. Chichester: Blackwell.
Kaufman, Alexander. 2018. *Rawls's Egalitarianism*. Cambridge: Cambridge University Press.
Kohlberg, Lawrence. 1973. "The Claim to Moral Adequacy of a Highest Stage of Moral Development." *Journal of Philosophy* 70 (18): 630–46.
Laden, Anthony. 2001. *Reasonably Radical*. Ithaca: Cornell University Press.
Locke, John. 1689. *Second Treatise of Government*. Open source material at https://www.gutenberg.org/files/7370/7370-h/7370-h.htm
Marx, Karl. 1844. "On the Jewish Question." [Written in 1843.] Open source material at http://fs2.american.edu/dfagel/www/Class%20Readings/Marx/Marx,%20_On%20the%20Jewish%20Question_Edited%20version%20from%20Tucker.pdf
Marx, Karl. 1872. "La Liberté Speech." Open source material at https://www.marxists.org/archive/marx/works/1872/09/08.htm
Marx, Karl. 1891. "Critique of the Gotha Programme." [Written in 1875.] Open source material at https://www.marxists.org/archive/marx/works/download/Marx_Critque_of_the_Gotha_Programme.pdf
Marx, Karl. 1932. *Economic and Philosophic Manuscripts of 1844*. [Written in 1844.] Open source material at https://www.marxists.org/archive/marx/works/download/pdf/Economic-Philosophic-Manuscripts-1844.pdf
Marx, Karl, and Friedrich Engels. 1848. *Manifesto of the Communist Party*. Open source material at https://www.marxists.org/archive/marx/works/download/pdf/Manifesto.pdf

Mason, Andrew. 2015. "Justice, Respect, and Treating People as Equals." In *Social Equality: Essays on What It Means to Be Equals*, ed. C. Fourie, F. Schuppert, and I. Walliman-Helmer. Oxford: Oxford University Press.

Meshelski, Kristina. 2019. "Rawls's Socialism and Pure Procedural Justice." *Ethical Perspectives* 26 (2): 343–47.

Miller, Richard. 1974. "Rawls and Marxism." *Philosophy & Public Affairs* 3 (2): 167–91.

Mills, Charles. 2005. "'Ideal Theory' as Ideology." *Hypatia* 20 (3): 165–84.

Nozick, Robert. 1974. *Anarchy, State, and Utopia*. New York: Basic Books.

O'Neill, Martin. 2008. "What Should Egalitarians Believe?" *Philosophy & Public Affairs* 36 (2): 119–56.

O'Neill, Martin. 2009. "Liberty, Equality, and Property-Owning Democracy." *Journal of Social Philosophy* 40 (3): 379–96.

O'Neill, Martin. 2012. "Free (and Fair) Markets without Capitalism: Political Values, Principles of Justice, and Property-Owning Democracy." In *Property-Owning Democracy: Rawls and Beyond*, ed. Martin O'Neill and Thad Williamson. Chichester: Blackwell.

Piketty, Thomas. 2013. *Capital in the Twenty-First Century*, trans. Arthur Goldhammer. Cambridge, MA: Harvard University Press.

Rawls, John. 1971. *A Theory of Justice*. Cambridge, MA: Harvard University Press.

Rawls, John. 1993. *Political Liberalism*. New York: Columbia University Press.

Rawls, John. 1997. "The Idea of Public Reason Revisited." *University of Chicago Law Review* 64 (3): 765–807.

Rawls, John. 1999. *The Law of Peoples*. Cambridge, MA: Harvard University Press.

Rawls, John. 2001. *Justice as Fairness: A Restatement*. Cambridge, MA: Harvard University Press.

Rawls, John. 2007. *Lectures on the History of Political Philosophy*, ed. Samuel Freeman. Cambridge, MA: Harvard University Press.

Reidy, David. 2017. "Moral Psychology, Stability, and the *Law of Peoples*." *Canadian Journal of Law and Jurisprudence* 30 (2): 363–97.

Roemer, John. 1994. *A Future for Socialism*. Cambridge, MA: Harvard University Press.

Scheffler, Samuel. 1982. *The Rejection of Consequentialism*. Oxford: Oxford University Press.

Schemmel, Christian. 2015a. "Social Equality—Or Just Justice?" In *Social Equality: Essays on What It Means to Be Equals*, ed. C. Fourie, F. Schuppert, and I. Walliman-Helmer. Oxford: Oxford University Press.

Schemmel, Christian. 2015b. "How (Not) to Criticize the Welfare State." *Journal of Applied Philosophy* 32 (4): 393–409.

Schweickart, David. 1993. *Against Capitalism*. Cambridge: Cambridge University Press.

Sen, Amartya. 1987. *Commodities and Capabilities*. Oxford: Oxford University Press.

Sen, Amartya. 1992. *Inequality Reexamined*. Cambridge, MA: Harvard University Press.

Tan, Kok-Chor. 2008. "A Defense of Luck Egalitarianism." *Journal of Philosophy* 105 (11): 665–90.

Thomas, Alan. 2012. "Property-Owning Democracy, Liberal Republicanism, and the Idea of an Egalitarian Ethos." In *Property-Owning Democracy: Rawls and Beyond*, ed. Martin O'Neill and Thad Williamson. Chichester: Blackwell.

Thomas, Alan. 2016. *Republic of Equals: Predistribution and Property-Owning Democracy*. Oxford: Oxford University Press.

White, Stuart. 2012. "Property-Owning Democracy and Republican Citizenship." In *Property-Owning Democracy: Rawls and Beyond*, ed. Martin O'Neill and Thad Williamson. Chichester: Blackwell.

Williams, Bernard. 1973. "A Critique of Utilitarianism." In *Utilitarianism: For and Against*, ed. J. J. C. Smart and Bernard Williams. Cambridge: Cambridge University Press.

Williamson, Thad. 2012a. "Realizing Property-Owning Democracy: A 20-Year Strategy to Create an Egalitarian Distribution of Assets in the United States." In *Property-Owning Democracy: Rawls and Beyond*, ed. Martin O'Neill and Thad Williamson. Chichester: Blackwell.

Williamson, Thad. 2012b. "Is Property-Owning Democracy a Politically Viable Aspiration?" In *Property-Owning Democracy: Rawls and Beyond*, ed. Martin O'Neill and Thad Williamson. Chichester: Blackwell.

Wolff, Richard. 2000. "Marxism and Democracy." *Rethinking Marxism* 12 (1): 112–22.

Wood, Allen. 1981. *Karl Marx*. London: Routledge and Kegan Paul.

CHAPTER 2

# Political Liberalism and the Dismantling of the Gendered Division of Labor

Anca Gheaus

## 1. Introduction

Women continue to be in charge of most child-rearing; men continue to be responsible for most breadwinning. There is no consensus on whether this state of affairs, and the informal norms that encourage it, are matters of justice to be tackled by state action. Nor is there any consensus that they are matters of justice sans phrase. One position is that it can also be incumbent on individuals to refrain from internalizing or acting on unjustified gender norms (henceforth, for simplicity, "gender norms"[1]), or from socializing children into them. The view I defend here illustrates this position by exploring the latter possibility.

Alongside normative disagreement, there is some empirical consensus among scholars: women's specialization in caregiving and men's in earning income explain, by and large, the inequalities of outcome between them: in all societies, compared to men, women hold a lesser aggregate share of wealth, political power, and status; they have lesser opportunities on the job market, less discretionary time, higher levels of dependency on potentially abusive spouses, and are at higher risk of poverty, especially as single parents after divorce or during old age.[2] For egalitarians, such disparities are prima facie concerning because the distribution of money, power, status, and, plausibly, of discretionary time, is generally regarded as a matter of justice. Further, feminists believe that this division of labor is gendered, meaning that it is, to a large extent, explained by gender norms, including norms that shape economic policies and employers' expectations. According to these norms, women should be nurturing and generally accommodating of other people's needs, in touch with their emotions, and self-effacing, and on the basis of these features, should be in charge of rearing their children and other caregiving. This is the caregiver role. Complementary gender norms require men to be generally unemotional, competitive, self-assertive, and protective, and thus in charge of their family members' economic security. This is the breadwinner role. I assume that the division of labor between women and men within the family is to some extent the result of individuals acting under the influence of such informal gender norms, and to the extent that it is so, I call it a "gendered division of labor" (henceforth: GDL). I remain agnostic, however, about the extent of this influence, which may be exercised in different ways: (a) through institutional coercion or incentive-setting, (b) through individuals' endorsement of the norms, (c) through the pressure exercised by other people's expectations, or (d) because the aggregate behavior of those who endorse gender norms or yield to gendered expectations makes it rational for others to conform to the GDL.

Feminists have criticized political liberalism for its alleged inability to embrace a full feminist agenda, an inability explained by political liberals' commitment to the ideal of state neutrality. The debate continues on whether neutral states can accommodate two feminist demands: first, to enact policies aimed at dismantling the feminization of caregiving, and especially child-rearing; second, to compensate women for some of the disadvantages they incur by being primary caregivers (Okin 1994; Lloyd 1995; Chambers 2008; Hartley and Watson 2018; Schouten 2019).

I contribute to this debate with three arguments in support of a range of individual duties and state action, including policies meant to degender caregiving and compensate caregivers, which political liberals can endorse. The first argument appeals to the principle of equality of opportunity to positions of advantage (henceforth: EO). It justifies policies that prevent or mitigate statistical discrimination and implicit biases. The other two arguments rely on several bodies of scholarly literature whose potential to advance the debate between feminists and political liberals has not yet been exploited: the tradition of psychoanalytical feminism, recent work on misogyny, and the philosophical literature on legitimate child-rearing. My second argument draws attention to a possible causal relationship between the specialization of women in early childcare and misogyny; since the latter is incompatible with political liberal justice, it yields the conclusion that political liberals ought to further investigate the causal hypothesis with the aim of establishing or refuting it. The third argument concludes that legitimate child-rearing prohibits adults from socializing children, or at the very least girls, into gender norms. It justifies duties of justice on parents, most likely unenforceable, as well as enforceable duties of justice on educators and economic agents, and justifies state policies meant to offset foreseeable breaches of some of these duties. My overall conclusion is compatible with the belief, held by many political liberals, that states shouldn't try to dissuade adults from endorsing gender norms and from leading gendered family lives. It therefore falls short of vindicating the feminist hope that political liberalism can deem the gendered division of labor illegitimate. It does, however, justify a prohibition against foisting gender norms on children, which significantly departs from the status quo, and rectificatory measures.

The next section clarifies my take on the feminist project and explains the demands of political liberalism. The third section explains why the GDL is responsible for women's diminished opportunities to attain positions of advantage, and for their higher risk of poverty and domination. Although it disadvantages women and, to a lesser extent, also diminishes men's opportunities,[3] the GDL endures due to the aggregate effect of many individuals' past engagement in it. Section 4 explains the difficulties of justifying state action aimed at dismantling the GDL. Sections 5–7—the normative core of the chapter—elaborate on so-far neglected reasons to resist GDL and its promotion through child-rearing. The last section explains the implications of my views on the permissibility of the state-enacted feminist policies.

## 2. "Feminism," "Justice," "State Neutrality"

The aims of the feminist project, as I understand it, are (a) to eliminate unjustified gender norms, and (b) to mitigate, or compensate for, the disadvantages generated by these norms. To understand "gender norms," one needs to rely on some version of the sex-gender distinction—although not necessarily on the traditional and contested (Mikkola 2017) version according to which there are (only) two sexes. On the one hand, there is the empirical fact that individuals have differentiated sexual characteristics, such as chromosomes, the kind of gametes that bodies can produce, hormonal makeups, and sexual morphology; for the present purposes, however, it doesn't matter whether there "really" are only two sexes, or more.

On the other hand, there are norms that create the "social meaning of sex," norms that sort people into two kinds (women and men) and hold them to different standards, by encouraging them to display different virtues and interests and to take on different social roles, and which sometimes assign them different rights and duties based on their sexual characteristics. These are gender norms.

I assume that the GDL exists by virtue of unjustified gender norms, and that it is therefore a central goal of the feminist project to undermine it. To the extent that policies to dismantle the GDL are effective, feminists have reason to endorse them; such policies include, for instance, parental leaves designed to encourage equal uptake by women and men, part-time jobs, and jobs that allow parents to work flexible hours without penalties in per-hour pay rates and other benefits (Schouten 2019). Other policies have been defended as better suited to serve the second aim of the feminist project, the elimination of disadvantageous outcomes generated by GDL-promoting norms. These might include split paychecks (Okin 1989) and maybe pension checks, caretaker resource accounts (Alstott 2004), a universal basic income (Baker 2008), and the creation of a sufficient number of jobs that allow parents to make ends meet while working flexible hours or part-time (Gornick and Meyers 2003). Some policies that feminists advocate are likely to accomplish both goals at once: good subsidized daycare centers, after-school programs, and systems of care for the frail elderly. While there are significant tensions between the aims of some of these policies—reflecting unavoidable tensions between trying to dissolve unjustified gender norms and trying to compensate those who are disadvantaged by them (Gheaus 2020)—feminists in general support a combination of such policies.

In liberal societies there is intractable disagreement about justice, yet, following John Rawls, I assume that reasonable citizens can converge on the view that justice demands both "a list of certain basic rights, liberties, and opportunities (such as those familiar from constitutional regimes)" and "measures ensuring for all citizens adequate all-purpose means to make effective use of their freedoms" (Rawls 1997). The first demand, which has special priority, guarantees among other things the conditions of equal citizenship, including individuals' equal power to shape the policies of their societies. On Rawls's own understanding of justice, all-purpose means give individuals the ability to pursue their conception of the good, and include money, opportunities for social positions, the social bases of self-respect, and possibly also discretionary time (Goodin et al. 2008; Rose 2016). For the present discussion, I assume these goods constitute the metric of justice.

A central tenet of political liberalism is that the legitimate exercise of state power requires state neutrality. A main assumption here is that liberal societies harbor deep and unresolvable disagreements about the best way to lead one's life; such societies are unavoidably characterized by a plurality of incompatible conceptions of the good. Because citizens are free and equal, having the moral power to choose, revise, and pursue their own idea of a good life, they are owed justification for the use of state power. Thus, state policies must be justified by appeal to considerations whose authority can be accepted by all. Such considerations may not appeal to controversial beliefs, such as those that are internal to disputed conceptions of the good life. For instance, policies may not be defended by appeal to divisive religious or metaphysical beliefs, or to particular ethical values that some reasonably reject. Hence, the required state neutrality is of justification, not of effect: policies need not make the pursuit of all conceptions of the good life equally costly; they pass the test of neutrality irrespective of consequences as long as they are justified by considerations acceptable to all reasonable citizens (Rawls 2005, 191–94).

"Reasonable" here is a technical term. There is considerable disagreement about how to interpret it, but for the purpose of this chapter it is enough to note that reasonable citizens may endorse views that many comprehensive liberals, and various egalitarians, including gender egalitarians, will think are based on mistaken metaphysical or ethical accounts. What makes a person reasonable is their recognition of others as free and equal, their acceptance of unavoidable disagreement, and a willingness to cooperate on fair terms, i.e., terms that they can reasonably expect others, who do not share their comprehensive views, to accept. Ethical and metaphysical beliefs about gender are notably contentious, and this fact rules them out as justification for state policy. Yet not all those who endorse gender-conservative views can be deemed unreasonable by virtue of their sexism. Rather, as long as they don't seek to limit women's basic liberties, they count as reasonable in the technical sense. People who endorse sexist, but reasonable, views are owed justification for state policies in terms that avoid assuming the truth of comprehensive feminist conceptions of the good life. This explains why political liberals who hold comprehensive feminist conceptions of the good and would like to see the GDL-promoting norms gone, can nevertheless disagree about the legitimacy of state policies aimed at dismantling such norms (Lloyd 1995).

## 3. The Gendered Division of Labor

A division of labor is gendered to the extent that the specialization in different roles is the result of gender norms. A host of discrete norms contribute to the GDL. Some are explicit and have to do with encouraging people to develop GDL-conforming skills and ambitions. Others are implicit, often unconscious, and operate by (sometimes intentional) shaping of women's and men's expectations about themselves and others. The influence of both typically starts in childhood. In short, gender norms prescribe the evaluation of women and men according to different standards. It is possible that in addition to gender norms, other factors, such as women's and men's different natural preferences, explain the specialization of women in caregiving and of men in breadwinning. Therefore it is possible, although hard to establish, that in a world free of any gender norms, we would continue to see some degree of specialization along these same lines. In that case, however, there would be no GDL. The GDL is not merely a pattern of specialization of women and men in different occupations; rather, it is a pattern of specialization inasmuch as it is determined by gender norms. Without gender norms, there would be no GDL. Feminists, I assume, object to the GDL, and not to the pattern of specialization in itself.[4] The objection is manyfold.

The first complaint is that GDL-promoting norms unjustly limit women's, and to a lesser extent men's, freedom of occupational choice. The norms are pervasive in private interactions, in the labor market, and more generally in the public sphere. In the labor market, they can result in discrimination, whether overt, driven by conscious stereotypes, or based on unconscious biases (Brownstein 2019). For instance, field experiments find that identical résumés are evaluated more favorably by potential employers if the applicant is believed to be a man rather than a woman (Steinpreis, Anders, and Ritzke 1999). At times, individuals inadvertently limit their own freedom by becoming subject to stereotype threats, themselves a by-product of gender norms.[5] A well-known example concerns women's math performance, which is lower when they are made aware of gender stereotypes about women being worse at math (Spencer, Steele, and Quinn 1999).

A version of the freedom complaint against GDL-promoting norms is that they are responsible for encouraging different preferences and abilities in women and men. For this complaint, the etiology of the norms has normative relevance: until recently, many of them were inscribed in laws and regulations that denied women's full legal status and prevented, to different degrees, their access to education, politics, and the labor market. Although liberal democratic states no longer overtly promote such norms, the legacy of sexist legislation probably explains, in part, their endurance as socially operative norms, and therefore grounds a moral presumption against them. In general, norms that encourage people to cultivate different preferences based on morally arbitrary differences can be justified—perhaps, for instance, those that encourage people to develop those skills for which they have greater talent. And, indeed, gender norms are sometimes defended by appeal to the good of encouraging people to get better at what they are already good at. Such considerations run against many feminists' belief that inborn differences between women and men are not significant enough to justify GDL-promoting gender norms as encouraging the development of inborn talent. More likely, these norms unduly limit individuals' free development, by making their central life goals depend on their sexual characteristics. This strikes many as being as arbitrary as a feudal economic system that requires people to join particular trades merely because they happen to be born to parents who already belong to the trades in question, or as arbitrary as a schooling system that encourages children to only purse the abilities attributed to them by racial stereotypes.

Freedom-based complaints don't fully capture the disadvantages inflicted by the GDL on women. Gender norms encourage them to care about meeting other people's needs, sometimes at the expense of their own, and discourage them from pursuing public ambitions, thus making them economically dependent on their partners. This explains the higher feminization of poverty in old age, the high rates of poverty among single parents, who are usually single mothers, and women's lower lifetime earnings compared to men's. Lower participation in paid employment also means less status and power, and less access to the most interesting, stimulating, intrinsically rewarding jobs, because the jobs that usually come with these kinds of advantages require full-time, highly committed workers. Moreover, jobs in feminized sectors tend to pay less than jobs in other sectors requiring the same level of qualification; according to some, the explanation is that women's general association with domesticity (and, hence with unpaid work) leads to a general devaluation of women's work (Okin 1989), which may be erosive of self-respect (Shiffrin 2004). When they combine employment and child-rearing, women are also poorer than men in discretionary time. Finally, women have lesser opportunities on the labor market; the GDL creates a path-dependent development of many women's careers: women take leaves for pregnancy, childbirth, and caregiving, and the longer they stay away from full-time jobs, the lower their employment opportunities compared to men's. Money, the social basis of self-respect, discretionary time, and opportunities are all part of the metric of justice, at least in Rawlsian terms according to which the metric contains all-purpose goods (Rawls 2005).

Gendered specialization is difficult to undo for parents; it is economically rational for fathers to continue to work full-time because women tend to earn less (Okin 1989; Allen 2008; Schouten 2019). Some feminists argue that life partners ought to defy the GDL and engage in egalitarian sharing of both domestic and paid work.[6] But whether or not individuals have duties to undo the GDL, a full account of justice must also establish whether states are permitted, or required, to intentionally dismantle gender norms and to compensate women for disadvantages incurred as a result of the GDL.

## 4. Feminism and Political Liberalism: The Difficulty

The GDL has many expressions, from ultraconservative religious views that deny women any independent access to public spaces, to the tendency, shaped by lighter social pressures and by economic rationality, that women rather than men raise children. Some of these expressions are clearly inimical to political liberal justice. First and foremost, justice protects basic freedoms; the infringement of women's freedom of conscience, speech, movement, association, or occupational choice, or of their political freedoms to vote and run for office, is ruled as illegitimate by political liberals (Lloyd 1995).

Further, political liberalism requires that citizens have sufficient shares of all-purpose means, including money, to make use of their basic liberties. As such, a prosperous society would have no involuntary poverty; in such a world, the GDL would not mean (risk of) poverty for women, let alone for their children. Further, Rawls identifies the social bases of self-respect as an important all-purpose good. Given that caregiving is essential to the well-being of every individual,[7] and indeed a socially necessary form of work, those who perform it in a just society would be protected from the devaluing that caregivers experience in the real world.[8] As Elizabeth Brake (2013) notes, not only women's, but also girls', treatment according to ultraconservative gender norms is probably prohibited by political liberalism: parents telling girls that their interests are less important than boys' is incompatible with a fair distribution of the social basis of self-respect. (A further question is whether such prohibition can result in a legal ban, since it is not clear whether one can enforce such a ban by legitimate means.) And if all able citizens should be in the position to support themselves economically, justice requires that girls be imparted the skills needed to effectively participate in the labor market (Lloyd 1995).

Other policies can be defended on political-liberal grounds as protecting women from some unjust consequences of an unregulated GDL, for instance overt discrimination driven by sexist prejudice. But it is less clear that state neutrality is compatible with policies meant to mitigate other disadvantages that women incur as a result of the GDL, including lower lifetime earnings due to lesser participation in the labor market, fewer opportunities for the most advantageous jobs, less discretionary time, and diminished access to the top tiers of political life. Particularly difficult to justify are policies attempting to eradicate women's specialization in caregiving, which is the core of the GDL. For these reasons, political liberalism has been said to be incompatible with the full feminist demand that the GDL be dismantled.[9]

Political liberalism protects people's pursuit of their reasonable conceptions of the good, including sexist ones. The family is an association that adults enter willingly and can exit at will (at least legally), and some forms of the GDL are compatible with the basic freedoms of family members. Consider a heterosexual couple engaging in a GDL, with the usual consequences for the woman's career, life-time earnings, and job opportunities, but free from risk of poverty and social stigma, thanks to adequate unemployment benefits and social respect for care workers. Assume that this instance of the GDL is driven by gender norms that the couple has internalized and endorses; political liberalism cannot deem their situation illegitimate by appealing to the superiority of a feminist account of morality or justice. Indeed, if it could, it should also classify as illegitimate the many religious views that mandate the GDL. Some such views depict women and men as different but complementary not only in their inborn abilities but also in their virtues: men are supposed to lead good lives by being protective, innovative, courageous, and public-spirited, while women do so by being nurturing, caring, and supportive. In this view, women and men flourish in different ways. Call this "the gender complementarity view." This view is a conception of the good—not a mere set of empirical beliefs about sexual difference, but also a metaphysical and ethical doctrine. When it takes forms that don't deny women's basic liberties, including their liberty to reject the view, it is also reasonable in Rawlsian terms. A political liberal state must be able to justify policies aiming to dismantle the more benign forms of the GDL, or at least undo its effects, to those who hold a reasonable version of the gender complementarity view.

Several answers to this challenge have been provided (Okin 1989; Chambers 2004; Hartley and Watson 2018; Schouten 2019). But I believe that more can be said on this matter. Below I discuss three promising, yet so far insufficiently considered, reasons that justify state action meant to constrain the effects of the GDL (the argument from equality of opportunity), to investigate the causal connection between feminized early child-rearing and misogyny, and, if the connection is established, to adopt policies that defeminize child-rearing (the argument from misogyny and feminized early childcare) and to degender child-rearing (the argument from legitimate child-rearing). To the extent that the state is unsuccessful in these aims, the same reasons justify policies that rectify certain disadvantages incurred by women due to the GDL.

## 5. The Equality of Opportunity Argument

Consider again the spouses depicted above. They endorse a version of the gender complementarity view and live in a society that is just at the bar of political liberalism: caregivers are socially respected and not at risk of poverty or domestic abuse. In case of divorce the wealth accumulated during marriage is fairly shared.[10] Caregivers also have enough discretionary time and are eligible for training to (re)enter the labor market to a degree sufficient to make them economically independent. However, specializing in caregiving has opportunity costs—diminished opportunities for well-paying, interesting, and prestigious jobs, as well as lower lifetime earnings—and, inevitably, fuels the sexist assumptions embedded in the gender complementarity view. Further, the GDL is sufficiently widespread that it warrants a general expectation, on the side of employers, that women will be less present in the workplace, and this partly explains a gender pay gap. Like in existing societies, good jobs require freedom from private care responsibilities, making the GDL economically rational for most parenting couples, while some also endorse it for principled, noneconomic reasons. Under such circumstances, what justifications are there for state interventions meant to tamper with the GDL or with its effects on individuals, justifications that don't assume that gender egalitarianism is morally superior to the gender complementarity view and that can therefore be accepted by our couple?

The first answer, which I consider in this section, is grounded in the widely endorsed principle of EO, which demands that the allocation of positions of advantage—such as good jobs—track only talent and ambition. When the GDL is sufficiently widespread, it generates statistical discrimination and implicit biases against women. The former refers to employers' rational tendency, other things being equal, to prefer male employees on account of their lower likelihood of taking long care leaves, requesting to go part-time, or even quitting their jobs to care for children. Statistical discrimination in access to the more desirable jobs is to be expected whenever staff turnover is costly for employers. It doesn't depend on employers being prejudiced against women in any way; but of course, employers often are prejudiced, and to the extent that they are unaware of their prejudices, discrimination against women is very difficult to (self-) police. Employers can and often do harbor implicit biases—that is, "relatively unconscious and relatively automatic features of prejudiced judgment and social behaviour" (Brownstein 2019). An (admittedly controversial) wealth of literature indicates that virtually everybody holds implicit biases against women by expecting them to conform to gender stereotypes.

Statistical discrimination and implicit biases against women undermine EO by letting considerations other than talent and ambition bear on people's access to positions of advantage. More generally, many believe that statistical discrimination against women offends against justice qua discrimination, although there is disagreement as to precisely how (Lippert-Rasmussen 2011).

If a critical mass of people engage in GDL, statistical discrimination and implicit bias can be generated even under conditions that are otherwise in full compliance with justice—that is, in circumstances in which employers are free from, or abstain from acting on, any conscious sexist stereotypes against potential employees. Importantly, statistical discrimination and implicit biases don't operate only against women who (will at some point) engage in the GDL, but against all women—or, at least, against all women of childbearing age, assuming it is care for children that is primarily responsible for women's lower attachment to the labor market. Women whose partners raise their children, as well as women who do not have children, are subject to statistical discrimination and implicit biases to the same extent as women who take on caregiving roles. Feminists regularly note that gender norms set back women's opportunities in the labor market by discouraging their professional ambitions or by imposing opportunity costs on them; in contrast, my focus is on the setback of opportunities of women whose ambitions do not reflect, and whose market behavior does not comply with, gender norms. Political liberals must be more concerned about this case than about the discrimination of women who comply, and identify, with gender norms. This is because in the case of the latter, lower opportunities for positions of advantage might be justified as the cost to be paid for one's life-work choices.[11] But the same justification is not available in the case of women who do not adopt caregiving roles. This group of women is most obviously required to pay the cost of diminished opportunities in the labor market, merely because they happen to have certain sex characteristics; this is an unfair situation, one that is not obviously justifiable to women who are victims of implicit biases and statistical discrimination.

Formally, the argument is:

P1 Positions of advantage should be allocated by EO.
P2 The GDL generates statistical discrimination and implicit biases.
P3 Statistical discrimination and implicit biases are incompatible with implementing EO.
C1 Therefore, some of the consequences of the GDL are incompatible with implementing EO.[12]

Political liberals find it easy to accept this conclusion as policy justification, but the policies that can be justified by appeal to it are very limited. The EO-undermining effect of the GDL is reason to combat the two specific consequences of the GDL that are the culprit—statistical discrimination and implicit biases—for instance by requiring employers to undergo anti-bias trainings if these are effective, or creating and possibly subsidizing institutional care that workers can use if they have children. But such measures are unlikely to be sufficient as long as the GDL remains in place, and sufficiently comprehensive measures, such the full institutionalization of childcare—say, by rearing children in well-run orphanages—are, I assume, illegitimate (Munoz-Darde 1999; Brighouse and Swift 2014). The source of the problem is the combination of child-rearing in the family and the GDL. Yet the GDL-undermining effect on EO is not sufficient to legitimize attempts to uproot the GDL itself: although EO is a widely endorsed principle of justice, the freedom to pursue a reasonable conception of the good is likely to have priority according to a wide range of conceptions of justice. (For instance, in Rawls's own conception of justice as fairness, FEO has lexical priority over the first principle protecting basic freedoms.) People who endorse the gender complementarity view cannot be required to live against their metaphysical and ethical convictions in order to prevent the creation of EO-disrupting biases.

This is to say that EO has less priority than the protection of people's basic freedoms, such as the freedom to enact the gender complementarity view. If so, the argument from EO cannot justify policies aimed at implementing the first feminist goal: the elimination of the GDL itself.

## 6. The Argument from Misogyny and Feminized Early Childcare

At least under Rawls's conception of justice as fairness, the first demand of justice, that citizens enjoy equal basic liberties, guarantees not only formal rights, but also the fair value of political liberties. In the case of citizenship rights, it doesn't merely protect women's legal rights to participate in politics on an equal footing with men, but also their ability to make use of these rights. One of the prerequisites for this is that women can participate in political debates and run for election without being impeded by widespread animosity, hatred, or irrational mistrust. In cultural environments in which women's voices are silenced with impunity, their opinions are devalued and routinely ridiculed, and they are mistrusted (in bigoted ways), women don't enjoy the fair value of their political liberties. In other words, widespread misogyny undermines their citizenship. By "misogyny" here I understand a cluster of attitudes that includes hostility toward women, the tendency to disvalue their abilities, and the tendency to see women as less entitled to participate in decision-making by discounting their interests or their ability to give reasons (what is sometimes called "epistemic injustice"), or by seeing them as unfit for positions of power merely because they are women. Because misogyny is often nested in micro-interactions, I also assume that it is impossible, let alone permissible, to effectively police most of it.

Presumably, prejudice against and devaluation of women as political subjects exists in all societies, albeit in different ways and to different extents. Two recent books that have been enjoying much public acclaim illustrate this thesis; one looks at misogyny in the public sphere throughout the history of Western civilization, the other at misogyny, public and private, in the contemporary US. The first, by historian Mary Beard (2017), explores the silencing of women in public settings; we are told that, since Homer, this practice has been seen as permissible and, moreover, as a desirable way to affirm one's masculinity. Beard's book is about vilifying women who dare to affirm their views on public matters, and especially in politics. The second book, by Kate Manne (2017), is an examination of men's sense of entitlement to women's attention, validation, care, and nurturing and its consequences for women. In particular, it claims that women who assume public functions traditionally reserved for men are being perceived as refusing to offer these emotional and relational goods to men, and so they become targets of misogyny.

Neither Beard nor Manne offers any thoughts on how to uproot misogyny, or any grand theory that could explain it. Manne is explicitly hopeless on the first count: "What could possibly change any of this? . . . I give up. I wish I could offer a more hopeful message" (2017, 300). However, a feminist explanation of misogyny has long been on offer, and, with it, a possible solution. The feminist psychoanalytical tradition provides several versions of an explanation of the pathologies discussed by Beard and Manne; the origins of this family of theories go back to Freud and understand misogyny as a revulsion against women, rooted in the facts that, as infants, we see our primary caregivers as overpowering figures and we eventually revolt against such power.

Dorothy Dinnerstein (1976), Jessica Benjamin (1988), and Rozsika Parker (2005) have all drawn on the same main insight, explaining widespread misogyny as a by-product of early child-rearing done almost exclusively by women. The assumption is that babies perceive their primary parental figure as entirely instrumental to the baby's needs. When the vast majority of primary figures are women, we tend to identify womanhood with the only source of essential goods such as affection, nurturing, safety, kindness, and compassion; this fuels an unconscious, lifelong resentment against women when they fail to provide such goods. Further, the enormous (perceived) power of the primary figure tends to become a target of resentment, especially during the process of the child's individuation, which requires her gradual emancipation from dependency on the primary figure. Growing up in societies where women are in charge of the domestic world, but have much less power than men in the public sphere, is an aggravating factor that leads to a general devaluation of womanhood. As we grow up, we equate women with caregiving and nurturing because this is what we see them doing, when we are in great need of their care and are incapable of moral judgment, and then expect—often unconsciously—that they will carry on doing it. We then resent their holding political power because, unconsciously, we feel threatened: even as adults, we are never fully independent, and continue to occasionally need care. Because we are primed to expect it from women, we respond with criticism and blame when women deny it to us, whether or not these attitudes are warranted.

If this psychoanalytical feminist analysis is correct, then a significant part of the cluster of bigoted attitudes that constitute misogyny can be explained by the GDL. As long as only women are raising children, they alone are the target of individuation-advancing resentment. Misogyny is incompatible with equal citizenship because it makes it difficult, if at all possible, to be receptive to what women have to say about public matters, and to accept them as legitimate holders of power. An obvious solution then is to ensure that a majority of infants have both women and men as primary figures—as all the feminists working in this tradition have advocated. This, of course, would mean ending the GDL, or, at the very least, abolishing its core: having most of the hands-on rearing of children done by women. (Another solution would involve overcoming adults' resentment, for instance via generalized psychotherapy. I don't consider this possibility further, since much of the resentment—on this account—is unconscious and not recognizable as such by most individuals. Eradicating it from the minds of adults seems an even more utopian enterprise than de-gendering early childcare.)

Formally, the argument is:

P4 Child-rearing by women only, which is the main element of the GDL, unavoidably generates widespread misogyny.
P5 Widespread misogyny is incompatible with equal citizenship.
C2 Therefore, women's overwhelming specialization in childcare is incompatible with equal citizenship.

Unlike in the conclusion of the argument from EO, the conclusion of this argument could indeed justify policies aimed at realizing part of the first feminist goal: dismantling GDL. In fact, it could justify more than that: if women were to overwhelmingly specialize in child-rearing even in the absence of GDL-promoting norms, C2 would be a political liberal reason to object to such specialization. Assuming that a strong causal connection between child-rearing by women only and misogyny could be established with a high level of confidence, this would of course not necessarily entail a prohibition of adults living in accordance with the gender complementarity view—or what is left of it after bracketing child-rearing. It would merely require a reform of child-rearing whereby the state offsets the disproportionate involvement of mothers in the care of their young children by strongly encouraging fathers to care, or more generally, by supplementing (and possibly partly replacing) care by women with care provided by men within and outside of the family.

There are two obstacles to reaching this conclusion, at least at the present moment. The first is that the first premise relies on a metaphysical view that is controversial and likely to remain so. Many disagree with the Freudian conception of the person. I return to this problem after addressing the second.

The second obstacle is that the first premise is highly speculative and difficult to test. A straightforward way to test it—as John Stuart Mill (1869) has noted—would entail comparing levels of misogyny in existing societies, which are dominated by the GDL, with those in societies where women and men share equally the hands-on childcare during children's first years of life. But the latter has never existed, and so this straightforward test is unavailable. However, given the importance of equal citizenship, political liberals should take seriously the possibility that child-rearing only by women generates misogyny, and seek permissible methods to test it. For instance, there may be ways to establish a causal connection between feminized child-rearing and widespread misogyny by using statistical regression to provide social-scientific evidence that more gender-neutral child-rearing ameliorates misogyny.[13] The level of feminization of early childcare differs across societies and social groups, so it should be possible to gather such evidence. In the presence of appropriate evidence, the existence of such a causal connection could be accepted without also accepting the causal mechanism postulated by the theory—or, indeed, any particular explicative mechanism.

The last claim should also provide the key to solving the first problem. As long as psychoanalysis remains controversial, it is not a theory on the basis of which one can give public reasons; but for the purpose of justifying gender-egalitarianism, it might be enough to test the empirical claim put forward by feminist psychoanalysts. Political liberals can take such evidence as authoritative without also endorsing psychoanalytic theory, whose value in this case would be merely to signal the potential causal relation—a relation that, if established, is highly relevant to the issue of equal citizenship. Doing this—i.e., distinguishing the empirical evidence from the background theory that inspired it—is not without precedent. For instance, reasonable citizens may disagree about the truth of Darwinian theory and yet agree that states may subsidize the development and distribution of vaccines on the grounds that they benefit individuals and serve public health aims.[14] Similarly, the status quo of some states subsidizing mental health therapies that rely on psychoanalytical theory as long as they prove sufficiently effective (relative to alternatives) does not seem problematic. If this proposal is plausible, then the argument proposed in this section really is an argument for a very particular kind of state action: pursuing a thorough investigation of the putative causal connection between feminized early childcare and misogyny.

## 7. The Argument from Permissible Child-Rearing

The political liberal explanation of why states cannot legitimately interfere with the GDL starts from the observation that domestic arrangements between consenting adults should be—and in liberal societies usually are—voluntary. Within such associations, people are free to pursue their conception of the good even if, as under the gender complementarity view, it imposes significant material and opportunity costs on women who endorse it. This is the same kind of protected freedom as being able to live according to one's religious views, which also restricts one's (labor market) opportunities.

But when families are voluntary associations, they are voluntary only for adults: children are assigned particular parents, whose parental rights are guaranteed by the state. Children are not asked for consent and have no exit rights from the relationship with their parents. This is not in itself objectionable: children lack the normative power to give, or withhold, consent. Paternalism over them is legitimate, and justice requires that some adults be assigned authority over them; yet such authority must be justified by appeal to the interests of the child. Children, I assume here, are rightholders; they may not be used as mere means to secure other people's interests. For this reason, parental authority may not be exercised to advance parents' interests—for instance, to make it possible for the parent to pursue a particular conception of the good, or put children in the service of controversial ethical values endorsed by the parent (Clayton 2006; Brighouse and Swift 2014). This view is not (yet) widely endorsed, and it is at odds with the current toleration of parental attempts to foist their own values on their children. I think, however, that it is the only view compatible with recognizing children's full moral status as ends in themselves: allowing parents to express their controversial values through their children is akin to letting them use the children as a means to either honor the values themselves, or to serve their own interest in self-extension or self-expression. This is not to deny that good parents usually wish that their children will adopt their values for the sake of the child's own well-being; this justification, however, is not available to them within the remit of public reason as long as the values at stake are controversial among reasonable citizens. Moreover, the claim that children may not be used as vehicles for adults' controversial values extends beyond parental authority, to the legitimate exercise of authority over children by other adults who have influence over particular children, and to adults as a whole.

On this basis, two different arguments can be brought to the conclusion that particular adults, and adults collectively, lack the permission to foist GDL-promoting norms on children. By "foisting" here I mean, for now, intentional enrollment, such as explicitly asking children to conform to controversial ethical ideals, as well as merely nudging or encouraging them to do so intentionally but in nonexplicit ways. The two arguments are rooted in alternative views about permissible child-rearing, one of which requires full neutrality, the other limited neutrality. The first version of the argument rests on the more general claim that adults lack permission to foist any conception of the good on children. The second version rests on the less demanding claim that adults lack permission to foist on children conceptions of the good that are detrimental to children's future access to goods that are part of the distribuendum of justice.

Both arguments accept the desiderata of political liberalism: that states ought to display neutrality of aim between different conceptions of the good pursued by adults. Matthew Clayton (2006) extends this requirement to relationships between adults and children, arguing that neutrality in upbringing is justified on grounds of the relevant similarities between the relationship between citizens and their states and that between children and the adults who have authority over them. In his account, parents and other adults who are in the position to influence children's values and how their lives go ought to refrain from attempting to influence children's formation of a conception of the good.

The reasons are similar to those that support state neutrality: in both cases, a powerful agent—the state, respectively parents—is in a relationship with a much weaker party—citizens, respectively children—who cannot exit the relationship without paying a very great cost. Just as states can and may coerce their citizens to implement justice, parents can and may coerce their children to ensure their development into future autonomous individuals endowed with the two moral powers, namely a capacity to form, revise, and pursue their idea of the good life and a sense of justice. Parents' role is to teach their children about their and other people's rights and duties, and to equip them with the knowledge and skills necessary to eventually make up their own minds about how to lead their lives. But respect for children as future autonomous agents forbids parents from intentionally transmitting their own ideas about what makes life good—including ethical values. In Clayton's view, parents are even barred from revealing their enthusiasms to their children, lest they put undue pressure on children to embrace their views. Clayton provides two reasons why children's future autonomy is violated by parental behaviors that intentionally steer the children's lives toward particular virtues and life goals (Clayton 2006, 104–5). The first is that most children grow up into autonomous beings who can make retrospective claims concerning their treatment during the times when they were not yet (fully) autonomous. An adult looking back at her parents' attempts to instill certain traits or values in her has reason to complain that, as a child, she had once been made to serve a conception of the good life that she is now rejecting. If she were required to live according to this conception of the good, she can complain that her ethical independence has been compromised, because under others' undue influence part of her life has been led according to a conception of the good that she has come to reject once in possession of full autonomy. Because children lack the wherewithal to resist adults' attempt to influence them, all intentional enrollment into controversial conceptions of the good counts as undue influence (Clayton, forthcoming). Second, children whose parents try to steer them toward particular virtues and goals are likely to face unwarranted psychological costs in reassessing their commitments to the goals in question, i.e., in revising their conception of the good (Clayton 2006, 104–5). Since GDL-promoting norms are a contested element of a conception of the good life, a principle of neutrality in child-rearing makes it impermissible for parents and other authority figures to foist such norms on children.

Formally, the first version of the argument is:

P6 State neutrality: it is morally impermissible for states to encourage their citizens to adopt any controversial conceptions of the good.

P7 The relationship between some adults and children is similar to that between states and citizens in respects that are relevant to the exercise of power.

C3 Therefore, child-rearing neutrality: it is morally impermissible for adults to foist on children any controversial conception of the good.

P8 GDL-promoting norms represent a controversial conception of the good.

C4 Therefore, it is morally impermissible for adults to foist GDL-promoting norms on children.

The extent to which respecting C4 would prevent the intergenerational transmission of gender norms is an empirical question, and one very much open to debate. If children's acquisition of norms were merely a matter of copying what parents and other adults do, in the absence of any instruction and nudging, this would perhaps be a modest conclusion. But it is more plausible that gender norms would wither over time if children were never instructed into gender norms, never expected to conform to their parents' and teachers' sexist standards, and never had their curiosity met with sexist explanations. Further, Clayton's account could be extended to argue that, since adults who exercise authority over children have a duty to protect children's autonomy formation, they are required to equip children with the means to resist undue influence. Parents and teachers ought therefore to draw children's attention to others' attempts to coercively instill gender norms in them and empower them to resist. Both peer pressure from other children and aggressive gendered advertising are likely to count as coercive influences because children have very limited opportunities to choose their social environments.

Few are fully persuaded by Clayton's views about the translation of the neutrality requirement to the case of children. As Norvin Richards (2018) noted, one difference between the state-citizen relationship and the parent-child relationship seems crucially relevant: while the state is not responsible for the well-being of its citizens, parents or perhaps adults more generally are partly responsible for how well their children's lives go.

For this reason, many will find it tempting to relax C3 to a requirement that adults not foist on children conceptions of the good that are detrimental to children's well-being. Where the previous version of the argument embraced neutrality in child-rearing, this one is perfectionist. Perfectionists believe that it is, in principle, permissible to try and encourage people to pursue conceptions of the good that are conducive to flourishing. When the people in question are adults, and the foisting agent is the state, there are powerful reasons to resist perfectionism, which seems incompatible with respect for autonomy (Quong 2011). But—against Clayton—it is less likely that the same worry applies to children in their relationship with authority figures.[15]

Is it coherent to require states not to interfere with, or pass judgments about, adults' pursuit of reasonable conceptions of the good, and at the same time require them to refrain from intentionally enrolling children in conceptions of the good that are detrimental to their flourishing? I am not convinced that there is a principled tension between the two requirements. A restriction of parental rights, according to which parents are not permitted to rear their children in (reasonable) conceptions of the good that set back children's interests, is a direct consequence of the requirement to treat children as right-holders whose interests cannot be sacrificed for the sake of advancing other people's conception of the good. That is, taking children's personhood seriously is not compatible with allowing adults to instill in them detrimental values, whether in the name of allowing adults to pursue their conceptions of the good or in the name of serving those values.

More worrying, for this argument, is the thought that in a diverse, liberal society, there is no authority that may publicly adjudicate which reasonable conceptions of the good are true, and hence conducive to flourishing, and which are not. Some people, of course, claim that gender roles themselves are conducive to flourishing, yet this is precisely what gender traditionalists deny. Hence, knowledge of true flourishing—or at least of conditions that are detrimental to it—is necessary if children are to be protected from false, pernicious conceptions of the good. If states take a stand on this matter, the worry is that they will thereby, implicitly and unavoidably, pass judgments about the value of their citizens' conceptions of the good. Whether doing so for the sake of protecting children from wrongful enrollment in certain conceptions of the good does or doesn't violate the spirit of political neutrality may depend on particular interpretations of the neutrality requirement. I hope that one version of the perfectionist account of child-rearing can successfully meet Clayton's changes, namely one that requires children to be exposed, in their value-formation, to several influential adults who hold different views of the good life (Gheaus 2024); but since I cannot properly make that case here, I revert to a more modest argument in the remainder of this section.

Even if political liberalism turned out to be inconsistent with perfectionism for children, for the purpose of this paper it is enough to note that political liberals can accept a more modest claim that perfectionist parenting must also endorse: that intentionally socializing girls into GDL-promoting gender norms is impermissible because it is detrimental to their future interests by political liberals' own lights. Namely, it is detrimental to the extent that gender norms impair girls' access to primary goods, which political liberals themselves identify as part of the metric of justice: opportunities for positions of advantage, income, discretionary time, and in societies like ours that often disrespect caregivers, the social bases of self-respect. This is an argument that political liberals can accept. (Further, if the feminization of early childcare turns out to be responsible for widespread misogyny, as the discussion in the previous section suggests, GDL-promoting gender norms are also detrimental to girls' future enjoyment of the fair value of their political rights.) If so, even if they would be wrong to require full neutrality in child-rearing, political liberals can support a demand that parents, other influential adults, and maybe adults collectively refrain from intentionally enrolling girls in GDL-promoting norms. Formally, the second version of the argument is:

P9 It is morally impermissible for adults to foist on children conceptions of the good that are detrimental to their equal access to primary goods.
P10 GDL-promoting norms represent a conception of the good that is detrimental to girls' equal access to primary goods.
C4 Therefore, it is morally impermissible for adults to foist GDL-promoting norms on girls.

Since the reason for C4 is to protect girls' equal access to the primary goods to which they are entitled, it warrants a more generous interpretation of "foisting," one that is not restricted to children's intentional gender socialization. Assuming, for instance, that children tend to emulate their parents' behavior and beliefs even when not explicitly instructed to do so, the setback in women's interest in all-purpose goods justifies active attempts to dissuade girls from copying gendered behaviors.

C4 is silent about the permissibility of adults themselves engaging in a GDL. It merely prohibits adults from (intentionally) socializing girls in GDL-promoting norms. However, these two realities may be impossible to separate in practice, if children ought to be raised in the family and if people who embrace the GDL have a right to raise children.[16] It is beyond the scope of my chapter to discuss these complications, which are nevertheless crucial to the implementation of the ideal I defend here. I limit myself to noting that the conclusions of the third argument can most readily justify states' attempts to prevent, offset, and mitigate the current influence of gender norms in children's or, at the very least, girls', socialization. In societies where enough parents and other adults involved in child-rearing breach their duty and use their authority to intentionally encourage children to internalize gender norms, states have a remedial duty to counterbalance such influences. It can discharge this duty by providing institutional rearing—in day care, kindergartens, and schools—that is not only free of gender norms itself, but is intended to help children reflect on, and possibly reject, the undue influence being exercised over them. The regulative ideal, as far as neutrality in child-rearing indicates, is a society in which adults who endorse GDL-promoting norms don't teach them to children, and that protects children from others' attempts to gender them.

Appeal to the same reason—providing children with the conditions needed to adopt or reject gender norms without undue influences—shows that children are also entitled to protection from intentional gendering that is ultimately driven by different aims. Markets in toys, educational materials, or clothes that unjustifiably differentiate their products according to gender, and the advertisement of these and other products in gendered ways, are ultimately motivated not by an intention to foist gender norms on children, but by economic reasons. Nevertheless, given that children are not in the position to protect themselves from advertisements or to avoid the markets in toys, educational materials, and clothes of their societies, they are owed protection from the powerful gendering messages carried by such markets and advertisements. One possible example of such protection is banning advertisements with gendering messages; the endorsement of any specific measure would, of course, require further argument.

## 8. Conclusions: Two Aims of Gender Justice

The overall conclusion of this chapter is moderately optimistic with respect to the convergence of political liberalism and the feminist commitment to dismantling the GDL. As far as the arguments I propose go, political liberals may be right that states should not try to dissuade adults from leading lives informed by gender norms. I provided no justificatory ground for making it harder, or costlier, for adults who endorse the gender complementarity view to follow their conception of the good (although this conclusion would be significant should we be able to establish that the feminization of early childcare unavoidably generates misogyny). Yet children, who by assumption have not yet formed their own conception of the good, must be protected from adults' or, indeed, market institutions', encouragements that they adopt gender norms. If this is correct, then political liberals must acknowledge two aims of justice concerning GDL-promoting norms.

The first aim is forward-looking and states that children are owed protection from undue influence in the formation of their ambitions and values. In particular, they have a right to be free from authoritative adults' attempts to make them comply with, and internalize, gender norms, and from the powerful gendering influence of markets of advertisements and toys, educational materials, and clothes. It is difficult to imagine the extent of institutional reform required to accomplish this aim in its entirety; this chapter is merely concerned with its principled justification.

Because it is hard to imagine that the first goal could be achieved, at least in the foreseeable future, the second, backward-looking aim is particularly important: it requires that individuals who have been wronged by a failure to implement the first aim are owed, at least in some cases, reparation. In particular, women are owed policies that offset certain disadvantages incurred as a result of gender norms, even if the women in question have internalized and even endorse these norms. As I mentioned in the introduction, such policies include split paychecks and pension checks, and caretaker resource accounts meant to compensate for caregivers' disadvantages in terms of wealth and discretionary time.

More specifically, individuals who came to endorse gender norms as a result of wrongful child-rearing are owed compensation for those disadvantages that are not integral to their pursuit of a gendered lifestyle. Here the assumption is that it would be disrespectful to offer compensation for costs that are integral to values that people endorse, but not for costs that are merely incidental to pursuing those values (Cohen 1999). For instance, one may expect women who endorse the GDL to also endorse the lesser opportunities they have for jobs that require very high time commitments and flexibility, as a justified and integral consequence of devoting much of one's life to caring for others. But, presumably, there is no presumption that they should endorse being economically dependent on abusive spouses, or being at high risk of poverty during old age, or even having, overall, lesser shares of primary goods such as income and the social bases of self-respect.

One important question that would need to be settled by a full account of gender justice in non-ideal circumstances is which agents owe compensatory duties to women who, while children, have been wrongfully socialized in gender norms and to all the women who are victims of statistical discrimination and implicit biases as a result of other people's socialization in gender norms. To the extent that these individuals incur disadvantages as a result of breaches of duties by the adults who raised them, or by market practices, it is tempting to think that the primary duty of reparation is born by the wronging agents: parents, but also schools and possibly other authority figures in children's lives, as well as those who are (perhaps, collectively) responsible for gendering advertisement and markets. Yet a proper treatment of the matter would require an elaborate view of duties to protect children from wrongful exercises of power over them. Such a view may include an account of whether, for instance, states themselves must ensure that schools do not function as gendering agents, or whether state interference is justified in the marketing of clothes, toys, and pastimes as being "for boys" or "for girls." If it is, then many more agents beyond parents and educators wrong children by foisting gender norms on them, although the precise ascription of duties and liabilities may not be straightforward.

All this, of course, allows for the possibility that some people will endorse the gender complementarity view in spite of having been successfully protected, as children, from intentional enrollment in sexist beliefs. Imagine a society in which the gender complementarity view is just one among several available accounts of how one's sexual characteristics matter, or don't matter, to living a flourishing life, and the society doesn't encourage any child to adopt it. Adults who adopt the gender complementarity view as autonomous choosers, without any history of undue influence, have no claims to compensation for the disadvantages integral to their pursuit of a life shaped by gender norms. (This is similar to the way in which an adult who had no religious upbringing, and who embraces a particular religion, cannot claim compensation for the various lifestyle limitations they thereby incur.) It is also possible that some people who live in sexist societies would have endorsed the gender complementarity view—counterfactually—even if they had been raised free from gender roles and beliefs. To the extent that they have in fact been subjected to such socialization, they come under the remit of the feminist project's second goal: the compensation of disadvantages that people suffer as a result of gender norms.

ACKNOWLEDGMENT

This is a slightly edited version of the paper with the same title, published in *Oxford Studies in Political Philosophy*, vol. 9, edited by David Sobel and Steven Wall (Oxford: Oxford University Press, 2023). For helpful feedback I am grateful to Constanze Binder, Elizabeth Brake, Matthew Clayton, Christina Easton, Tweedy Flanigan, Christie Hartley, Louis Larue, Holly Lawford-Smith, Christian List, Erik Malmquist, Gloria Mähringer, Andrew Mason, Tim Meijers, David O'Brien, Tom Parr, Georg Schmwerzeck, Gina Schouten, Adam Slavny, Adam Swift, Laura Valentini, Steven Wall, Lori Watson, and audiences in Umea, Utrecht, London, Rotterdam, Stockholm, Kingston, Gothenburg, Arizona, and Munich, and also to an anonymous reviewer.

NOTES

1. Elsewhere (Gheaus 2023) I explain the difference between gender norms that are justified and those that aren't. The present argument concerns only the latter.

2. Throughout this chapter I make a number of claims about the GDL and the ways it generates disadvantages for women. For an overview of recent empirical literature substantiating these claims as applied to both developed and developing societies, see Schouten (2019).

3. For instance, they are expected to be the main breadwinner, leaving them with less time and, possibly, fewer skills for flourishing personal relationships. They also face discrimination in child-rearing professions.

4. Although some defend, as "gender justice," the view that we ought to mitigate, when possible, some of the alleged inborn shortcomings in people's ability to realize (to some extent) the central goods of the opposite gender role. So, for example, if men are for biological reasons less able to nurture others than women, we owe them more training in this respect. See Gheaus (2012).

5. To be subject to a stereotype threat is to tend to conform to the negative stereotypes associated with your socially salient group in those situations in which you are reminded that you belong to the group in question. See, for instance, Stricker and Ward (2004).

6. At least when they raise children; see Okin (1989), who calls the family "the first school of justice."

7. That is, at least in infancy and during periods of sickness, and for some people, during frail old age or while afflicted by disability. Care is, in this sense, an all-purpose good, one that individuals have reason to want no matter what other things they desire. For this reason, some feminists have argued that it should be on the list of primary goods—i.e., part of the metric of justice. See Kittay (1999) and Brake (2010). It is a disturbing anomaly that the production of such an essential good fails to attract social respect for those who provide it.

8. Harley and Watson (2018) in particular make a convincing case that political liberalism requires the dismantling of gender hierarchies, as incompatible with equal citizenship. I assume—like Schouten (2019)—that the GDL may survive

such hierarchies and remain objectionable for some of the reasons explained in section 3.

9. For a defense of this view see Lloyd (1995). For literature overviews by authors who ultimately defend the thesis that political liberals ought to enact GDL-undermining policies, see Hartley and Watson (2018) and Schouten (2019).

10. Which, as Neufeld (2009) notes, political liberals should support as long as marriage is a state-regulated institution, and welfare policies and economic institutions function on the assumption that domestic and care work is largely performed informally by women.

11. Many feminists reject this justification, because they believe that justice requires an opportunity to combine attractive careers with child-rearing (Fraser 1994; Gornick and Meyers 2003; Gheaus 2012; Hartley and Watson 2018). But this conception of justice cannot be accommodated by political liberalism, on account of its likely perfectionist nature.

12. If implicit biases against women as workers and statistical discrimination against them are unavoidable consequences of the GDL, then the GDL itself is incompatible with EO. I don't think the stronger conclusion is supported.

13. I am grateful to several readers and members of audiences for this suggestion: Elizabeth Brake, Louis Larue, Erik Malmquist, Christian List, and Tweedy Flannigan have independently made it, with encouraging confidence in the prospects of this strategy.

14. Thank you, Steven Wall, for this example.

15. See Fowler (2014, 2020). Another view that attempts to combine the requirements of state neutrality and perfectionism toward children is implicit in Brighouse and Swift (2014), who believe that parents are morally responsible for the well-being of children *qua* children.

16. It may be for this reason that both Schouten (2019) and Fowler (2020) seem to assume that their arguments concerning a tension between the GDL and children's acquisition of autonomy require parents to abstain from engaging in a GDL. By contrast, I don't reach this conclusion.

## REFERENCES

Allen, Anita. 2008. "Rationalising Oppression." *Journal of Power* 1 (1): 51–65.

Alstott, Anne. 2004. *No Exit: What Parents Owe Their Children and What Society Owes Parents*. Oxford: Oxford University Press.

Baker, John. 2008. "All Things Considered, Should Feminists Embrace Basic Income?" *Basic Income Studies* 3 (3).

Beard, Mary. 2017. *Women and Power. A Manifesto*. London: Profile Books.

Benjamin, Jessica. 1988. *The Bonds of Love: Psychoanalysis, Feminism, and the Problem of Domination*. New York: Pantheon Books.

Brake, Elizabeth. 2010. *Minimizing Marriage*. Oxford: Oxford University Press.

Brake, Elizabeth. 2013. "Rereading Rawls on Self-Respect: Feminism, Family Law, and the Social Bases of Self-Respect." In *Feminist Interpretations of Rawls*, ed. Ruth Abbey. University Park: Penn State University Press.

Brighouse, Harry, and Adam Swift. 2014. *Family Values*. Princeton: Princeton University Press.

Brownstein, Michael. 2019. "Implicit Bias." *Stanford Encyclopedia of Philosophy*, ed. Edward N. Zalta, https://plato.stanford.edu/archives/fall2019/entries/implicit-bias

Chambers, Clare. 2004. "Are Breast Implants Better than Female Genital Mutilation? Autonomy, Gender Equality and Nussbaum's Political Liberalism." *Critical Review of International Social and Political Philosophy* 7 (3): 1–33.

Chambers, Clare. 2008. *Sex, Culture, and Justice: The Limits of Choice*. University Park: Penn State University Press.

Clayton, Matthew. 2006. *Justice and Legitimacy in Upbringing*. Oxford: Oxford University Press.

Clayton, Matthew. Forthcoming. *Independence for Children*. Oxford: Oxford University Press.

Cohen, G. A. 1999. "On the Currency of Egalitarian Justice." *Ethics* 99 (4): 906–44.

Dinnerstein, Dorothy. 1976. *The Mermaid and the Minotaur: Sexual Arrangements and Human Malaise*. New York: Harper & Row.

Fowler, Tim. 2014. "Perfectionism for Children, Anti-perfectionism for Adults." *Canadian Journal of Philosophy* 44: 305–23.

Fowler, Tim. 2020. *Liberalism, Childhood and Justice: Ethical Issues in Upbringing*. Bristol: Bristol University Press.

Fraser, Nancy. 1994. "After the Family Wage." *Political Theory* 22 (4): 591–618.

Gheaus, Anca. 2012. "Gender Justice." *Journal of Ethics & Social Philosophy* 6 (1): 1–24.

Gheaus, Anca. 2020. "The Feminist Argument against Supporting Care." *Journal of Practical Ethics* 8 (1): 1–27.

Gheaus, Anca. 2023. "Feminism without 'Gender Identity.'" *Politics, Philosophy & Economics* 22 (1): 31–54.

Gheaus, Anca. 2024. "Enabling Children to Learn from Religions while Respecting Their Rights: Against Monopolies of Influence." *Journal of Philosophy of Education* 58 (1): 120–27.

Goodin, Robert, J. M. Rice, A. Parpo, and L. Eriksson. 2008. *Discretionary Time: A New Measure of Freedom*. Cambridge: Cambridge University Press.

Gornick, Janet, and Marcia Meyers. 2003. *Families That Work: Policies for Reconciling Parenthood and Employment*. New York: Russell Sage Foundation.

Hartley, Christie, and Lori Watson. 2018. *Equal Citizenship and Public Reason: A Feminist Political Liberalism*. Oxford: Oxford University Press.

Kittay, Eva. 1999. *Love's Labor: Essays on Women, Equality, and Dependency*. New York: Routledge.

Lippert-Rasmussen, Kasper. 2011. "'We Are All Different': Statistical Discrimination and the Right to be Treated as an Individual." *Journal of Ethics* 15: 47–59.

Lloyd, Sharon. 1995. "Situating a Feminist Criticism of John Rawls's Political Liberalism." *Loyola of Los Angeles Law Review* 28: 1319–44.

Manne, Kate, 2017. *Down Girl: The Logic of Misogyny*. Oxford: Oxford University Press.

Mikkola, Mari. 2017. "Feminist Perspectives on Sex and Gender." *Stanford Encyclopedia of Philosophy*. First published May 12, 2008; substantive revision, January 18, 2022. Available at https://plato.stanford.edu/archives/sum2024/entries/feminism-gender/

Mill, John Stuart. [1869] 1994. *Subjection of Women*. London: Longmans, Green, Reader, and Dyer.
Munoz-Darde, Veronique. 1999. "Is the Family to Be Abolished Then?" *Proceedings of the Aristotelian Society* 99 (1): 37–56.
Neufeld, Blain. 2009. "Coercion, the Basic Structure, and the Family." *Journal of Social Philosophy* 40: 37–54.
Okin, Susan Moller. 1989. *Justice, Gender, and the Family*. New York: Basic Books.
Okin, Susan Moller. 1994. "Political Liberalism, Justice and Gender." *Ethics* 23 (105): 23–43.
Parker, Rozsika. 2005. *Torn in Two: The Experience of Maternal Ambivalence*. London: Virago.
Quong, Jonathan. 2011. *Liberalism without Perfection*. Oxford: Oxford University Press.
Rawls, John. 1997. "The Idea of Public Reason Revisited." *University of Chicago Law Review* 64 (3): 765–808.
Rawls, John. 2005. *Political Liberalism*, expanded ed. New York: Columbia University Press.
Richards, Norvin. 2018. "Raising a Child with Respect." *Journal of Applied Philosophy* 35: 90–104.
Rose, Julie. 2016. *Free Time*. Princeton: Princeton University Press.
Schouten, Gina. 2019. *Liberalism, Neutrality, and the Gendered Division of Labor*. Oxford: Oxford University Press.
Shiffrin, Seana. 2004. "Race and Ethnicity, Race, Labor, and the Fair Equality of Opportunity Principle." *Fordham Law Review* 72: 1643–75.
Spencer, Steven, Claude Steele, and Diane Quinn. 1999. "Stereotype Threat and Women's Math Performance." *Journal of Experimental Social Psychology* 35 (1): 4–28.
Steinpreis, Rhea, Katie Anders, and Dawn Ritzke. 1999. "The Impact of Gender on the Review of the Curricula Vitae of Job Applicants and Tenure Candidates: A National Empirical Study." *Sex Roles* 41: 509–28.
Stricker, Lawrence, and William Ward. 2004. "Stereotype Threat, Inquiring about Test Takers' Ethnicity and Gender, and Standardized Test Performance." *Journal of Applied Social Psychology* 34: 665–93.

CHAPTER 3

# Democratic Equality and Basic Social Institutions

Alexander Kaufman

John Rawls describes a society whose institutions are effectively regulated by the principles of its public conception of justice as *a well-ordered society*. The institutions of a well-ordered society must, in Rawls's theory, satisfy a set of demanding requirements. These requirements operate *jointly* and together define the substance of Rawls's conception of social justice (*justice as fairness*). Since these requirements apply collectively "as a unit" (TJ[1] 73, JAF[2] 46n10[3]), no single criterion determines the nature of just social institutions. Rather, just institutions are the product of a complex process of reasoning.

Against a background of social arrangements that guarantee the protection of basic liberties, institutions that satisfy the requirements of justice as fairness must ensure the provision of a basic social minimum, guarantee real equal economic and social opportunity, and require that remaining inequalities in the distribution of social and economic goods are to everyone's advantage. Rawls emphasizes that each of these requirements interacts with and qualifies the character and proper application of the other requirements. A set of institutions that satisfies these requirements realizes the principles of democratic equality and—Rawls argues—generates social conditions that are well designed to realize a social ideal of reciprocity. Such a social arrangement ensures to each person real freedom to choose what form of life to lead, but also requires that each person be responsible for generating his or her own just share of social goods.

The form of reasoning that is to govern the process of designing institutions for a well-ordered society under justice as fairness remains incompletely understood. Even after forty-five years of careful study, the literature of distributive justice has yet to provide a clear specification of the institutions of a well-ordered society under justice as fairness or of the process of reasoning that could define such a set of institutions. In this chapter, I attempt to clarify both the underlying justification and the general structure of Rawls's account of just institutions. First, I discuss Rawls's general approach to moral and political justification. Second, I discuss the nature of institutional arrangements that satisfy the joint requirements of Rawls's principles of distributive justice under ideal conditions.

## Rawls and Contractualist Justification

Rawls designs his approach to moral and political justification to be sensitive to a wide range of considerations relevant to moral judgment. His approach therefore contrasts sharply with influential consequentialist approaches to political judgment that focus narrowly on one kind of information—the kind of value associated with states of affairs to be realized in the future. Consequentialist approaches assume that moral action should be designed to realize certain states of affairs. These states of affairs are the primary bearers of value, and moral reasoning tells us to realize valuable states and to prevent the occurrence of states of affairs that minimize such value. According to this view, the value of an action is always determined by the value of its consequences.[4]

Contractualists such as Rawls reject such a consequentialist account of moral value and argue that many moral considerations relevant to the justification of the choice to perform a particular act concern not the desirability of the consequences but rather the eligibility of reasons relating to the act (TJ 509). In particular, as Amartya Sen notes, agency considerations constitute relevant reasons that consequentialist theories tend to overlook.[5] The state of affairs in which Brutus has killed Caesar, for example, is morally distinct from a state of affairs in which Caesar has died from natural causes. A moral theory that ignores distinctions of this type, Sen argues, misdirects moral judgment.

When Rawls writes that "justification is a matter of many considerations, of everything fitting together in one coherent view" (TJ 507), then, he is offering a precise criticism of consequentialist approaches to moral reasoning. Such approaches assume the authority of basic moral principles requiring pursuit of a "best" outcome defined in terms of utility, preference satisfaction, or some other measure of well-being. As Rawls notes, however, "there are great obstacles to maintaining that [such principles] are necessarily true, or even to explaining what is meant by this. . . . There is no set of conditions or first principles that can be plausibly suited to be necessary or definitive of morality and thereby especially suited to carry the burden of justification" (TJ 506). A plausible approach to moral justification must avoid relying on the truth of postulated principles, and must instead "look for possible bases of agreement where none seem to exist" (TJ 509).

T. M. Scanlon offers the following example to illustrate the practical significance of this distinction between consequentialist views of moral reasoning and an approach that focuses on the eligibility of a wider range of reasons relating to an act or policy. Suppose that a consequentialist assumes that the reasons to prevent murder consist of the need to avoid disutility associated with two kinds of undesirable consequences: (i) the disutility of the occurrence of a death, and (ii) the special intrinsic disutility of the occurrence of a murder. According to such a view, the value of preventing a murder will necessarily outweigh the value of preventing an accidental death, since the combined disutility of the occurrence of a death *plus* the occurrence of a murder would necessarily outweigh the single source of disutility deriving from the occurrence of a merely accidental death.[6]

Such a perspective, however, presents an implausible view of the bases of moral judgment. Suppose that the prospective murder victim is terminally ill, while the prospective accident victim is robustly healthy. Any number of reasons other than the intrinsic badness of murder might be relevant to moral judgment, but the consequentialist approach will minimize or disregard these reasons. The view that moral judgment must be determined exclusively by the value or disvalue of states of affairs thus appears to misrepresent the structure of moral judgment (see Scanlon 1998, 79–87).

A more attractive approach would identify and respond to the various eligible reasons bearing on an action. To achieve this goal, contractualist approaches assess moral and basic political questions by bringing all identifiable relevant reasons to bear on moral judgment. The constructivist form of contractualism—familiar from the social contract tradition—designs a decision procedure that represents the various relevant reasons in structural features of the decision procedure. The task of moral reasoners, in employing this decision procedure, is to explore and articulate the practical implications of demonstrably relevant reasons.

Rawls's constructivism is notable for its representation of moral propositions in the structure of the decision procedure employed. The decision procedure that Rawls employs in *A Theory of Justice* represents the proposition that *justice must be impartial* by requiring that the choosers of moral principles must form their judgments behind a veil of ignorance that filters out all information regarding their special interests, so that choices formed in the procedure literally cannot be affected by information that could lead to a self-interested judgment. Similarly, Rawls's procedure represents the idea that *justice must respect the inviolability of the person* by assigning to each chooser the power to veto any judgment or choice proposed by other choosers within the choice process; this veto power gives each chooser the power to protect all of his or her fundamental interests, thus ensuring that all judgments formed will respect the inviolability of the person. Finally, Rawls's procedure represents the considered judgment that *justice must not be arbitrary* by depriving the choosers of all information that is "irrelevant from the standpoint of justice" (TJ 17)—thus ensuring that arbitrary factors do not affect the process of judgment.

The employment of a decision procedure that represents relevant considerations in its structure exemplifies the character of the contractualist approach to reasoning. Rather than aiming to maximize some value identified as "the good," contractualist moral theory aims to bring relevant reasons fully to bear. Rawls's justification of the principles of justice therefore develops, not an account of the *value* of goods or social surplus to be realized through application of the principles, but rather an account of the reasons that require the adoption of standards to regulate basic social institutions.

The reasons relevant to the justification of such standards relate to the protection of the fundamental interests of citizens. Rawls identifies two sets of fundamental interests corresponding to the "two coordinate roles"[7] of the basic structure of society: (i) securing equal basic liberties, and (ii) providing background institutions that secure social and economic justice (TJ 53).[8] In addition, the choosers consider the priority ranking that a proposed conception of justice establishes between conflicting claims grounded in these interests. Rawls emphasizes that a conception of justice is defined not merely by the principles it contains, but by the priority rules that determine the relative weight to be assigned to the requirements of each principle.[9] The priority that his conception establishes among citizens' fundamental interests is central to Rawls's argument that choosers in the original position would prefer that conception to utilitarianism.[10] Thus, a satisfactory conception of justice is satisfactory because of the relation that it establishes between content and structure.[11]

## Institutions of the Basic Structure under Ideal Conditions

Taking into account the full set of relevant reasons, what features does Rawls's theory of distributive justice require in just social institutions? What set of social and economic institutions will ensure the value of liberty, guarantee real equal opportunity, and secure fairness in the distribution of goods? Rawls argues that the social conditions that could jointly satisfy these conditions are to be determined by the joint application of his two principles of justice. The social minimum ensures the value of liberty interests, while the two requirements of the second principle—fair equality of opportunity and the difference principle, operating together as a unit—ensure equal opportunity and fairness in distribution. The requirements of fair equality of opportunity are particularly significant, requiring an effective guarantee that persons with equal abilities and motivation will enjoy equal prospects of success.

In this section, I first provide a sketch of the scope of the requirements of fair equality of opportunity, and of the form of reasoning about just institutions required by the joint application of the principle of fair equality of opportunity and the difference principle. In subsection 1, I discuss the scope of the requirements of fair equality of opportunity. In subsection 2, I discuss Rawls's claim that the principles apply as a unit. In subsection 3, I discuss Rawls's integrated approach to reasoning about distributive justice.

*(1) The Scope of Fair Equality of Opportunity.* The principle of fair equality of opportunity requires that persons "with similar abilities and skills should have similar life chances" (TJ 63). The principle requires not merely the enforcement of legal protections of formal equal opportunity, but "that all should have a fair chance" to attain success. The principle attempts to ensure that each member of society may enjoy the same effective opportunity to compete for advantageous positions by ensuring access to the services needed to ensure that each individual "acquire[s] the cultural knowledge and skills" (TJ 63) to ensure equal opportunity to compete for such positions. The life chances "of those with the same abilities and aspirations" (TJ 63), Rawls argues, should not be determined by their starting position and initial set of social endowments.

Rawls assigns the highest priority to "maintaining equal opportunities of education for all" (TJ 63). A just society must ensure "equal chances of education and culture for persons similarly endowed and motivated" (TJ 243, 245; see JAF 44). Initially, in fact, Rawls's discussion of the principle of fair equality of opportunity might seem to suggest that access to education constitutes the sole substantive guarantee required to assure equal opportunity. The discussion of means to realize the principle in section 12 of *A Theory of Justice*, for example, discusses only education as a policy tool. Rawls, however, clearly establishes that the guarantees under the principle are far more extensive. First, the fair opportunity principle requires guaranteed access to the training needed to give persons from less advantaged backgrounds the skills to compete effectively for advantageous positions (TJ 270). Fair equality of opportunity ensures that "many more people receiv[e] the benefits of education and training" (TJ 270) in order to secure "open competition between . . . greater numbers of the well-trained and better educated" (JAF 67). In addition, equal opportunity requires equal access to medical care: "provision for medical care . . . to meet the needs of citizens as free and equal . . . falls under the general means necessary to underwrite fair equality of opportunity" (JAF 174). Special provisions of family law are necessary to ensure that "the burden of bearing, raising, and educating children does not fall more heavily on women, thereby undermining their fair equality of opportunity" (JAF 11). To ensure that the recipients of education, training, and other services have the effective opportunity to employ their skills, the stabilization branch must aim to ensure "reasonably full employment in the sense that those who want work can find it and the free choice of occupation" (TJ 244).

While these guarantees are generally viewed as describing the full scope of the requirements of fair equality of opportunity, Rawls makes clear that those requirements extend far beyond the limited set of guarantees that he discusses explicitly. Rawls provides only a sketchy explicit account of the principle and its requirements, he notes, because he assumes that "the elements of this framework are familiar enough" (TJ 63). The opportunity principle, he assumes, embodies liberal notions of egalitarian justice discussed in the work of nineteenth and early twentieth century liberal philosophers and theorists such as Henry Sidgwick and R. H. Tawney. For a more thorough account of the nature and necessary conditions of equal opportunity, he refers the reader to specific passages in Sidgwick, Tawney, and Bernard Williams (TJ 63n11). An accurate understanding of the scope and substance of the guarantees required under the principle therefore requires an examination of these passages, which Rawls incorporates by reference.

In discussing the guarantee of equal opportunity in education, Rawls cites a passage from Sidgwick's *The Method of Ethics* in which Sidgwick argues that "ideal justice" would require the removal of "the inequalities that are attributable to circumstances *by bringing the best education within the reach of all classes*, so that all children might have an equal opportunity of being selected for any functions for which they seem to be fit."[12] Ideal justice does not require *merely* policies to improve the quality of public schools or to provide access to private schools. Equal opportunity is not realized while the less advantaged are denied the equivalent of the "best education" that is available to the more privileged. Any set of institutions that fails to meet this standard allows arbitrary inequality of opportunity to determine the distribution of social goods and opportunities.

Tawney argues that the effects of unequal education are powerfully reinforced by unequal access to other essential goods and services that affect life chances profoundly. Tawney cites, for example, reports that a significantly larger percentage of the children of working class families than of the children of privileged families suffer from serious health problems.[13] In addition, he notes, only a small minority of these children are adequately nourished.[14] Finally, these working class children are "exposed to [environmental] conditions in which health, if not impossible, is necessarily precarious."[15] Such disparities in access to healthcare, adequate nourishment, and safe environments, Tawney argues, "are more powerful as instrument[s] of social stratification even than the difference of income of which they are the consequence."[16]

Such disparities in healthcare, nutrition, and environment reinforce the enormous disparity in educational opportunity that exists between children of the working class and children of the privileged classes. Working class children are educated in environments "which would not be tolerated for an instant in the schools attended by the well-to-do."[17] The defective quality of the early years of education provided to this class is reinforced by their lack of access to higher education: "the proportion of children leaving the elementary schools who enter . . . secondary schools is, in England and Wales as a whole, less than one-seventh, and in some areas less than one-tenth."[18] Thus, working class children "end their education just at the age when their powers are beginning to develop."[19] To the extent that similar conditions in contemporary societies undermine the ability of disadvantaged students to develop their abilities, those societies fail to realize equal opportunity.

The passage Rawls cites from Williams's paper "The Idea of Equality" provides the clearest account of the full scope of the requirements of fair equality of opportunity. Equal opportunity, Williams argues, is best understood as requiring "that a limited good shall in fact be allocated on grounds which do not *a priori* exclude any section of those that desire it."[20] A proper understanding of equal opportunity therefore requires that "people from all sections of society have an equal chance of satisfying" the necessary conditions for the acquisition of any particular social good.[21] If education at an expensive elite school is a necessary condition of entry into certain careers (e.g., medicine, law, investment banking), Williams argues, a society that allows elite schools to allocate positions in their classes on the basis of ability to pay fails the test of equal opportunity. Under such an arrangement, children who are not born into wealthy families will clearly not "have an equal chance of satisfying" the necessary conditions of achieving a particular social good—the opportunity to compete for advantageous positions.

If children from privileged homes have a greater opportunity to succeed than children from less advantaged homes because of qualities specifically associated with privileged homes, then the society fails to satisfy the requirements of equal opportunity. The difference in opportunity to succeed is simply the product of "environmental factors" whose effects could be eliminated or reduced by "imaginative social reform."[22] To give two persons equal opportunity, then, "involves *regarding their conditions*, where curable, *as themselves part of what is done*" to the persons:[23] "Their identity, for these purposes, does not include their curable environment, which is itself unequal and a contributor of inequality."[24] A social system fails to secure equal opportunity if the distribution of a social good is unequal and those who receive less advantageous shares "are under a disadvantage which could be removed by further reform or social action."[25] A society that fails to undertake the necessary reforms, Williams argues, "falls short of equality of opportunity."[26] In incorporating Williams's account of equal opportunity by reference as an account of the concept of equal opportunity that is "familiar enough," Rawls indicates that fair equality of opportunity, if fully implemented, would require "imaginative social reform" to address *any* deficits of education or training and any inequalities of access to healthcare or advantageous environmental factors that might result in unequal ability to compete for advantageous positions.

Rawls's understanding of the requirements of equal opportunity is far from limited to the requirement that the government must attempt to eliminate overt discrimination and reduce disparities between the quality of education available to the privileged and the less advantaged. Rather, a society fails to achieve fair equality of opportunity *if any person or group suffers from a deficit in skills, education, or other capacity required to compete effectively for a desirable position, and that deficit (i) is the product of environmental factors and (ii) could be removed by social policy*. Under this standard, more effective and extensive versions of the Head Start program, manpower training programs such as those authorized under CETA (the Comprehensive Education and Training Act), manpower policies of the sort pursued by Sweden and Denmark, housing subsidies, and universal health insurance—as well as any other programs required in order to compensate for deficits in education, skill, or capacity to compete—are all potential elements of a set of requirements of equal opportunity that must be implemented *before* distributional issues under the difference principle are to be considered.

The passages from Sidgwick, Tawney, and Williams provide information that is essential to adequately understand the requirements of fair equality of opportunity. The passage from Sidgwick establishes that fair equality of opportunity imposes a demanding standard of equality of educational opportunity. The passage from Tawney suggests the wide range of environmental factors to which the principle applies. And the passage from Williams establishes the full scope of the obligation to equalize opportunity under the principle—if a deficit in capacity to compete is the product of an environmental factor, a *just* government *must* employ imaginative social policy to anticipate and address that environmental impediment to equal opportunity.

*(2) The Principles Apply as a Unit.* Precisely what form of reasoning does Rawls recommend when he emphasizes that fair equality of opportunity and the difference principle must apply as a unit? The integration of the principles relates to both their meaning and their implementation. Rawls argues that the two principles, taken together, express an understanding of *genuine* equal opportunity in which the difference principle transforms both the operation of the fair opportunity principle and the proper understanding of its aims.

Implementation of the fair opportunity principle, Rawls asserts, ensures that the system of cooperation realized is characterized by *a form* of pure procedural justice (TJ 76). Full implementation of the fair opportunity principle, in the context of a background political culture in which basic liberties are secured, ensures that social endowments do not determine life chances, so that opportunities are distributed fairly, all enjoy free choice of occupation, and economic institutions in general satisfy the fundamental requirements of fairness. Thus, a certain conception of pure procedural justice is realized once the fair opportunity principle has been implemented.

A conception of pure procedural justice will not be *acceptable*, however, unless other conditions are satisfied so that the resulting distribution of social goods is just, whatever it happens to be. As Rawls notes in section 13, while a conception of distributive justice that combines the requirements of the principle of fair equality of opportunity and the principle of efficiency secures pure procedural justice "to some extent at least," such a conception "still leaves too much to social and natural contingency" (TJ 69). To address these remaining contingent influences, it is necessary to ensure that the distribution realized also satisfies the difference principle. In imposing this requirement, Rawls addresses two concerns. First, as he notes, implementation of the fair opportunity principle in combination merely with the principle of efficiency will allow arbitrary factors—in particular, the distribution of natural endowments—to influence life chances decisively. Such an interpretation of the two principles, then, fails "to mitigate the influence of . . . contingencies . . . on distributive shares" (TJ 63). Second, Rawls is concerned to ensure that "the democratic equality interpretation of the two principles[27] will not lead to a meritocratic society" (TJ 91; see TJ 86[28]). In a meritocracy, the arbitrary distribution of a particular natural endowment—talent—determines or significantly influences life chances. A meritocracy therefore allows natural contingency to play a large and unjustifiable role in determining the distribution of social goods and opportunities. In addition, the existence of conditions of meritocracy encourages an unattractive social understanding of equal opportunity: "[e]qual opportunity [merely] means an equal chance to leave the less fortunate behind in the personal quest for influence and social position" (TJ 91). The view that distributive justice requires merely a meritocracy, therefore, constitutes "a danger for the . . . interpretations of the principles of justice" (TJ 91), since a meritocratic view understands equal opportunity to require nothing more than opportunity to compete for individual advantage in a zero-sum economy.

Rawls argues that the two principles of justice as fairness, taken together, express an understanding of *genuine* equal opportunity in which the difference principle transforms both the operation of the principle of fair opportunity and the proper understanding of its aims. While the fair opportunity principle focuses primarily on addressing inequalities of opportunity at every level of income and wealth, the factors that justify the difference principle justify the conclusion that "to provide genuine equality of opportunity, society must give more attention to those with fewer native assets and to those born into the less favorable social positions" (TJ 86). The difference principle therefore requires that in providing education and other services to ensure equal opportunity, society should devote more attention to the needs of the least advantaged. Since "inequalities of birth and natural endowments are undeserved," Rawls argues, "greater resources should be spent on the education" of the less well endowed and less fortunate, "at least over a certain time of life" (TJ 86).

In addition, the difference principle "transforms the aims of society" (TJ 91) in a manner that fundamentally changes public understanding of the goals and meaning of equal opportunity. Equal opportunity no longer means equal opportunity "to leave the less fortunate behind" (TJ 91). The difference principle "transforms the aims of the basic structure so that the total scheme of institutions no longer emphasizes social efficiency and technocratic values" (TJ 87) to the exclusion of reciprocity and fraternity. In particular, the difference principle's requirement of priority for the claims of the least advantaged to receive education and other services under the fair opportunity principle "expresses a conception of reciprocity" (TJ 88) implicit in the difference principle's transformation of the notion of opportunity (see TJ 88). Similarly, the difference principle qualifies the fair opportunity principle to ensure that the least advantaged realize an adequate share of the social bases of self-respect. Policies designed to enhance opportunity must also aim to secure conditions in which the least advantaged are able to realize "the confident sense of their own worth" (TJ 92). To facilitate the realization of such a sense, the difference principle requires not only that the education provided under fair equality of opportunity must be directed first to the least advantaged, but that such education not be limited to functional training judged according to the "return as estimated in productive trained abilities" (TJ 92); furthermore, the value of such training should not "be assessed solely in terms of economic efficiency" (TJ 87). Rather, resources for education must be allotted "according to their worth in enriching the personal and social life of citizens" (TJ 92). Each citizen must enjoy equal opportunity with all others to acquire the culture and knowledge necessary to permit each to participate equally in society's social and cultural life.

In this context, while all enjoy equal opportunity to prosper, all also "gain from their good fortune only on terms that improve the situation of those who have lost out" (TJ 87). The difference principle thus provides an interpretation not only of the notion of reciprocity, but of the principle of fraternity—"the idea of not wanting to have greater advantages unless this is to the benefit of others who are less well off" (TJ 90). Public affirmation of the second principle thus constitutes affirmation of the notion of fraternity. In acknowledging the conception, the more favored acknowledge that they "are not to gain merely because they are more gifted," but rather "in ways that help the less fortunate as well" (TJ 87).

*(3) Just Institutions.* The structure of Rawls's account of distributive justice is clearly ascertainable. First, the liberty principle's guarantee of basic needs requires the provision of a social minimum as a constitutional essential (PL 228–29). Constitutional essentials are elements of the basic structure that "specif[y] and [secure] citizens' equal basic rights and liberties" (PL 229; see TJ 243). Rawls, in fact, seriously considers preceding the liberty principle with a lexically prior principle requiring the guarantee of a social minimum: the liberty principle "may be preceded by a lexically prior principle requiring that basic needs be met" (JAF 44n7).

The fair opportunity principle then applies to require guarantees of employment, free choice of occupation, "similar chances of education and culture for persons similarly motivated" (TJ 245), real equal access to high-quality education and training, all other forms of "imaginative social reform"[29] required to ensure real equal opportunity, and policing of the conduct of firms to prevent "restrictions and barriers to the more desirable positions" (TJ 243). State institutions must aim to achieve "reasonably full employment" (TJ 244) so that "the free choice of employment . . . [is] supported by strong effective demand" (TJ 244). They must also offer fair equality in education (TJ 247); policies providing job training (TJ 270); medical care (JAF 67); and protections designed to ensure that "the burden of bearing, raising, and educating children does not fall more heavily on women" (JAF 11). Such policies would presumably include subsidized jobs, apprenticeship programs, public service employment, case management, and the remaining repertoire of programs associated with labor policy in the United States and Western Europe. Finally, state institutions must keep the price system competitive and prevent the "formation of unreasonable market power" (TJ 244) that might allow privileged economic elites to monopolize opportunity.

The economic relations established under such institutions would, however, still allow arbitrary factors to exercise an undue influence over life chances and might establish conditions that could lead to a meritocratic society. Basic economic institutions must also, therefore, satisfy the difference principle, which ensures that (i) institutions assign priority to realizing opportunity for the least advantaged persons; (ii) opportunity is understood in terms of the chance to realize equal citizenship, not the opportunity to leave others behind; and (iii) the inequalities permitted to the more fortunate under circumstances that satisfy the preceding conditions are to everyone's advantage.

While a conventional view has assumed that the difference principle primarily employs income transfers to perform these functions, Rawls emphasizes that the difference principle operates to a significant extent to make "all-purpose means available to the least advantaged members of society to achieve their ends" (PL 326). Like the fair opportunity principle, then, the difference principle creates conditions within which persons are free to pursue their own ends and have the capacity to exploit that freedom. The difference principle interacts with the fair opportunity principle by (i) requiring that policies designed to realize equal opportunity assign priority to the needs of the least advantaged, but also (ii) providing assistance in the form of all-purpose means designed to improve the capacity of the less fortunate to realize equal opportunity (not primarily in the form of income assistance). In addition, as discussed above, the difference principle requires that assistance to the less advantaged under the fair opportunity principle must provide opportunity to obtain culture and education in the liberal arts, not merely training that generates skills rewarded in the market.

The conventional understanding of the requirements of justice as fairness thus represents an unacceptable distortion of Rawls's theory. According to the conventional view, a well-ordered society must (i) secure basic liberties, (ii) prevent overt discrimination, (iii) ensure that the school system is designed "to even out class barriers" (TJ 63), and then (iv) maximize the position of the least advantaged through tax and transfer policy. According to this view, Rawls's theory requires that officers of the state must determine in advance the distribution of social goods required by justice and must use tax and transfer policy to secure that distribution. The conventional view, that is, presents Rawls's account of distributive justice as a theory designed primarily to allocate "a given collection of goods . . . among definite individuals" (TJ 77). This picture bears very little resemblance to the requirements of justice as fairness.

Rawls explicitly rejects the idea that a centralized decision process should determine the shares of goods that individuals receive. Rather, he argues for a conception of justice under which the justice of a distribution "cannot be judged at all apart from the claims (entitlements) of individuals earned by their efforts within the fair system of cooperation" (JAF 50; see TJ 76) so that "what a person is entitled to depends on what he does" (TJ 74). A just distribution cannot be identified until persons have actually participated in the market and have generated their legitimate claims.

The conventional view that justice as fairness requires that social institutions secure a just distribution primarily through tax and transfer policy misrepresents Rawls's theory precisely because the conventional view describes justice as fairness as an *allocative* conception of justice—a conception that aims simply to divide a given collection of goods "among definite individuals with known desires and needs" (TJ 77). Rawls *rejects* allocative approaches to theorizing justice "as incompatible with the fundamental idea by which justice as fairness is organized: the idea of society as a fair system of cooperation organized over time" (JAF 50). Allocative justice applies, Rawls asserts, in conditions in which (i) the goods to be allocated are not the product of the individuals who are to receive the goods, and (ii) "there are no prior claims on the things to be distributed . . . [since] [t]he collection is not the product of these individuals" (TJ 77). Rawls's theory, in contrast, requires that "[a] distribution cannot be judged in isolation from . . . [consideration of] what individuals have done in good faith in light of established expectations" (TJ 76). To paraphrase Robert Nozick, the conventional understanding of Rawls's view presents justice as fairness as a theory defined by end-state principles—principles that consider only the distribution of goods when assessing the justice of a situation.[30] In fact, however, justice as fairness assigns central significance to historical information: determination of the justice of present claims must—in Rawls's account of distributive justice—assign decisive importance to claims of entitlement that have been generated in the past. Like Nozick's theory, as Rawls notes, justice as fairness "give[s] a fundamental role to . . . pure adjusted procedural justice. It follows that neither of these doctrines are end-state views."[31]

In rejecting allocative conceptions of justice, Rawls presents a theory of distributive justice that is designed to achieve a *form of social relations* that realizes an ideal of equality. Rawls thus anticipates Samuel Scheffler's argument that the most compelling account of distributive justice will be an account "whose source in an ideal of genuine social equality can be vividly and convincingly demonstrated."[32] Scheffler intends to criticize theories of egalitarian justice that present equality as an "essentially distributive ideal."[33] Such theories, Scheffler argues, support judgments inconsistent with reliable moral intuitions. For example, some theories of equality that present equality as a distributive ideal assign decisive importance to individual responsibility for disadvantage and would therefore accept the conclusion that an indigent defendant should be denied access to legal counsel if her inability to afford such counsel is "the result of poor financial planning on her part."[34] To avoid such implausible conclusions, Scheffler argues that egalitarians need to connect their arguments regarding justice in the distribution of goods to a plausible ideal of equality.

The value of anchoring distributive justice in an ideal of equality, Scheffler argues, is that such an approach captures the normative ideal of equality that the notion of a society of equals represents. The normative ideal of justice that grounds any acceptable account of distributive justice requires not mere equality in the distribution of goods, but also that relations among members of society "should have a certain structure and character."[35] An acceptable conception of distributive justice, then, must—in addition to providing an account of justice in distribution—provide an account of this structure.

Rawls's account of justice addresses Scheffler's concern. It goes beyond an account of justice in distribution and sets out a normative ideal of justice that incorporates an account of the character of relations that are appropriate for members of society viewed as free and equal moral beings. While the fair opportunity and difference principles determine the nature of the just institutions within which individuals will generate a just distribution of goods, the liberty principle ensures that the basic rights and liberties of citizens enjoy full and unconditional protection. The liberty principle performs important work in realizing the idea—implicit in social contract—that in a just social order, the laws must be incapable of doing wrong to anyone. In addition, the second principle—in transforming social goals and social understandings of the meaning of success—ensures that all persons are guaranteed equal citizenship, not merely equal opportunity to leave others behind in a zero-sum form of economic competition. Thus, as Scheffler notes, Rawls's theory "shows how. . . . a plausible form of distributive egalitarianism can be anchored in a more general conception of equality as a social and political ideal."[36]

Scheffler's conclusion—that the more general conception of equality provided by Rawls's theory provides a necessary anchor for discussions of egalitarian justice—was, in essence, the view that resolved a controversy in the egalitarian literature of the 1970s involving Bernard Williams, Robert Nozick, and Amy Gutmann. In "The Idea of Equality," Williams argued that the idea of equality, properly explicated, requires that people should be treated alike under relevantly similar circumstances. Egalitarian justice therefore requires that for every difference in the way people are treated, some general ground of differentiation must be given. Such a ground will not justify unequal treatment unless it shows why the stated basis for unequal treatment (e.g., race, gender, class) is relevant to the distribution of goods. The requirements of equality are satisfied only if a relevant reason can be provided that justifies differential treatment.

Williams's application of this standard, however, exposes a weak point in his argument. Applied to the sphere of healthcare, Williams suggests, his approach requires that inequality in the provision of medical services can be justified only if such inequality is a necessary element of a policy that reduces ill health more effectively than a policy that does not require such unequal provision. It is "a necessary truth," Williams claims, that "the proper ground of distribution of medical care is ill health."[37] According to this view, then, any argument offered to justify the unequal distribution of medical care must demonstrate that the unequal distribution effectively serves the goal of reducing ill health. The relevant reason capable of justifying inequalities in the provision of healthcare, Williams suggests, can be identified simply through an assessment of the character of the social practice of medicine.

In response to this argument, Nozick notes that the process of identifying a relevant reason to regulate a particular practice—in Williams's approach—is more dependent than Williams concedes on assumptions regarding the character of the practice. For example, Williams asserts that it is "a necessary truth" that the character of the practice of medicine requires the distribution of medical services on the grounds of ill health. But suppose, Nozick suggests, that medical services are also distributed through another social practice—"schmoctoring"—in which the relevant reason for distributing medical services is profit.[38] If both practices exist, Nozick inquires, how could one justify the claim that the only relevant reason capable of justifying inequalities in the provision of medical services is ill health? On what grounds could one justify privileging the practice of medicine over the practice of schmoctoring?

While Nozick's critique of Williams initially appeared to present a strong case against Williams's attempt to generate precise practical extensions of the idea of equality, it is more plausibly viewed, as Gutmann notes, as an indictment of Williams's narrow focus on particular applications of the idea of equality without careful consideration of the concept's connection to more general social principles. The internal purposes of a practice, Gutmann notes, are often properly construed in light of broader social purposes. To provide defensible accounts of relevant reasons to regulate particular practices, Williams's account of equality must therefore be "situated within a theory of justice that reconciles these purposes when they conflict."[39]

Situating Williams's account of equality within the structure of Rawls's theory of justice would thus provide the basis for a response to Nozick's objection. Suppose an individual urgently requires a medical service that he cannot afford, and that his society's medical practitioners—who endorse the schmoctoring interpretation of their practice—refuse to provide him with the service unless he pays for it in full. If the society is in general regulated by justice as fairness, then members of that society will affirm the considered judgment that access to valuable social goods should not be determined by arbitrary factors such as level of income or wealth. In a society well ordered by justice as fairness, members of the medical profession would—on reflection—recognize that the schmoctoring interpretation of their practice as inconsistent with the considered judgments of justice that they affirm, and would therefore cooperate to generate an acceptable arrangement providing urgently needed medical services to poor patients. Rawls's account of justice thus provides the required justification for privileging the practice of medicine over the practice of schmoctoring.

More generally, a general theory of justice sets out criteria that provide the basis for assigning priority to certain interpretations of practices and thus facilitates the identification of relevant reasons that could justify or require the rectification of inequalities in distribution. The identification of relevant reasons and development of criteria of distribution based on those reasons could also ensure rejection of the view that an indigent defendant should be denied access to legal counsel because poor financial planning left her unable to afford such counsel. Thus, consideration of the Williams/Nozick controversy and Rawls's contribution to the resolution of that controversy illustrates the specific character of the contribution to ethical thought that a general theory of justice performs in regulating more specific analyses of moral questions.

## Conclusion

A fully balanced account of Rawls's conception of distributive justice must provide an account of the process of reasoning through which the two constitutive elements of Rawls's second principle—fair equality of opportunity and the difference principle—are jointly brought to bear on the problem of designing institutions for a well-ordered society. The specific character of Rawls's conception is determined not merely by the content of its constitutive principles, but also by the structural relation between these principles and the consequences of their interaction. While the two principles are ranked in lexical order, Rawls specifies that the principles operate as a unit; each principle necessarily interacts with and qualifies the character and proper operation of the other principle. Interaction between the two principles ensures that implementation of the principle of fair equality of opportunity does not establish a meritocracy; the joint operation of the principles provides the basis for a form of social life in which social institutions are constituted in a manner than abstains from exploiting the contingencies of nature and social circumstance.

The interaction between the difference principle and fair equality of opportunity transforms the aims of the basic structure so that the total scheme of institutions no longer emphasizes social efficiency to the exclusion of reciprocity and fraternity. In particular, in qualifying the requirements of the fair opportunity principle to require priority for the needs of the least advantaged, the difference principle expresses a conception of reciprocity implicit in that principle's transformation of the notion of opportunity. Similarly, the interaction between the difference principle and the fair opportunity principle ensures that the least advantaged realize an adequate share of the social bases of self-respect. The conception of distributive justice realized through the interaction of these principles, viewed as a whole, thus seems likely to "transform our perspective on the social world and to reconcile us to the dispositions of the natural order and the conditions of human life" (TJ 448).

Finally, Rawls's theory addresses the concern—expressed by Scheffler and others—that an acceptable account of egalitarian justice must go beyond an account of justice in distribution and must set out a normative ideal of justice that incorporates an account of the character of an egalitarian society. In particular, the function of the second principle in transforming social goals and social understandings of the meaning of success ensures that all persons are guaranteed equal citizenship, not merely equal opportunity to leave others behind in a zero-sum form of economic competition. Rawls's theory, as Scheffler notes, "shows how . . . a plausible form of distributive egalitarianism can be anchored in a more general conception of equality as a social and political ideal" (199).[40]

NOTES

1. John Rawls, *A Theory of Justice* (Cambridge, MA: Harvard University Press, 1999 [1971]). This work is cited in the text in parentheses and preceded by TJ.

2. John Rawls, *Justice as Fairness: A Restatement* (Cambridge, MA: Harvard University Press, 2001). This work is cited in the text in parentheses and preceded by JAF.

3. The two principles "are designed to apply in tandem and to work as a unit" (JAF 46n10).

4. See Scanlon (1998), 84.

5. "Acts are as much a part of a state of affairs as the resulting consequences and utility" (Sen 1985, 177).

6. Scanlon (1998), 83.

7. Rawls (2001), 48.

8. See Rawls (2001), 48. Rawls provides the clearest statement of this point in *Justice as Fairness: A Restatement*, when he writes that the parties in the original position act to secure the "fundamental interests [of the persons that they represent] in their freedom and equality—in the conditions adequate for the development and exercise of their moral powers and effective pursuit of their conception of the good on fair terms with others" (JAF 85).

9. "The assignment of weights is an essential and not a minor part of a conception of justice" (TJ 37).

10. The assignment of priority "beyond the calculus of social interests" to the first principle, Rawls argues, supplies the quality of justice as fairness that ensures that the choosers will recognize that that conception is "more effective than the principle of (average) utility in guaranteeing the equal basic liberties." See JAF 115.

11. Rawls emphasizes that "justification rests upon the entire conception," it is a matter "of everything fitting together into one coherent view" (TJ 507). Justice as fairness constitutes the most satisfactory conception of justice because it "combine[s] into one conception the totality of conditions that we are ready on due reflection to recognize as reasonable in our conduct with regard to one another" (TJ 514).

12. Sidgwick (1981 [1907]), 285, my emphasis.

13. Tawney (1952), 73.

14. Tawney (1952), 74.

15. Tawney (1952), 74.

16. Tawney (1952), 73–74.

17. Tawney (1952), 73.

18. Tawney (1952), 73–74.

19. Tawney (1952), 74.

20. Williams (1962), 125.

21. Williams (1962), 125.

22. Williams (1962), 127.

23. Williams (1962), 127, my emphasis.

24. Williams (1962), 127.

25. Williams (1962), 127.

26. Williams (1962), 127.
27. The *democratic equality* interpretation of Rawls's second principle combines fair equality of opportunity with the difference principle.
28. "I should like to forestall the objection to the principle of fair opportunity that it leads to a meritocratic society" (TJ 86).
29. This requirement is discussed in the preceding chapter.
30. Nozick (1974), 153–55.
31. Rawls, J. *Justice as Fairness: A Guided Tour* (unpublished ms.), 57.
32. Scheffler (2010), 207.
33. Scheffler (2010), 200.
34. Scheffler (2010), 201.
35. Scheffler (2010), 202.
36. Scheffler (2010), 199.
37. Williams (1962), 121.
38. Nozick (1974), 235.
39. Gutmann (1980), 102.
40. Scheffler (2010), 199.

## REFERENCES

Freeman, S. 2018. *Liberalism and Distributive Justice*. Oxford: Oxford University Press.
Gutmann, A. 1980. *Liberal Equality*. Cambridge: Cambridge University Press.
Nozick, R. 1974. *Anarchy, State, and Utopia*. New York: Basic Books.
Rawls, J. 1999 (1971). *A Theory of Justice* Cambridge, MA: Harvard University Press.
Rawls, J. 1996 (1993). *Political Liberalism*. New York: Columbia University Press.
Rawls, J. 2001. *Justice as Fairness: A Restatement*. Cambridge, MA: Harvard University Press.
Rawls, J. *Justice as Fairness: A Guided Tour*. Unpublished manuscript.
Roemer, J. 1994. *Egalitarian Perspectives: Essays in Philosophical Economics*. Cambridge: Cambridge University Press.
Scheffler, S. 2010. *Equality and Tradition: Questions of Value in Moral and Political Theory*. Oxford: Oxford University Press.
Tawney, R. H. 1952. *Equality*. Reprint, Totowa, NJ: Rowman & Littlefield, 1989.
Williams, B. W. 1962. "The Idea of Equality." In *Politics, Philosophy, and Society: Second Series*, ed. P. Laslett and W. G. Runciman, 110–31. Oxford: Basil Blackwell.

CHAPTER 4

# What's Left of Luck Egalitarianism?

Shlomi Segall

Is there anything left to say about luck egalitarianism? There is more than a suggestion that the topic has exhausted itself. Some have pointed to a sense of fatigue with luck egalitarianism.[1] Still, if to judge by citation numbers, things may point in the other direction. In the decade since luck egalitarianism was likened to mustard, there have been three times as many citations as in the decade prior.[2] Whatever the case, the feeling is growing that the debate about egalitarian justice has either been settled or exhausted itself.

In this chapter I shall not challenge that assessment. Instead, I want to use this space to take stock of the current status of luck egalitarianism as a theory about egalitarian justice. I want, in particular, to assess whether there are any loose ends that could be tied up at this point in time. I say "loose ends" because in a sense the critics are correct; luck egalitarianism has been extensively debated and defended. What's left, I want to concede, are a bunch of fringe questions. Still, I believe these residual questions are worth discussing, even if in a speculative and tentative manner.

Let me outline what I see as some of those questions, and allow the reader to judge for herself. It has been said that:

1. For luck egalitarians to appeal to a "second-person standpoint" (SPS) is untenable, partly because SPS is itself a deontological mechanism, and thus unsuited to explain the badness of inequality.
2. Luck-egalitarian talk of "natural" inequalities makes no sense.

3. The egalitarian conversation, imagined by the "second-person standpoint," can only ring true in a very specific social setting, such as G. A. Cohen's camping trip.
4. Luck egalitarians criticize the view known as conditional egalitarianism, and yet offer a view that is also of conditional nature.
5. Luck egalitarians offer an account of equality of opportunity pretending to be "radical," yet hide behind "value pluralism" every time it runs into trouble.
6. Luck egalitarians are harsh because they abandon caregivers and other do-gooders.
7. Luck egalitarians' reliance on a "moment" of equality of opportunity spells disproportionate, and therefore extremely harsh, burdens to individuals making choices that are only slightly different in terms of prudence.

This list is obviously not meant to be exhaustive. Still, addressing these outstanding issues could further our understanding of luck egalitarianism, its strengths, and its potential weaknesses.

## I. Luck Egalitarianism and the Second-Person Standpoint

Many defining features may separate Rawlsian justice from its bitter rival, luck egalitarianism. One of those is the common view that while the latter is an "impersonal view," the former is grounded in a "dialogical" mechanism of how persons stand vis-à-vis each other.

It may also be the case, however, that, contrary to first appearances, they have some features in common. Here is something of this sort that I have in mind. In the axiological version of luck egalitarianism, the unfairness of being worse off than another through no fault of one's own is the source of evil that makes inequality bad. To draw this out, some luck egalitarians (Temkin most notably, but also myself) allude to complaints that worse-off individuals might have against better-off individuals, and the corresponding duties that the latter might have to answer those complaints. But this second-person standpoint (SPS), some feel, is more at home in a deontological framework than an axiological one. Moreover, it is a hallmark of the rival view to luck egalitarianism, namely relational egalitarianism. After all, it is philosophers such as Elizabeth Anderson and Samuel Scheffler who look at the value of equality through the narrow prism of how each individual relates to another in a society of equals. It is for people like

Anderson and Scheffler to imagine conversations between different members of the political community, and specifically the well-to-do versus the trodden-upon. It is that imaginary conversation that generates relational egalitarianism's all-too-powerful emphasis on oppression and subjugation, which is so conspicuously missing from the more *cosmic* luck egalitarianism.

There are at least two types of complaints about luck egalitarians alluding to SPS embedded here that I would like to address. Some critics have raised concerns about the *content* of that complaint, whereas others have raised concerns about the overall legitimacy of alluding to the SPS. Let me take those in turn.

### *The Content of Egalitarian Complaints*

Some critics may express puzzlement over the very nature and content of the egalitarian complaints and the corresponding obligations they give rise to. Specifically, do individuals have complaints about being worse off with regard to some index of *social* goods, or do they also have a claim when disadvantaged with regard to natural goods? The latter, of course, is the familiar luck-egalitarian view. But that, some critics have pointed out, is a little odd, because what is there to complain about with regard to the mere fact of having a worse talent, *independently* of this generating a socioeconomic inequality? Notice that this is not your ordinary relational refrain about luck-egalitarian preoccupation with the arbitrariness of the natural lottery. Rather, the puzzle over that preoccupation is made all the more pronounced in light of the imaginary conversation brought on by the SPS. What, exactly, are the untalented complaining about if not some unfair distribution of wealth, social standing, or any other social good, the critic asks. Imagine two individuals who are equal to each other in all social respects, but are unequal only in some nontrivial talent. What, then, is the content of the egalitarian complaint? What case must the talented individual answer? What fault of hers is this difference between them?

I think there is a point to this worry. But I also think that the luck-egalitarian account of the badness of inequality is well placed to meet that challenge. Consider the following account. Suppose there is no egalitarian complaint (or badness) in the absence of *inequality* in that which ultimately matters. Individuals being *equal* to each other with respect to whatever it is that the final currency of egalitarianism is (say, welfare) can never be bad in itself. It is therefore bad for one person to be less talented than another (obviously, something neither of them has a control over), *when* and only when this leads one person's welfare to be worse than another's. Imagine two individuals who are identical in all but their basketball skills. Neither of them, however, has the inclination to play the game, either professionally or even as a means of recreation (whereby the skill may be a harbinger of social esteem and acceptance). Suppose, as per stipulation, that the inequality in innate talent does not lead to an inequality in welfare. In that case, the luck egalitarian may suggest, there is *no* complaint to be had by the untalented player, and therefore no case to answer by the more talented player. I believe critics are right that this particular nuance has not been adequately stressed.

But that does not yet solve all the puzzle surrounding the content of the luck-egalitarian complaint. Clare Chambers, for example, criticizes the possibility of a luck-egalitarian complaint borne by people who are "unlucky in love." Her objection is not just the usual one about the expansion of the scope of justice that this implies. Rather, more specifically, she is puzzled by the fact that it is actually the beneficiary (the loved one), rather than the person bestowing it (the lover), who is identified as the bearer of the duty. "How could anyone reasonably justify—as opposed to merely explain—why their partner loves them and not another equally worthy person?"[3]

It is a fair question, and a legitimate criticism of luck egalitarianism. Still, it (the criticism) betrays some misunderstanding of the luck-egalitarian deployment of the SPS. Individuals incur obligations of justification when two conditions obtain cumulatively. First, they must be better off than others. They must be better off, mind you, not just with respect to a "local" good (say affection or love), but with regard to the overall currency of egalitarian justice (e.g., welfare). Second, they incur a duty when they are better off through no choice or merit of their own. Return to our person who is lucky in love. She has, among other things, an interpersonal duty to justify her position to other, worse-off individuals. Romantic love, one would venture, far from being an idiosyncratic good, is actually one of the chief constituents of happiness; of what makes our lives go well. Why should some people be, as a consequence, better off overall than others, and moreover through no choice of their own? There is nothing odd about this claim. "Look how much attention he gets from other men; life is so unfair!" sounds like a common enough refrain. Critics of luck egalitarianism may well think this has nothing to do with "political" justice. But importantly, that is not the question here. Rather, what's at stake is Chambers's implication that such bad luck has nothing to do with fairness, and as a consequence, does not generate a duty of justification. But that of course is nowhere near self-evident. Moreover, is it so crazy to suggest that the world would be better if individuals got a decent shot at meaningful relationships *independently* of, say, some Hollywood idea of good looks and other features for which they are not responsible?[4] Are we not, in fact, already witnessing some modest social movement in that direction (ads with models of more varied body types, for example)? Now the critic might reply that what I am pointing out is a duty *by the relevant industry* (e.g., media) to address this unfairness. There may well be such a duty. What the luck egalitarian is emphasizing, though, is that such a duty does not negate the interpersonal duty on behalf of the better-off loved one. After all, if there is no responsibility on the part of those individuals, why should the media be held responsible alone for catering to individuals' tastes? ("My ads contain only thin people, that's true, but it is not my fault that that is virtually what everybody likes to see in a partner of the opposite sex!")

If you thought moving the media as well as individuals to a greater variety in love interests (in terms of race, body-mass index, and so forth), Chambers's reading, according to which the "lucky in love" have absolutely no case to answer, cannot be credited with moving us in that direction.

### *The Structure of Egalitarian Complaints*

Here is a different concern. Is it consistent for luck egalitarians to offer an account of the badness of inequality that is explicitly axiological (or "telic"), *while* making use of a deontological tool, namely the "complaint model"? Put differently, can a luck egalitarian allude to the SPS and at the same time adhere to G. A. Cohen's notion of a "fact-insensitive" account of justice?[5]

First, then, how can an axiological account make use of a tool that is most recognizable as a deontic one? The answer lies in the dual use of the SPS within luck egalitarianism. It performs an instrumental, heuristic role and at the same time a non-instrumental one. Let me explain. In one sense luck-egalitarian allusion to the SPS is purely instrumental. Whether or not individuals have a complaint that is of an egalitarian nature is a *litmus test* for the prevalence of the disvalue of inequality. Suppose Tom has a complaint against Harry for being better off than him, as a result of no choice or fault of his (Tom's) own. Harry's advantage might be justified, all things considered (his advantage might in some way benefit Tom, say). But the existence of such a complaint, and the corresponding duty to explain it away, is the litmus test for bad inequalities (or inequalities that are bad). As is obvious, this is *not* some mixing of deontology with axiology (suppose we concede for the moment that that would be an illegitimate move). It is a legitimate use of a thought experiment (the existence of an egalitarian complaint) to determine the existence or absence of the disvalue of inequality. Harry has an obligation to explain why it is right for him to be better off than Tom. Notice that it is an obligation to explain why it is right (or just) for him to be better off, not an obligation to explain why it is justified, all things considered, for him to be better off. (The retort "Yes I am a more talented brain surgeon than you, and through no effort or choice of mine, but you stand to benefit from this, if God forbid the need will arise" belongs in the latter category; the reply "because I worked harder" belongs in the former one.)

The luck-egalitarian allusion to SPS can be instrumental in nature. There is therefore no inconsistency in offering an account that is axiological (or telic), while employing the SPS the nature of whose obligations is deontic. Within that telic account, the notion of duties of justification does not perform a justificatory role but only a heuristic one, and is therefore kosher. So far so good. But in a different way, I want to insist, the luck-egalitarian allusion to the SPS is also non-instrumental. The point is this: it is my view, following Larry Temkin and others, that the badness of inequality *is* made up of individual egalitarian complaints. Those individuals' complaints *constitute* the badness of inequality. Do not confuse those with some contingent, fact-sensitive grievances. Rather, inequality is bad when individuals have cause for egalitarian complaints, that is, when they are worse off than others through no fault or choice of their own.

## II. The SPS and the Value of Community

I have been discussing the conversational mechanism as emphasizing and illustrating the badness of inequality and the absence of luck-egalitarian justice. This mechanism is nothing new in luck-egalitarian thought. In his essay *Why Not Socialism?*, G. A. Cohen famously used the metaphor of a camping trip to illustrate the desirability of the socialist model. But he did more than that. In that little book, Cohen made vivid use of conversational tools to illustrate the core principles of luck-egalitarian justice. To give just one example: in one incident the camping party stumbles on an apple tree, and Henry protests that this tree was planted by his father and so he should get all the apples, or at least a greater share, or be excused from dishwashing duty. The members of the group retort: "Henry, you yourself have done nothing to deserve any of these things. Don't be such a schmuck." To be sure, the latter clause is not your standard philosophical argument. But it is compelling nevertheless. The conversation taken as a whole proves to be a useful litmus test.

Now, many have since objected to the content of such egalitarian complaints. But some have also objected to the use of this conversational mechanism, particularly in the way it is carried out by Cohen. It does not matter how true and compelling such conversations sound, or how true the egalitarian complaints and array of unsatisfactory answers they betray are, these critics say. And that is because, put simply, life is not a camping trip.

To say that life is no picnic is in one way, of course, a rather cheap argument. But in a different way, it conveys the following claim, and one that has implications for our use of the SPS. A camping trip is a special social context. And norms of behavior that apply there may not apply elsewhere or more generally in life. Miriam Ronzoni has made that rather obvious observation. But she couches it in slightly fancier terms, by speaking of a camping trip as "goal-monistic," whereas ordinary life, and especially market society, is characterized by goal-pluralism.[6] To put this simply, one cannot deduce from the type of claims that individuals press on one another in a very specialized setting such as a camping trip, what they owe each other in market society. If Ronzoni is right about the validity of the camping trip, this may have repercussions for luck-egalitarian use of the SPS. Individuals may have a duty to justify themselves in the type of special setting imagined by Cohen, but not in ordinary life and market society.

In one sense Ronzoni is surely right. Life is no picnic. Let's call this the "cheap" argument. Indeed, the whole point of Cohen's thought experiment is to use the uniqueness of the cooperative settings of the camping trip (fishing, cooking, washing dishes, all done communally) to illustrate a point. It is because a camping trip is such an isolated experience that it generates the communo-egalitarian sentiments that Cohen draws on. In that trivial (or cheap) sense, Ronzoni is surely correct. The more interesting question, though, is *in what sense* life is not a camping trip, and what this may imply for the validity of the conversations imagined by Cohen.

*Why*, then, is life not a camping trip, according to Ronzoni? In a nutshell, because unlike life, a camping trip is a goal-monistic voluntary expedition. By going on a camping trip, one voluntarily removes oneself from ordinary life and goes on a voluntary, joint, and isolated venture, with one particular unifying goal (be it general, such as "camping out in the woods together for two nights," or more specific, "going bird watching in the Kazbegi"). It stands to reason that one would acquire all sorts of special obligations on account of her decision to join such a venture. It is because life is very different from this specialized venture that the whole sound of Cohen's conversations ("Henry, don't be such a schmuck") rings true.

In a trivial way life is not a camping trip, I have already conceded. But is Ronzoni correct in diagnosing key features in which the two are different, and moreover, in a way that invalidates the strength of the egalitarian complaints and corresponding obligations? Let me raise three points of skepticism. Ronzoni says that the camping trip is unique by virtue, among other things, of being voluntary, whereas one's participation in market society is not. But some camping-trip-like ventures can be involuntary. Individuals may well find themselves on something like Cohen's camping trip, and for reasons that are far from voluntary. Arguably, on those occasions (when the trip is not voluntary), one would be an even greater schmuck if she excused herself from dishwashing duty on account of her greater fishing skills or the apple tree her father may or may not have planted. Think of victims of shipwrecks or a group caught in a blizzard or something of this sort. The egalitarian conversation that Cohen imagines would not weaken but only gain strength from the involuntary nature of the setting. Thinking of shipwrecks and blizzards is hardly stuff of Hollywood or science fiction. The literature on future generations and the earth's carrying capacity often makes use of the shipwreck metaphor. Life on planet earth in the twenty-second century might not be a picnic, but it seems likely that it will resemble managing a shipwreck more than taking a stroll in a shopping mall.

Voluntariness does not distinguish the SPS-generating camping trip. What about mono-goalism? On reflection that is hardly a better argument. Different people may join a camping trip in pursuit of different goals. One comes along for the laughs and company, another for the scenery, a third to add species to his Western Palearctic birding list, and a fourth to collect mushrooms (and this is just my immediate family I draw on). Indeed, one of the nice things about camping trips is that they allow this plurality of goals. People join in one unified venture, but within it each is free to pursue her own vocation, hobbies, and life projects. Take one of the most extended and exciting camping trips in human history, the kibbutz. No one dared shirk a mess-hall duty, and yet individuals were free to pursue individual projects. In fact, some hypothesize that it is no coincidence that many of

Israel's top novelists, poets, songwriters, and artists came from kibbutzim. The ride was a joint one, but it allowed the passengers to meaningfully pursue many individual vocations.

Mono-goalism and voluntariness are not invalidating features of the camping trip. I already said that you might find yourself on one of those trips against your will. But even in less extreme scenarios you may go on a camping trip and not even enjoy it. Even Cohen, while extolling the type of conversation that no one would challenge while on a camping trip, was at pains to stress that he himself doesn't even like camping! It is therefore to miss the point completely to complain that life is not a camping trip. The camping trip rather, is there to make obvious something that our market societies obscure. And that is, that anyone seeking differential pay for something for which she is not responsible is a schmuck. A Rawlsian veil of ignorance masks this fact; luck egalitarianism gives it center stage.

## III. Is Luck Egalitarianism a Version of Conditional Egalitarianism?

Luck egalitarianism is at odds with the egalitarian account provided by Andrew Mason and Thomas Christiano known as *conditional egalitarianism* (CE). On that view, roughly, equality is good, but only when it benefits at least one person. The great advantage of such an account is, of course, that it averts the leveling down objection (LDO). By providing a person-affecting account of egalitarianism, CE averts the age-old egalitarian problem of recommending an outcome that is to the benefit of no one. People have criticized CE citing objections that target its slide into intransitivity, and more importantly, its ad hoc nature. You may think that equality is valuable, and you may believe in the principle of beneficence (that more of a good thing is better than less). But why think that one conditions the other? It is a bit like saying, to quote Nils Holtug, that equality is good, but only on Wednesdays.[7]

I invoke CE and the leveling down objection for the following reason. Critics have pointed out that while luck egalitarians reject CE, they at the same time offer an account of egalitarianism that is itself *conditional*. Adina Preda, for example, has pointed out that while luck egalitarians object to inequality, they typically don't object to all inequalities, only to undeserved ones.[8] Preda also points out that this conditionality may conflict with the description of inequality as intrinsically bad.[9] For an intrinsic value cannot, she says, be a conditional one.

Let me start with the latter point. One thing to note is that whether

Preda is correct about the incompatibility of conditionality with intrinsic value, it is an objection that equally affects the CE view (that luck egalitarians object to). For according to Mason, at least, on his account, which is indeed conditional, equality may well be intrinsically valuable.[10] But setting that aside, I do think we should concede that bit of Preda's criticism. Perhaps she is correct that the luck-egalitarian account of the badness of inequality indeed does not establish it as of intrinsic (dis)value. And it is probably not of intrinsic value precisely for the reason outlined by Preda (namely, that of placing a condition on which inequalities are bad and which are not). Notice, though, that while inequality may not be bad in an intrinsic way, it could still be bad in a *noninstrumental* way.[11]

With that bit of the criticism conceded, how to respond to the more general (and in my view, important) worry about luck egalitarianism being conditional after all (while all the while criticizing CE)? We want, first, to set aside the merely linguistic objection. It should not bother us, terminologically, whether luck egalitarianism could or could not be described as "conditional." The real worry, of course, is whether luck egalitarians criticize the account known as conditional egalitarianism for something of which their own account is also guilty. Here is one way to see that the debate cannot be about mere terminology. Luck egalitarians readily concede that in one important way their view about the value of equality is indeed conditional. Luck egalitarians do not object to inequalities in the number of letters in people's surnames (unless it leads to some disadvantage in alphabetic waiting lists), or in the number of freckles on their upper arms (unless, of course, the latter leads to greater vulnerability to melanoma, say). The luck-egalitarian ideal of the value of equality is conditioned by the *minimal person-affecting proviso of inequality*.[12] According to that proviso, inequality can only be bad when pertaining to a *currency* that impacts how well people's lives are going. That is a very minimal condition indeed.

Accounts of the value of equality are therefore bound to be conditional in one way or another. We need to move beyond that linguistic quibble and examine whether they are conditional in a problematic or benign way. The luck-egalitarian objection to CE is that it conditions the value of equality in *a hopelessly ad hoc* manner. It avoids a major objection to egalitarianism (LDO) by placing a person-affecting proviso (and not at all a "minimal" one) on the value of equality. To avoid being ad hoc, proponents ought to explain why conditioning the value of equality on it improving the life of at least one person is different from conditioning the value of equality on which day of the week we happen to be talking about. When pressed on this, the justification provided by Christiano is that "[a] necessary condition for equality mattering is that the thing being equalized is such that more is better than less."[13]

I have already distinguished a sense in which person-affecting considerations *do* affect the value of equality. Equality must obtain for a currency that matters to individuals, and one for which more is better than less. But importantly, this is a constraint on the *currency* of equality, not on the *pattern* of distribution. We care about inequalities with regard to things (currency) that matter as opposed to inequalities with regard to things that don't (freckles, letters in one's surname). From this to the suggestion that we care only about *patterns of distribution* (inequalities) that matter to people's welfare is a great leap indeed. Even on the logic given by proponents of CE themselves, the person-affecting proviso constrains the currency of inequality, not its pattern. To put this differently, it *is* true that we want more of a good thing rather than less. But it is far from obvious that we want this for reasons of equality. (In fact, it is the exact opposite.)

CE's account of the value of equality is hopelessly ad hoc. The luck-egalitarian account is not. Some inequalities are non-instrumentally bad. Which inequalities? Those that are arbitrary. Does this mean that luck egalitarians object to any pattern of distribution that is the product of luck? Of course not. It is an unfortunate misinterpretation to think that they object to luck as such.[14] Luck egalitarians object to luck *in the service of* inequality. Luck egalitarians do not object to inequality *and* luck. They object, rather, to *undeserved inequalities*. So yes, luck egalitarianism can be characterized as a conditional view, but no, it is nowhere near conditional in an ad hoc manner.

## IV. Value Pluralism

Many critics, mostly of Rawlsian bent, object that whenever luck egalitarians are in a tight spot, they resort to value pluralism. Whenever the luck-egalitarian radical account, especially of equality of opportunity, leads to counterintuitive results, they resort to some other value or consideration to rescue their view. We have no justice-based reason to hire qualified brain surgeons; it is unjust for well-off parents to read bedtime stories to their children; it is a breach of equality of opportunity to not invite people of color to your dinner parties. Many see these as intrusive and unsavory policy implications. And the luck-egalitarian response is to avoid them by alluding to "autonomy," "promotion of overall well-being," "promotion of family relationship goods," and more. What a cop-out![15]

Once again, we may begin with a concession. But it is a concession about the content of the move, not about its very nature. Perhaps luck egalitarians have been too quick to concede the implausibility of some of the policy implications of their views (this might be true especially with regard to radical equality of opportunity). For example, some luck egalitarians have alluded to the value of "adequacy" in education,[16] which in hindsight may have been a mistake.

While luck egalitarians may concede that some of the values alluded to as part of their value pluralism have been picked up in haste, they need not concede the more general point, about the *strategy* as a whole. Value pluralism need not be a cop-out. Let me try to explain why. The distinction between principles of justice and rules of regulations is of course one of the more important legacies left to us by Jerry Cohen. But it seems that critics still don't fully grasp its importance. Let me put it in rather blunt terms. Few luck egalitarians think parents, of whichever strata, should cease reading bedtime stories to their children. But luck egalitarians do typically think that these well-off parents should not feel too smug about doing so. I personally think it would be a good thing if the thought that by doing so they are exacerbating already unjust inequalities occasionally flickered in their mind. I know it does in mine. I do think people should marry for love rather than for social justice (wouldn't that be something?). But I also think it is not a bad thing if they once in a while questioned their taste in romantic partners, and how it might reflect traditions of social biases. I do not think the police should monitor dinner parties. But I do think you should occasionally look around your dinner table, and notice who is there, and more importantly, who is not. I do think the best qualified should be appointed as brain surgeons. But I also think they should not be smug, or ungrateful (to the rest of us) about it. You get the point.

You might think justice is only relevant when it guides social policy. Good for you. But two things: be open to the possibility that some people think differently, and see justice as guiding also the way each individual should evaluate her conduct in the world. And second, be open to the possibility that social policy is not only that brute instrument of regulatory power, but also the more nuanced ways by which social conventions and norms morph and change.

## V. Luck Egalitarianism and the Harshness Objection

Luck egalitarianism mandates helping victims of brute luck, but not those of option luck. But this has harsh consequences. Think of the following case pressed by Re'em Segev and Ofer Malcai.[17] Suppose that in Pond, Ann and Ben each encounter a drowning child (on separate occasions). Rescuing that child would result in muddy pants, a detour back home on the way to the office (to change clothes), and a couple of lost hours of work. Weighing these costs, Ben decides against the rescue, and the child drowns. Ann rescues the child and incurs the said costs. Surely, Ann is entitled to compensation (and Ben to eternal condemnation), but allegedly luck egalitarians would deny her that, because it was her choice and so a matter of option luck. That is highly unattractive, and paints luck egalitarianism in an unbearably harsh light.

One thing luck egalitarians could do to address this is to slightly modify their principle, and specify that option luck excludes heroic or laudable choices, and that, in turn, option luck is best understood as "culpable choices."[18] (Or perhaps more accurately, that brute luck excludes heroic and laudable choices.) I personally think this is too strong a solution. More specifically, this solution brings luck egalitarianism very close to the ideal of desert, from which I think it ought to keep its distance.

Instead, I think it would be more accurate to say the following. Ann's actions bear the marks of brute luck rather than option luck, and so she ought to be compensated for the costs incurred in saving the boy. But how can this be? It was her choice to do so. Well, not really. We ought to believe, I think, that Ann actually did not have a choice in the matter. No decent person could have stood idle and watched. If so, saving the boy was a matter of brute luck. But how can you say, the critic would pounce, that Ann had no choice, where we have the example of Ben who, faced with the exact same dilemma, chose a different course of action? We can say so very easily, once we realize that Ben is a sociopath. Ben's sociopathic conduct only serves to show that Ann did *not* have a choice. Indeed, after she has a minute to collect herself from the stress of witnessing such a drama, and from the uplift that the rescue surely must have given her, Ann may well have had the following passing thought. "I am privileged to have saved a life, although I had no choice in the matter. But look at my pants. Like, what a bummer. I have an important meeting at work, and I cannot show up like that." This monologue rings completely true to me. With respect to the muddy pants, Ann is the victim of bad brute luck. *Stumbling* across a drowning boy, the rescue of whom requires muddying your pants, was neither her choice nor fault.

Still, wouldn't you say that the luck-egalitarian treatment of victims of option luck is harsh and, more particularly, disproportionate? More than one critic has invoked an often-cited example raised by Clare Chambers to illustrate the disproportionate punishment meted out by luck egalitarians toward victims of option luck. I refer to the oft-repeated story of Jason and Jeremy, who are identical in all but the fact that the night before an important high-school exam, Jason decided to study an extra hour while Jeremy opted to take a break and watch an episode of Ken Burns's *Civil War*. This slight turn of events, in Chambers's telling, produces a momentous result. For Jeremy, as a consequence, did slightly worse in the test. Consequently, he got into a slightly less prestigious university, and as a consequence landed a job that paid substantially less. Because luck egalitarianism relies so heavily on equality of opportunity, and a radical one at that, so much of its consequences depend on the *moment* when opportunities are supposed to be equalized. It ends up being harsh because it metes out a disproportionate "punishment."

This is a nice little story, and I concede that it does tell us something interesting about equalizing opportunities. But I also think it misses an important element of what luck-egalitarian justice is about (if it is meant as a criticism, that is). Here is the bottom line of it. Jeremy is indeed responsible for opting to study slightly less diligently for the test. But he is *not* responsible for *all* of the chain reaction and the enormous consequences that this has brought about. Jeremy, to put it simply, is not responsible for how the capitalist society he happens to live in is set up. He is certainly not to blame for the way a small difference in how you do in one exam generates an enormous difference in life prospects.

Fair enough, some critics have said, but doesn't it then follow that in luck egalitarians' implausible account, *nothing* is ever just? For realistically, choices that vary in their prudence always end up causing chain-reactions of this type, leading to disproportionate punishments. My own contribution in replying to this line of criticism is "Not so fast." Luck egalitarianism is distinct in the fact that it allows unequally good fates to result from unequally prudent undertakings. It is precisely the *latitude* of this inequality that it objects to. It is fine, under luck egalitarianism, for Jeremy to end up with a worse-paying job (and somewhat lesser marriage options). It is *not* fine for Jeremy to end up with a grossly worse-paying job (and all the ensuing disadvantages). Notice, this is not due to some ad hoc mechanism of reasonableness in punishment or something of that sort. Rather, this limitation of the range of eventual inequality between Jason and Jeremy is rooted in the very luck-egalitarian idea of finding what one is responsible for and what one is not. Jeremy, to reiterate, is responsible for studying less hard; he is not responsible for all the ills of capitalist society.

The implications of pinning down what individuals are responsible for are as familiar as they are radical. A proper reading of luck egalitarianism calls for contracting the accordion of differential wages. They need not be contracted all the way down, but they certainly need to be narrowed down radically in most of today's societies. Cohen's discussion alluded to this, of course, when he gave as an example a comparison between salaries of the managerial level in Germany and the US. Luck egalitarianism does not oppose inequality in wages, but it certainly has tools in its kit to oppose the range of these inequalities. If you find yourself still struggling with this, do what I sometimes do, and imagine a conversation about responsibility and luck, say between the provost of your university and the last of the cleaning ladies on your campus. You never know; it might help.

NOTES

1. Waldron famously derided the "57 different varieties of luck egalitarianism." Jeremy Waldron, "Political Theory: An Inaugural Lecture," *Journal of Political Philosophy* 21 (2013): 21.

2. Interestingly, Google Scholar citations of "John Rawls" have dropped 15 percent during the equivalent period.

3. Clare Chambers, "Review of Shlomi Segall, *Equality and Opportunity*," *Ethics* (2016): 851–52.

4. Surely, this is a sentiment someone like Chambers would be on board with. See her *Intact: A Defence of the Unmodified Body* (London: Penguin, 2022).

5. Blain Neufeld, "Review of Shlomi Segall, *Equality and Opportunity*," *Notre Dame Philosophical Review* (2015): 6.

6. Miriam Ronzoni, "Life Is Not a Camping Trip," *Politics, Philosophy & Economics* 11 (2012): 171–85.

7. Nils Holtug, *Persons, Interests, and Justice* (Oxford: Oxford University Press, 2010), 196–97.

8. Adina Preda, "Review of Shlomi Segall, *Why Inequality Matters*," *Ethics* (2017): 279.

9. I commit to that in *Why Inequality Matters*, 14.

10. Andrew Mason, "Egalitarianism and the Leveling Down Objection," *Analysis* 61 (2001): 248.

11. I therefore want to retract the claim I make on page 8 of *Why Inequality Matters* according to which ex post inequalities (as opposed to ex ante ones) are *intrinsically* bad. I should have said that they are non-instrumentally bad and left it at that.

12. *Why Inequality Matters*, 30.

13. Thomas Christiano, *The Constitution of Equality: Democratic Authority and Its Limits* (Oxford: Oxford University Press, 2008), 34.

14. Neufeld in his review of my second book is a notable exception as someone who gets this right. See his review in *Notre Dame Philosophical Review*.

15. Neufeld, "Review," 4; Chambers, "Review."

16. *Equality and Opportunity*, 143.

17. Ofer Malcai and Re'em Segev, "A Dilemma for Luck Egalitarians," *Journal of Value Inquiry* (forthcoming).

18. Nir Eyal, "Egalitarian Justice and Innocent Choice," *Journal of Ethics and Social Philosophy* 2, no. 1 (2006). Some have called this version "Luck Eyalitarianism."

CHAPTER 5

# Why Kant Is Sooner Socialist than Toronto Liberal

Nicholas Vrousalis

According to an influential "Toronto" interpretation of Kant's political philosophy, the Kantian objection to economic dependence is fundamentally about poverty. Eliminate poverty—read: propertylessness—and you have eliminated economic dependence. So Kant's political economy of independence *just is* the dialectic of property and propertylessness under the modern state. This paper argues that crucial passages in the *Doctrine of Right* presuppose an account of Kantian economic dependence broader than mere propertylessness. Economic independence, for Kant, is co-extensive with self-standing (*selbstständig*) production for a competitive market—that is, independent commodity production. Kant's political economy of independence is therefore not just about property and propertylessness, as the Toronto interpretation holds, but also about the independent exercise of the productive purposivenesses of free and equal people. This makes Kant's politics sooner socialist than Toronto liberal.

This chapter is structured as follows. In section 1, I explain the polemical thrust of the Toronto interpretation. In section 2, I elaborate on the Toronto position on redistribution and the welfare state, drawing from Chris Essert, Arthur Ripstein, and Ernest Weinrib. In section 3 I briefly review relevant passages from Kant on economic independence. In section 4 I show that these passages do not support the narrow Toronto focus on property and argue that they support a broader, productive purposiveness reading. And in section 5 I highlight some contrasts on the topic of economic dependence between Kant and Marx on the one hand, and Kant and Rawls on the other.

## 1. The Antilibertarian Gambit

Suppose Rishi Sunak, the former British PM, decided to privatize the roads and sidewalks. And suppose that the reason for this policy was not efficiency, but ostensibly equal freedom: perhaps the British government consisted of tough-minded luck egalitarians, who thought that everyone should own an equal share of road and sidewalk. What could one object to this policy, on Sunak-type grounds? A devastating objection is that it would make every commuter subject to the private will of each individual road owner. That is, even if every citizen owned an equal road share, that ownership would make the purposiveness of all subject to the purposes of each: I am not free to move around if my movement depends on your permission, even if you're inclined to grant it. So the Sunak policy would undermine equal freedom.

This kind of objection is central to the debate between G. A. Cohen (1995) and Robert Nozick (1974) on the nature of property rights. One of Cohen's dialectical arguments against Nozick's promiscuous use of the term "liberty" in *Anarchy, State, and Utopia* asks whether Lockean self-ownership protects individual autonomy. To show that it does not, Cohen imagines a system of joint ownership, in which everyone must get permission from others to perform any external action, including occupying physical space. Cohen then asks whether such a system would be compatible with the form of self-ownership prized by Nozickian libertarians. If, on the one hand, self-ownership and joint ownership *are* compatible, then self-ownership is no freedom at all, for it is compatible with having to ask permission from others to set and pursue any possible end. If, on the other hand, self-ownership and joint ownership are *not* compatible, then capitalist private property draws exactly the same objection as joint ownership—the value of being able to set and pursue ends independent of alien permission requires a state more extensive than a minimal state, that is, a state that provides poverty relief and redistributes wealth.[1]

This argument has a distinctly antilibertarian flavor, because it starts from a premise about the external *freedom* of the poor, not about their needs or welfare. It has been revived in the work of Ernest Weinrib (2003) and Arthur Ripstein (2009)—the "Toronto Kantians." One of their contributions to that debate has been to add more flesh to Cohen's barebones argument against libertarianism, this time on the basis of Kant's political philosophy. I begin by elaborating on this social-democratic—"liberal"—strand in Kant exegesis.

## 2. Taking Toronto Roads Seriously

The Toronto Kantians, especially Ripstein, think there is something special about roads. The term "roads" doubles up in meaning here: it signifies roads, but also any all-purpose means. So here is Ripstein, discussing the problem of the landlocked commuter:

> Private ownership of land does not simply foreclose some particular purpose that you might happen to have, but also forecloses the entire formal class of purposes involving voluntary interaction with others. The problem is formal, because it does not depend on the particular purposes for which any two persons might wish to interact, but rather on the fact that they are subject to a third person from whom they must secure permission to interact. (Ripstein 2009, 247)

As his fellow Toronto Kantian Chris Essert puts it, lacking a road is unlike lacking a boat; roadlessness is unlike boatlessness in that having a boat serves a relatively narrow set of ends (Essert 2017). Roadlessness, by contrast, deprives you of access to *any* end involving other people; it deprives you of end-setting capacity *tout court*. So "[t]he solution to this problem is obvious: roads, understood as a system of public rights of way, guaranteeing that there is a path from every piece of privately held land to every other" (Ripstein 2009, 248). Indeed, the contrast between boatlessness and roadlessness can be extended further. Consider homelessness. This is not just lack of a home, because a homeless person can consistently have access to shelter. So her problem is not lack of housing, but lack of an enforceable *right* to a home (see Essert 2017). In lacking such a right, she is subject to the permission of *some* landowner or other, even if they are each individually, or collectively, inclined to grant it.

One of the ambitions of this Toronto reading is to show that private property requires, for its justification, a system of omnilateral rights that guarantees each her independence. Ripstein argues that this requires economic redistribution:

> This argument for economic redistribution is *internal* to the idea that acquisition must be authorized and disputes resolved through public procedures that can be accepted by all. Absent institutions of public justice, the rich person's claim to exclude the poor from her property would just be a unilateral imposition of force. Those who have property have the right to exclude provided that their holdings of property are consistent with a united will shared by all—that the system of private rights really is part of a system of equal independence of free persons. (Ripstein 2009, 283)

It follows that the Kantian state must provide *publicly funded* poverty relief. Kant's argument, on this interpretation, starts from the premise that you cannot give yourself laws that would make you into the servant of another. And since a system of laws that allowed poverty—propertylessness—would make the propertyless servants of property, poverty is not in conformity with right. More succinctly: nobody can covenant her way into poverty, not even the possibility of poverty. It follows that the Kantian state must include *mandatory* coercive redistribution from the propertied to the propertyless. I will call the Toronto Kantians who affirm this conclusion "Toronto liberals."

The Toronto liberal position is stronger than Cohen's, because it asserts the necessity of redistribution *coerced by public laws*. It would not, in other words, suffice if some philanthrocapitalists got together and offered poor relief equal to what a state would offer: Oprah-funded poverty relief is *necessarily* unjust when Leviathan-funding is available. Cohen's joint-ownership scenario, by contrast, allows private persons to accommodate the external actions of others. The problem, once again, is that Oprah's permission is always revokable *by Oprah's private will*.[2] I now explain how Kant's discussion of work shows his views of economic independence to be more demanding that Toronto liberalism allows.

## 3. Kant on Economic Dependence

Toronto liberalism is compelling, both substantively and as an interpretation of Kant. But the way it construes the omnilateral will is too weak. The rest of this paper argues that Toronto liberalism is too lenient on private property and that Kant is not so lenient.[3] The basic idea is that Kant's discussion of Public Right problematizes economic dependence in a way that goes beyond property. But to make good on this idea, I must first rehearse some basic ideas from the *Doctrine of Right*.[4]

Kant's *DR* attempts to deduce the idea of the liberal state—including the full panoply of coercively enforceable individual rights, from the basic liberties to property rights to equality of opportunity and poverty relief—from a single right to freedom as independence (*Unabhängigkeit*) from the choices of others. Kant's argument has two movements. The first movement, Private Right, proceeds from a premise about the "innate right"[5] of independence, to the justification of a provisional set of property rights (*DR* 6: 261f.). This is a move from a preinstitutional, natural right, to private property as a condition of the possibility of everyone's independence. But Kant also thinks that, in the absence of a universally legislating public power, these private rights are indeterminate, nonbinding, and unenforceable.[6] The second movement, Public Right, is designed to correct these defects in the state of nature: enter omnilateral rule by a powerful and united will that creates, applies, and enforces law (*DR* 6:312ff). This establishes a "rightful condition" under universal laws of right.[7]

Kant discusses specifically economic dependence in the context of an attempt to defend certain qualifications on citizenship in the section on Public Right. His theory of citizenship replaces the French revolutionary triptych of liberty, equality, and fraternity with freedom (*Freiheit*), equality (*Gleichheit*), and civil self-sufficiency (*Selbständigkeit*). These are grounded in *DR* §46, where Kant offers an original-position-type argument. He argues that the state's legislative authority belongs to "the concurring and united will of all," where "each decides the same thing for all and all for each." He adds that, since one "can never do wrong in what he decides upon with regard to himself," it follows that the legislation of such a united will must be consistent with the demands of right. Kant's co-legislating citizen has three normative attributes (*rechtliche . . . Attribute*): he[8] enjoys freedom (*Freiheit*), "the attribute of obeying no other law than that to which he has given his consent"; equality (*Gleichheit*), the attribute of "not recognizing among the people any superior with the moral capacity to bind his as a matter of right in a way that he could not in turn bind the other"; and civil self-sufficiency (*Selbständigkeit*),[9] the attribute of "owing his existence and preservation to his own rights and powers as a member of the commonwealth, not to the choice of another among the people." (*DR* 6: 314) Freedom, equality, and civil self-sufficiency, then, are the ideal expression of Kantian independence.

A preliminary elaboration of these conditions follows Kant's account of the franchise. After suggesting that "the only qualification for being a citizen" is "being fit to vote," Kant adds that this:

> presupposes the self-sufficiency of someone who, as one of the people, wants to be not just a part [*Teil*] of the commonwealth but also a member [*Glied*] of it, that is, a part of the commonwealth acting from his own choice in community [*Gemeinschaft*] with others. The quality of being self-sufficient, however, requires a distinction between active and passive citizens, though the concept of a passive citizen seems to contradict the concept of a citizen as such. The following examples can serve to remove this difficulty: an apprentice in the service of a merchant or artisan; a domestic servant (as distinguished from a civil servant); a minor; all women and, in general, anyone whose preservation in existence (his being fed and protected) depends not on his management of his own business but on arrangements made by another (except the state). All these people lack civil personality and their existence is, as it were, only inherence [*Inhärenz*]. (*DR* 6: 314; translation amended)

Kant's passive citizens[10] enjoy freedom and equality if they possess legal standing as parts (≠ members) of the commonwealth and if they can work their "way up from this passive condition to an active one" (*DR* 6: 315). Both conditions are satisfied, he implies, in the case of apprentices, domestic servants, minors, and women, albeit *passively*. Minors, for example, enjoy a right "to the care of their parents until they are able to look after themselves" (*DR* 6: 280), a right entailed by their innate right to independence. It follows that enjoyment of innate rights is compatible with de facto lack of control over its conditions of exercise. What is the significance of this inference?

In Vrousalis (2022), I argued that Kant could not have thought that dependents should be disenfranchised, unless he thought that, in legislating, they would be making "arrangements about another." Economically dependent citizens, for example, would be legislating not for *themselves* as citizens, but only for their bourgeois masters as citizens.[11] In this interpretation, you enjoy civil self-sufficiency if and only if you enjoy unsubjected exercise of your rights and powers, including your productive powers,[12] as a member of the commonwealth. In a nutshell, Kant's disenfranchising exclusions are not about *how* citizens are disposed to vote, but rather about the nature of the object of universal legislation in the Kantian state. The idea is that only economically independent citizens can, in legislating, *self*-legislate, that is, make arrangements about their own agency.

By way of further elaboration, Kant follows up on these examples with a set of contrasts:

> The woodcutter I hire to work in my yard; the blacksmith in India, who goes into people's houses to work on iron with his hammer, anvil and bellows, as compared with the European carpenter or blacksmith who can put the products of his work up as goods for sale to the public; the private tutor, as compared with the school teacher; the tenant farmer as compared with the leasehold farmer, and so forth; these are mere underlings of the commonwealth because they have to be under the direction or protection of other individuals, and so do not possess civil self-sufficiency. (*DR* 6: 314–15; translation amended)

The Indian traveling blacksmith[13] contrasts with those who are subject to fiduciary relationships, in that he is merely contractually bound to "let and hire" his productive powers to his employer(s) (*DR* 6: 285).[14] But the blacksmith's position is similar to those subject to fiduciary relationships in that he, too, lacks civil self-sufficiency. According to Kant, the Indian blacksmith enjoys freedom and equality insofar as he *could* come to own enough iron and thereby come to bind his employer to him as much as the employer actually binds him. This is the significance of Kant's equal-opportunity proviso, that "anyone can work his way up from this passive condition to an active one" (*DR* 6: 315). But the blacksmith presently lacks iron ownership, which means that *he lacks independent use of his productive powers*: to exercise these powers, he must get permission from the iron owner(s) to use the iron they own, which means he must put his powers at their disposal. He therefore lacks civil self-sufficiency. Like the minor, the Indian blacksmith remains subject "to the choice of another among the people" (*DR* 6: 314), quite independently of a supervening fiduciary relationship.

So Kant's discussion of work under the rightful condition generates a *discriminating position*: the European blacksmith is independent, whereas the Indian blacksmith is not. What explains this position? One Toronto-friendly explanation is that only the latter is poor. I now show that Kantian economic dependence extends beyond poverty, in the sense that poverty is only a sufficient, but not a necessary condition for economic dependence. Kant is, in this sense, sooner socialist than Toronto liberal.

## 4. Kant beyond Toronto

Suppose the European and the Indian blacksmith share a qualitatively identical productive power of working iron into hammers. Both produce, say, an equal output per hour out of equal inputs; both serve the commonwealth by making it richer by some hammers. Suppose further that both enjoy the same set of commonwealth-conferred legal rights to exercise these productive powers, in addition to the right to own iron. Kant implies that the Indian blacksmith owns no iron, such that if he is to exercise his productive powers by working iron, he must ask permission from the iron owner(s).[15] The Indian blacksmith's ironlessness thereby gives the iron owner(s) discretion over the exercise of the blacksmith's productive powers—his ability to work iron into hammers. According to Kant, it follows that he lacks *Selbständigkeit*, since his labor process, and *therefore the conditions of exercise of his commonwealth-conferred legal rights and powers*, is de facto unilaterally controlled by others.[16] The Indian blacksmith, in other words, is economically dependent and therefore normatively disqualified from exercising his own agency. According to Kant, only those in independent possession and use of their powers, including their productive powers, can rightfully legislate on behalf of these powers.[17] And this also explains why he is wont to disenfranchise the poor.

Does the Toronto emphasis on poverty account for Kant's discriminating position? It does not, for one can imagine the Indian blacksmith possessing property equal to that of Kant's civil servant and craftsman, or even of the European blacksmith, all of whom are dubbed independent.[18] So Kantian economic dependence must be broader than poverty. More precisely: *poverty is a sufficient but unnecessary condition for unjust economic dependence*. So how exactly does Kant spell out the necessary condition? The answer, I argued above, has something to do with the independent possession and use of one's powers.

To insulate the rest of my exegesis from Toronto liberalism, I will hereafter assume that wage laborers are not poorer than the median public servant—because there is high demand for labor, or there is public poverty relief, or an unconditional basic income. Being empirical, these assumptions do not beg the question against Toronto. I now explain how economic dependence, for Kant, extends beyond poverty.

A central step toward understanding Kant's assertion of the discriminating position between the two blacksmiths must look to the role he assigns to the market. The contrast between being your own master and being someone's servant is central here. Indeed, Kant thinks that "being fit to vote," serving "no one other than the commonwealth," and "being [your] own master" are extensionally equivalent expressions of equal freedom; having to give others permission to use your powers, by contrast, is a form of servitude. He elaborates as follows:

> Someone who makes an *opus* can convey it to someone else by alienating it, just as if it were his property. But *praestatio operae* is not alienating something. A domestic servant, a shop clerk, a day laborer, or even a barber are merely *operarii*, not *artifices* (in the wider sense of the word) and not members of the state, and are thus also not qualified to be citizens. Although a man to whom I give my firewood to chop and a tailor to whom I give my cloth to make into clothes both seem to be in a quite similar relation to me, still the former differs from the latter, as a barber from a wigmaker (even if I have given him the hair for the wig) and hence as a day laborer from an artist or craftsman, who makes a work that belongs to him until he is paid for it. The latter, in pursuing his trade, thus exchanges his property with another [*opus*], the former, the use of his powers, which he grants to another [*operam*]. (*TP* 8: 295)[19]

The relevant contrast, for my purposes, is that between barber and wigmaker: the former, Kant says, is relevantly like domestic servants, shop clerks, and day laborers in that he must give others permission to use his powers to make a living. Not so in the case of the wigmaker, who can exercise his own powers independently of such use—he merely sells the *product* of that exercise. Crucially, Kant adds that the wigmaker enjoys such self-sufficiency "even if I have given him the hair for the wig." As I understand him, Kant is saying that *the concern with propertylessness is derivative of a more fundamental concern with the independent (although possibly joint) exercise of the human productive powers*, a proper subset of our powers as members of the commonwealth. Just like an orchestra of independent musicians, where each exercises her share of the musical powers unsubjected to alien control, so under legitimate public power each commonwealth member exercises her share of the productive powers unsubjected to alien control.[20] Each is simultaneously interdependent and independent.

How, then, are we to account for the discriminating position? On the present interpretation, the European blacksmith produces for the competitive market in a self-standing way, that is, not for a boss or a series thereof. This is what some Marxists call "petty commodity production," but a better name is *independent commodity production*. Independent commodity production, for Kant, guarantees the productive independence of interdependent people. Now notice that we are already outside Toronto territory: Kantian economic independence requires more than the absence of propertylessness. One might object that there is no discrimination to be had between the power of the market, as opposed to the power of bosses. If nobody wants to buy the European blacksmith's hammers, then he will starve. By the same token, if nobody wants to hire the Indian blacksmith's productive powers, then he will starve. There is therefore no sustainable discriminating position between the two cases—dependence on a series of consumers through the product market and dependence on a series of bosses through the labor market. Kant's response to this objection is to insist on the distinction between *opus* and *operam*—that is, between:

(a) private discretion over the use of your powers

vs.

(b) private discretion over the *product* of the use of your powers

Only (b) is in conformity with right, because only (b) is consistent with the producer legislating on behalf of her own agency. Kant of course grants that independent commodity production, such as the European blacksmith's, implies dependence on a competitive market and therefore on the will of consumers as a whole. But this is just shorthand for dependence on the material conditions of the state—the conditions for the freedom of all: "Thus a nation's wealth, insofar as it is acquired by means of money, is really only *the sum of the industry with which human beings pay one another* and which is represented in the money in circulation within it" (*DR* 6: 287, emphasis added). Such dependence on the mere "sum of industry" contrasts with the Indian blacksmith's dependence on the individual will of a (series of) private employers. So the European blacksmith, but not the Indian blacksmith, can self-legislate, in the sense that *he can make arrangements for himself with what is his*; the exercise of his powers is not permissionally conditional on someone else's—only the sale of his product is.

This defense of the discriminating position would be roundly criticized by Marx some sixty years later. In the *Grundrisse*, Marx argues that independent commodity production—independent, small-scale production for a competitive market—is compatible with a set of merchants, usurers, or protocapitalists coming to control the net product. This means that they possess an ownership-conferred power over the labor capacities of others, *even if they are not anyone's boss and even if markets are perfectly competitive.*[21] This very possibility arises when and because some market actors can command more labor than they give in its production—a possibility broached by Smith in *The Wealth of Nations* but hardly applicable to the port economy of eighteenth-century Königsberg, Kant's city.

Yet Kant's insistence on independent commodity production, although unrealizable under mechanized industry, suggests that he is not just interested in poverty as propertylessness, as the Toronto interpretation suggests. This transpires in the *production* of rightful institutions—the supply-side of Right, which is completely overlooked by the Toronto Kantians. Let me explain.

Suppose that omelets are the only means of consumption and that, if I am to nourish myself, I must produce an omelet. As long as you and others own the eggs, I can produce the omelet only by your permission, which makes my ability to set and pursue the end of omelet production—my productive purposiveness—subordinate to your unilateral will. Omelet redistribution will not solve this problem, insofar as it leaves the mode of omelet *production* untouched, no matter how much it ameliorates the mode of omelet *distribution* in my favor. Egalitarian egg *pre*distribution does better, but still subordinates my omelet production to your will, insofar as it does not preclude your ownership and control over the omelet-producing cookshop. Independent commodity production, Kant thinks, features neither form of subjection: in producing for the market with their own inputs, independent commodity producers are subject neither to poverty nor to the power of bosses.[22] Whether or not this is true, it implies that Kant's political economy of independence is not fundamentally about property and propertylessness, but about forms of discretion over the productive powers of the direct producers.

To sum up the argument so far: in *DR* §46 Kant says that those who cannot make arrangements about themselves, including the poor, cannot legislate on behalf of their own agency, and therefore cannot be enfranchised. But in Remark C he broaches another possibility: that they need not be disenfranchised if given enough property to legislate on behalf of their own agency. I have argued that Kant's examples evince the same ambivalence about wage labor: should it be abolished or should its agents be disenfranchised? The ambivalence arises because if nobody can covenant into property as her master, then nobody can covenant into *capitalist* property as her master. But then eliminating poverty (as general propertylessness) is only a subset of economic independence. So instead of a QED, Kant's disenfranchising exclusions can be read as a *reductio*. This seems to be the only reading consistent with Kant's own examples and contrasts.

## 5. From Kant to Rawls, through Marx

One way to read Kant's argument in *DR* §46f. is as providing a set of special justifications on power over the productive capacities of others.[23] One such justification is the power of public offices as such. That is, to produce under the direct authority of a public office, assuming it is geared toward the freedom and equality of all, is to serve the conditions of everyone's freedom. It is therefore to serve only the conditions of your own rightful freedom—to "make arrangements about yourself" as free and equal. Kant's contrasts between domestic and civil servant, private tutor and schoolteacher, etc., all seem to presuppose this exculpating condition on power: how else could the same labor content (delivering letters, teaching students, etc.) have different freedom valence in the contrasted cases?

But Kant's *DR* contrast between the two blacksmiths and his *TP* contrast between barber and wigmaker suggests another special justification for power over productive capacity, namely self-standing production for a competitive market—a market in which sellers are neither poor nor subject to the unilateral authority of (a series of) boss(es). In this market, consumers as a whole have power over producers as a whole, but that is unlike the power employers as a whole have over employees as a whole. Crucially, this is the only way to make sense of Kant's consistent assertion of the discriminating position in all of his writings on work. Marx's later criticism of the discriminating position, and his concomitant distinction between labor and labor power, shows that Kant's argument can only be sustained under more restrictive conditions than Kant himself thought. But both Kant and Marx may be right: the former was wrong only about the restricted applicability of an otherwise sound principle.

Now, the *DR*, as well as Kant's preparatory manuscripts for the *DR*, repeatedly feature an antinomy between citizenship and property. Kant needs civic status to justify property and not vice versa. But his assertion of civic independence covertly reintroduces property as a condition for citizenship. We're stuck in a circle, a circle first discovered by Rousseau and then highlighted by Marx in his critique of Hegel's theory of the state and his essay on the Jewish question. But, once again, the thought that political independence is insufficient for *social* independence is already in Kant, as is the idea that social independence requires more than universal property. So the reason Toronto liberalism is inadequate is that Kant takes production and social reproduction, as well as their material conditions—access to scarce productive assets—as themselves subject to the natural right to freedom.

Another corollary of my reading is that Kant has something resembling a dialectic of labor.[24] Although Kant does not say so explicitly, *DR* does advert to the form of *interdependent* independence that comes with independent commodity production. This dialectic is substantiated in Kant's discussion of the foundations of the state in the *Conjectural Beginning of Human History*, where he surmises that "the human being passed over from the period of comfort and peace into that of *labor* and *discord*, as the prelude to the unification in society" (*CB* 8: 118, emphases in original). Since the division of labor and the concomitant "discord" are indispensable to progress, the only way to humanize them is through the institutionalization of independence. Echoing Rousseau, Kant adds that this requires an "external lawfulness, [. . .] civil right," which obtains because "the human being was to *labor himself* out of the crudity of his natural predispositions by himself, and yet was to take care not to offend against them even as he elevates himself above them" (CB 8: 117, emphasis mine). My interpretation explains how the enfranchisement of human production might work as part of Kant's broader theory of justice.[25] Its application to the modern capitalist state, moreover, helps unearth a tension between citizenship and economic dependence, a project only fully realized in Marx's *Critique of Political Economy*, half a century after Kant.

I conclude by contrasting the Kantian picture I have sketched with Rawls's. Rawls (2001) criticizes welfare-state capitalism for being too lenient on inequality and therefore on the conditions for equal citizenship. Rawls's view is, in that respect, more demanding than Toronto liberalism and so more in line with Kant's, as I have presented him. Rawls endorses "property-owning democracy" and "liberal socialism"— property-owning democracy plus worker cooperatives—as the only two eligible institutional arrangements for justice as fairness. In making this move, Rawls enfranchises "powers and prerogatives of offices and authority" into the subject of justice. So, if these powers fall under the purview of the difference principle, and if work involves such powers, then there is no reason why a Rawlsian well-ordered society should not regulate the workplace to treat everyone as free and equal. Enfranchising powers and prerogatives under the difference principle would also allow self-esteem to come into play as a supplement to other maximinized primary goods, such as income and wealth. And all this would tell in favor of something stronger than property-owning democracy, such as liberal socialism.

Now, Kant was not and could not have been a socialist, any more than Plato could have been a Christian: like his contemporary Sieyès, Kant's main concern was to eradicate the juridical vestiges of feudalism. But Kant went further than Sieyès, by thinking of the modern state as an organism whose members are agents possessed of rightful (productive) powers, whose interdependent mode of *exercise* independent of unilateral permission matters for Right. So Kant's arguments are socialism-friendly. For the socialist Kant, the normative disempowerment of the poor—her inability to legislate universally because an alien will de facto controls the conditions of her agency—also afflicts the worker subject to a capitalist boss, *whether she is poor or not*. If this is correct, then one Kantian institutional remedy would be to endow workers with the requisite powers over work, that is, to create a system of worker control quite independent of rights to property. On this reading, Rawlsian property-owning democracy would also be insufficient for Kantian independence. And now we find ourselves, again, further to the left of Toronto liberalism.

To sum up: I have defended an interpretation of *DR* in which Kant's political economy of independence is not fundamentally about property and propertylessness, as the Toronto liberals argue. It is, rather, about alien control over productive purposiveness. I argued that such control is, in general, inconsistent with Right, unless it draws a special justification. One such justification, for Kant, is self-standing (*selbstständig*) production for a competitive market—that is, independent commodity production. Although independent commodity production is not possible under mechanized industry, Kant's normative theory, I argued, provides fruitful engagement with the topic of work that takes us beyond Toronto liberalism. It therefore provides an exciting avenue for future work on freedom at work.

## NOTES

1. I discuss and defend Cohen's argument in Vrousalis (2015).

2. What if Oprah has no such discretion, but retains beneficial ownership? By state mandate, for example, she does not legislate the permissions for receiving poor relief but retains rights to the residual (the state pays her rent from general taxation or gives her tax cuts). This seems equivalent to the state coercing me to pay

you not to kill me. The correct policy is to hinder your attempt to kill—not to get me to pay you not to do it. The Toronto view seems consistent with these powers remaining Oprah's, even if she is constrained to exercise them for public purposes.

3. Allen Wood has written that "Kant is sooner socialist than libertarian" (Wood 2014, 122). I will argue that Kant is, in addition, sooner socialist than Toronto liberal.

4. References are to *The Cambridge Edition of the Works of Immanuel Kant* (Kant 1996, 2013). Abbreviations are as follows: *DR* = *Doctrine of Right; TP* = *On the Common Saying: That May Be True in Theory But It Is of No Use in Practice*; *CB* = *Conjectural Beginning of Human History*.

5. Kant distinguishes between "innate" and "acquired right," rights possessed by nature versus rights possessed by virtue of some further act (*DR* 6: 237).

6. See Ripstein (2009) for a recent reconstruction along these lines.

7. It is important that this view is about the *external* freedom of persons, so not about the form of their *internal* motivation or maxims. Merely rightful obligations, for Kant, are externally individuated. It follows that Kant's political philosophy is orthogonal to his *ethics*: you can accept the former without accepting the latter. And that's a boon for the theory, because it does not depend on any comprehensive views about morality or the good life.

8. For Kant a citizen is, invariably, a "he." *DR* contrasts with *TP* in that the former does not ascribe to women a naturalized property of being unfit to vote. Rather, in *DR*, Kant seems to be saying that women are dependent just by dint of extant social conditions. See J. Weinrib (2008) for a defense of this interpretation and Kleingeld (1993) for an influential discussion of Kant's sexism.

9. Mary Gregor renders both *Unabhängigkeit* (as a feature of the innate right to freedom) and *bürgerlichen Selbständigkeit* (as a feature of civil status) as "independence," using the "civil" operator to distinguish the latter from the former. On the interpretation I will present, Kant uses *Unabhängigkeit* to refer to the content of right, whereas *Selbständigkeit*, along with freedom and equality, are the complete public expression of that content. In keeping with recent scholarship, I render *Selbständigkeit* as "self-sufficiency."

10. There is some evidence that Kant borrows the distinction between active and passive citizens from the French constitution of 1791 and the writings of Sieyès (Maliks 2014; Davies 2020). In Vrousalis (2022), I argue that Kant's interpretation of the distinction differs from Sieyès's in crucial respects.

11. Of the four possibilities—noninterdependent dependence, noninterdependent independence, interdependent dependence, and interdependent independence—the first is incoherent. Kant follows Rousseau in thinking that, of the last three, only interdependent independence counts as human freedom proper. I contrast noninterdependent and interdependent independence in Vrousalis 2022.

12. A productive power is a nonnormative ability to bring about an effect by making a physical object into a means to that effect. I possess a productive power when I can cook an omelet in my kitchen; I also possess that power when I can cook an omelet at the cookshop under a division of labor with other omelet producers. A productive power contrasts with a *productive choice*, which is intentional exercise of a productive power.

13. Moran (2021, 4) discusses the origins of Kant's example.

14. The labor contract normally counts as a status relation, what Kant calls *locatio (conductio) personae*, the granting of my powers to a principal as her agent in return for payment. The Indian blacksmith case seems to involve not a labor contract, but rather "granting another the use of my powers for a specified price," which Kant classifies as *locatio operae* (*DR* 6: 285). The argument that follows applies to both sets of cases.

15. Rafeeq Hasan elaborates: "What the Indian blacksmith lacks is not the ability to use what is his: his tools and labor power. Rather, what he lacks is iron, that is, the raw materials, which he can transform through his productive activity into something of exchange value" (Hasan 2017: 921).

16. Ripstein (2017: 211) argues that Kant's account of citizenship presupposes a distinction between the possession and exercise conditions of political rights, but does not discuss human productive powers or the relevance of interdependence.

17. Contemporary liberalism solves this problem by severing the link between franchise and independence, thereby enfranchising wage labor. But this move misunderstands the spirit of Kant's argument. Kant wants to make interdependent independence—unsubjected exercise of one's interdependent rightful powers—central to political life in the modern state. The rightful condition must therefore reflect more than free consent by juridical equals: this is what *Selbständigkeit* adds to the *Freiheit-Gleichheit* diptych. And this is also why the Indian blacksmith, lacking *Selbständigkeit*, cannot self-legislate: the way Kant sees it, his dependence means he would not be legislating on behalf of his own rightful powers, even if he had the right to vote.

18. Moran (2021) makes a more general point about the merely formal nature of the wage laborer's dependence, which implies that such dependence does not presuppose poverty.

19. This passage encapsulates the *Critique of Political Economy* in germanized, Kantianized Latin: Marx's distinction between labor and labor-power is already there (in Kant's distinction between *opus* and *operam*), as is the distinction between manual (*operarii*) and mental labor (*artifices*).

20. Crucially, these powers are *unownable*, since Kant is not a libertarian.

21. "[T]he merchant induces a number of weavers and spinners, who until then wove and spun as a rural, secondary occupation, to work for him, making their secondary into their chief occupation; but then he has them in his power and has brought them under his command as wage labourers" (Marx 1973, 510ff.).

22. I discuss variants of this idea in Vrousalis (2023).

23. More generally, the very existence of public power as a system of omnilateral authorization seems to presuppose certain powers, that is, certain necessary presuppositions for public power to even be *thinkable* as such. These powers must include powers of public officials over other public officials, the power of voters over public officials, a separation of jurisdictional power across different branches of government (*DR* 6: 313), and so on.

24. Readers may be familiar with Marx's dialectic of labor from the *Grundrisse*, where he discusses the primitive independence of the individual under precapitalist societies, distinguishing it from the subsumed interdependence of

the individual under capitalism, an antinomy resolved in the free individuality of communist society.

25. I defend this claim in Vrousalis (2022).

REFERENCES

Cohen, G. A. 1995. *Self-Ownership, Freedom, and Equality*. Cambridge: Cambridge University Press.
Essert, C. 2017. "Property and Homelessness." *Philosophy & Public Affairs* 44: 266–95.
Hasan, R. 2017. "Freedom and Poverty in the Kantian State." *European Journal of Philosophy* 26: 911–31.
Kant, I. 1996. *The Metaphysics of Morals*. In *Practical Philosophy*, trans. M. Gregor. Cambridge: Cambridge University Press.
Kant, I. 1998. *Critique of Pure Reason*. trans. A. W. Wood and P. Guyer. Cambridge: Cambridge University Press.
Kant, I. 2013. *Anthropology, History, and Education*, trans. Robert B. Louden and Gunter Zoller. Cambridge: Cambridge University Press.
Kant, I. 2018. *Lectures and Drafts in Political Philosophy*, trans. F. Rauscher and K. Westphal. Cambridge: Cambridge University Press.
Kleingeld, P. 1993. "The Problematic Status of Gender-Neutral Language in the History of Philosophy: The Case of Kant." *Philosophical Forum* 24: 142–68.
Marx, K. 1973. *Grundrisse*. Harmondsworth: Penguin.
Rawls, J. 1971. *A Theory of Justice*. Oxford: Oxford University Press.
Rawls, J. 2001. *Justice as Fairness: A Restatement*. Oxford: Oxford University Press.
Ripstein, A. 2009. *Freedom and Force*. Cambridge, MA: Harvard University Press.
Varden, H. 2016. "Rawls. vs. Nozick vs. Kant on Domestic Economic Justice." In *Kant and Social Policies*, 93–123. Cham, Switzerland: Palgrave Macmillan.
Vrousalis, N. 2015. *The Political Philosophy of G. A. Cohen*. London: Bloomsbury.
Vrousalis, N. 2022. "Interdependent Independence: Civil Self-Sufficiency and Productive Community in Kant's Theory of Citizenship." *Kantian Review* 27: 443–60.
Vrousalis, N. 2023. *Exploitation as Domination: What Makes Capitalism Unjust*. Oxford: Oxford University Press.
Weinrib, E. 2003. "Poverty and Property in Kant's System of Rights." *Notre Dame Law Review* 78: 795–828.
Wood, A. W. 2014. *The Free Development of Each*. Oxford: Oxford University Press.

# PART II

# Democratic Equality

CHAPTER 6

# Egalitarianism and Nordic Social Democracy

Richard Arneson

## Seeking to Justify Nordic Social Democracy—Two Egalitarian Approaches

To many, the political and economic arrangements that characterize the Nordic countries—including Norway, Denmark, Sweden, Finland, and to some extent Iceland—have long seemed to embody a gentler, kinder, better version of capitalist society. I shall refer to the core institutions shared by the first four mentioned countries as constituting Nordic social democracy (NSD). To many other observers, these countries appear in a quite different light, as dark and menacing. They epitomize the bogey of cradle-to-grave socialism or the nanny state. What many left-wingers love, right-wingers hate.

Although the Nordic countries quite obviously do not feature economies organized by centralized state planning and eschewing capitalist market exchange, I believe the popular right-wing characterization of them has a point. If we ask what moral principles might plausibly justify NSD arrangements and single them out as superior, the answer this essay seeks to defend is a set of commitments that merit the label "socialist principles," which left-wingers are likely to endorse and right-wingers to spurn. A simple though admittedly not compelling basis for this claim is that these abstract moral principles, when coupled with a set of empirical claims that social democrats are likely to believe, imply that NSD or some set of arrangements in this neighborhood should be implemented and sustained, and the same moral principles, coupled with a different set of empirical claims that traditional socialists were likely to believe, imply that an economy organized around centralized state planning ought to be implemented and sustained.

I am not claiming that NSD came about by some process in which a bunch of Scandinavians over time reflected about what fundamental moral principles should claim their allegiance, settled on what I call "socialist values," and set about applying egalitarianism to remake their institutions and their collective life. NSD arose and has sustained itself for well over a half-century as the contingent outcome of messy democratic politics driven by different social groups seeking to use state power to advance their interests (Jensen and van Kersbergen 2017; Sejerstad 2011). To what degree this unique process could be emulated in other nations now is to my mind an open question (for a positive response to it, see Kenworthy 2019 and 2022). My claim is that if you intuitively find the generous welfare state institutions and policies of Nordic countries morally inspiring, and ask what moral principles would best explain and justify those arrangements, a plausible answer is the egalitarian norms this essay will describe.

A complication is that these norms do not themselves speak with one voice; they come in two distinctively different versions—welfarist egalitarianism (WE) and relational egalitarianism (RE). WE consists of an imperative to bring about better-quality lives for people and distribute this good-quality life (welfare or well-being) more equally across persons. RE tells us that morality requires regarding and treating one another as equals, and this involves avoiding social relationships in which some dominate others, bringing about real freedom for all to live as they choose, and achieving a true democracy in which all citizens have equal opportunity to influence political decision-making (EOPI). So which egalitarian approach should command our allegiance if we wish to march under a broadly egalitarian banner? This essay mostly sets that important question to the side. This essay concentrates on WE, and tentatively suggests that it is a better fit with Nordic social democracy, better coheres with it, than RE. But that suggestion, even if correct, could just as well provide a reason to reject WE and NSD alike, and to uphold RE and seek to identify feasible institutions and policies (reformed NSD) that would best implement that egalitarian ideal. That's not my own view, but this essay leaves it an entirely open path.

In passing, notice that both WE and RE can be traced back to the critiques of early industrial capitalism raised by the likes of *both* Karl Marx and John Stuart Mill in the mid-nineteenth century. So to speak, there are two souls of socialism. (It is possible to mix and match these approaches rather than go whole-hog for either, but the differences are stark.)

The political and economic arrangements in place in Nordic countries vary from country to country, and within each country over time. By NSD arrangements I shall understand ones that combine (1) political democracy, (2) generous welfare-state policies that work to compress both pre-tax-and-transfer and post-tax-and-transfer inequality of incomes, and also to provide social insurance against common misfortunes by universal provisions that specially benefit the less wealthy, (3) forms of taxation and public spending and regulation that foster economic efficiency and growth and thereby avoid sharp equity versus efficiency conflict, (4) policies that promote women's employment and child welfare and, more broadly, equality of life prospects between men and women, and (5) fair treatment of people in successive generations, especially as regards young people starting their adult lives. Notice that the last three items on this list stipulate that the policies described are successful. If a country's policies aim to promote women's employment but fail to do so, the country would to that extent fail to qualify as NSD. The categories somewhat overlap. For example, policies that promote women's employment (as in 4) probably also foster economic productivity, efficiency, and growth (as in 3).

Perhaps the most salient feature of NSD is that its policies seek somewhat to equalize the post-tax-and-transfer income of adult members of society generation by generation. Obviously the egalitarian principles proposed as rationalizing and justifying NSD must be consistent with this core salient feature.

Consider a libertarian idea of equality attained when all enjoy the same freedom to live as they choose, so long as they don't wrongfully harm others in certain familiar ways, using whatever talents they possess and whatever property they legitimately obtain by gift and market exchange transactions (Nozick 1974; Brennan 2012). After all, NSD incorporates a capitalist market economy, so perhaps the libertarian understanding of what we all are equally owed by each other, incorporating a robust conception of capitalist market freedoms, is the backdrop norm in play that is the proper standard for assessing NSD policies. But whatever the substantive plausibility of this view, it rules out the many-sided exercises of state power, prominently featuring government coercive impositions that take the legitimately acquired property of some to help others, that are plainly central to NSD. Libertarian equality condemns NSD (but for a position that argues for reconciliation between certain libertarian claims and at least some NSD policies, see Miller 2018a, 2018b, 2019).

What might morally license the takings of people's private property (legitimately acquired according to core rules that structure and define a capitalist economy of free market exchange based on private ownership) that are routine and unproblematic in Nordic social democracy? Almost half of what people earn in NSD countries is taken from them by taxation. Much of what is taken goes to government programs that benefit all, and so do not necessarily impose net losses on any citizen. But about 30 percent of government spending is frankly redistributive, leaving the rich worse off and a large swath of the population better off. Forcing some to help others presupposes that those forced are under enforceable moral obligation to make sacrifices to help these others. Beyond this, the cleanest and simplest explanation of why rights of private ownership give way in response to others' needs is that rights of private ownership are not morally valuable to uphold for their own sake, but only if, and to the degree that, upholding such rights is an effective means to fulfill fundamental moral values. If it were the case that wide expropriation of private property or even eliminating private ownership better served these fundamental moral values, expropriation or elimination could be carried out without moral loss.

Regarding rights to engage in commercial transactions and rights to acquire and keep privately owned goods as mere tools to secure other values does not make the justification of these core capitalist rights insubstantial or frail. Empirical contingencies can be stable and robust. To get a quick glimpse of why upholding the core capitalist rights citizens enjoy is a robustly good means to fulfill moral goals we morally must fulfill, we can take a very brief detour to socialist philosopher G. A. Cohen's exploration of *Why Not Socialism?* (2009). Cohen proposes that egalitarians can and must favor abolition of capitalism and private ownership if that is feasible. ("Feasible" here means "can be done at acceptable cost to the other values we should care about.") But Cohen understates the instrumental value of private ownership for creatures like us, evolved in a certain way, with inborn dispositions to favor ourselves and those near and dear to us over fellow humans as such. To see this, it suffices to consider the case for private ownership of climbing ropes; this example generalizes. To highlight the case for socialism, Cohen has his readers imagine a camping trip among friends, and urges that the appeal of a good camping trip is that it is run in accordance with socialist principles of share and share alike. However, we should not want climbing ropes to be available on loan like books from the public library. Many of us would not climb with anyone who shared her rope indiscriminately with others. People differ in aspirations, risk preferences, skill, and other factors affecting what one needs a rope to do on particular occasions, and so what constitutes responsible rope care. There is also variety across people, and for any one person across time, in the diligence we can muster to treat a borrowed rope as if it were our own. This last factor might be the most consequential one. Not for any and all rational agents, including saints and angels, but for humans like us, public ownership is often inefficient.

A yet further qualification needs to be introduced here. Above, I have slipped into writing as though WE was the sole fundamental principle of an act-consequentialist morality. (Act consequentialism says one morally ought always do an act, among the available alternatives, that would bring about an outcome no worse than the outcome of anything else one might instead have done.) WE here provides the standard for the assessment of outcomes as better or worse. But a more ecumenical view holds that the fundamental moral divide, determining one's allies and what side of the barricades one should be fighting on, is not between those who accept and those who reject act consequentialism, but between those who accept and those who reject the idea that fundamental-level enforceable morality includes a significant principle of impartial beneficence. This says that each person is bound by a demanding duty to improve the world by bringing about outcomes that are morally better. This ecumenical view allows that fundamental-level morality might also include significant, demanding constraints (e.g., don't tell lies) and options (provided one is not violating moral constraints, one has a moral prerogative to act as one chooses to some considerable degree). WE then gives content to the principle of beneficence—balance the goals of increasing the total well-being that people attain and distributing that well-being more equally across persons.

Let's explore further the contrast between the families of egalitarian views I have labeled welfarist egalitarianism and relational egalitarianism as possible justifications of NSD. Recall that RE tells us that what we fundamentally owe to one another is regarding and treating one another as equals, and this involves avoiding social relationships in which some dominate others, bringing about real freedom for all to live as they choose (Anderson 1999), and achieving a true democracy in which all citizens have equal opportunity to influence political decision-making (EOPI). EOPI is satisfied just in case all those with the same ambition to be politically influential and the same political talent have the same chances to be politically influential in a democracy in which all citizens have an equal vote in elections that determine, directly or indirectly, what laws and public policies will be established. The eminent political philosopher John Rawls holds that equal opportunity for political influence (he calls it the "fair value of political liberty") is a necessary part of the right to a democratic say that is among the basic liberties (including freedom of speech and association) that take strict priority over all other justice values (Rawls 1999). If some citizens being wealthier than others (or having more access than others to the free time needed to become well informed about political matters and politically influential) threatens to conflict with fulfillment of EOPI, then either these resource inequalities must be eliminated or they must be prevented from conflicting with EOPI attainment. Niko Kolodny (2023) holds that democracy including EOPI is a crucial component of a society that avoids unequal social relationships. Fulfilling this social equality aim is in itself of great moral importance, according to Kolodny, but unlike Rawls, he does not rule out trade-offs between social equality and other justice values.

But however noble this EOPI aspiration might be, Nordic social democracy does not appear to be organized to achieve it. In Sweden, back in the 1970s, the Social Democratic Party proposed initiating a plan whereby business firms would gradually turn over shares of stock to their employees so that eventually most firms would become worker-owned and controlled. This Meidner Plan was swiftly abandoned and has not been revived since. People become millionaires and billionaires nowadays in Denmark, Sweden, Norway, and Finland. If you are talented, ambitious, hard-working, just plain lucky, or some mix of the above, you can strike it rich under NSD arrangements. NSD from its inception has aimed at class compromise, not class war. Of course, compressing the distribution of income will have some inevitable tendency to compress somewhat the post-tax post-transfer distribution of wealth, but the two aims are not at all close substitutes.

Also, actual NSD incorporates political democracy—each citizen has a vote that counts equally in determining the composition of the group that (roughly by majority vote) determines the content of the laws and also the set of public officials who issue coercive commands that all citizens are to obey, this political process taking place against a background of wide freedom of speech, assembly, and association. But this ordinary idea of political democracy does not incorporate the idea of equal opportunity for political influence, and it is hard to discern efforts in Nordic countries to achieve EOPI. There is more to say here. But at a first pass, a candidate set of moral principles that gives high priority to EOPI is a poor fit with NSD. Such a political morality condemns rather than endorses NSD arrangements.

However, striving to increase a society's EOPI fulfillment by equalizing the distribution of wealth and other resources across persons might not succeed, if equalizing wealth would induce further circumstances that would cause EOPI fulfillment to lessen. The same goes for striving to insulate possession of wealth from creating unequal opportunity to influence political decision-making. The obvious possibility is that reducing the political power of the wealthy might tend to increase the power of democratically elected lawmakers and top officials to entrench themselves in office, giving them greater nonaccountable opportunity for political influence and eventually for gaining authoritarian control over political decision-making. This scenario is studied under the label of "competitive authoritarianism" (Levitsky and Way 2002). If this was so, then RE would not condemn Nordic social democracy for failure to maximize EOPI fulfillment. That charge would not stick. On the flip side, if reducing the political power of the wealthy in NSD societies beyond its present levels worked to boost equality-weighted well-being without increasing EOPI fulfillment or even preventing lessened EOPI fulfillment, WE would on this score criticize present NSD arrangements while RE would not.

RE also requires bringing about real freedom for all to live as they choose. (You have real or effective freedom to travel to Paris just in case there is some course of action you can choose that will result in your getting to Paris, and you have formal freedom to go to Paris if no law prohibits your going there, and if you try to get to Paris, no one will wrongfully interfere with your attempt.) This component of RE might be interpreted as holding that all should have equal opportunity for lifetime desire satisfaction or life aim fulfillment. By contrast, WE is satisfied by attainment, not opportunity. Also, rather than the satisfaction of whatever desires/life aims you have, WE fulfillment might be measured by an objective, not subjective, welfare standard, often called an "objective list" view. To illustrate, suppose there are some types of things, such as friendship, love, worthwhile achievements under some construal of what is worthwhile to achieve, enjoyment, and knowledge, that are such that the more you gain instances of these types of things, the better your life goes for you. This will be so independent of your own subjective opinions or feelings about getting these types of things.

Against this backdrop, return to the question of what sort of egalitarian principles coheres best with supporting NSD. There is at least some reason to interpret some NSD arrangements as more strongly supported by the idea that we should be helping people to achieve and obtain objectively good-quality things, not merely things we subjectively believe to be valuable. To explore this, we need to describe NSD arrangements further.

Core NSD policies clearly and plainly aim to boost people's labor-force attachment, and especially women's labor-force attachment. The idea is that for most of us, sustaining productive paying employment is good for us, whether we think so or not. A job tends to put good structure in our lives, facilitates our forming valuable relationships and engaging in valuable teamwork with workmates, and tends to help us sustain reasonable self-esteem. (There may also be a duty falling on us to contribute to the productive economy that benefits us all [Kenworthy 2019, 113–21].)

Core NSD policies include generous unemployment benefits that losing a job makes us eligible for, along with active labor market services that provide retraining and advising to help match our skills with available jobs. In Denmark, an employed woman is guaranteed a year's paid leave if she bears a child, and a child on becoming one year old can access subsidized, affordable preschool care, and later, after-school care. The result of these and similar policies is higher women's labor force participation in Northern European countries compared to more conservative Southern European countries with welfare state policies tied to a male breadwinner model for families (Jensen 2021; Kenworthy 2019).

Welfarist egalitarianism favors the high rate of employment, and especially high women's employment, that NSD policies foster. Regarding women, a concern is that a woman who lacks job skills and steady paid work is likely to end up subordinate to some man. Such oppression of half of the population is, to put it mildly, extremely unlikely to be compatible with maximizing the welfare of all with a tilt toward boosting the welfare of those worse off. You could perhaps try to reconcile NSD policies with the RE view that the state should be neutral on what counts as the good life, and restrict itself to promoting fulfillment of all citizens' life aims except those aimed at injustice. But this reconciliation attempt would run into trouble. For example, RE will countenance (for example) a woman's self-abnegating preferences to serve the advancement of her husband's career at any cost to her own flourishing, so long as this sacrifice would not impede her fulfilling duties to others. WE implies criticism of preferences to sacrifice one's own fulfillment to benefit others when the sacrifice would not maximize equality-weighted well-being. Or consider a man's desire to be main breadwinner of his family, come what may.

Such NSD policies that foster sharing of child-rearing and outside-the-home careers between adult family partners (1) are hard to square with neutrality regarding the good that is built into RE, and (2) give off more than a whiff of paternalism. Paternalism here consists of treating a normal well-informed adult person on the basis of a judgment that this person is less than fully competent to manage her own affairs. At an extreme, paternalism might take the form of a coercive shove, constraining someone's liberty for her own good, but might also take the form of a noncoercive nudge, offering aid in a form that encourages some uses of it rather than others. To be sure, welfare egalitarians might have reason to reject many paternalistic intrusions, and relational egalitarians might have reasons to accept some.

More generally, NSD policies provide important in-kind benefits, including old age pensions, healthcare, and help with finding employment provided by active labor market policies, rather than general-purpose resources such as cash that could be used to help fulfill almost any life aim one might have. Key features of NSD policies mentioned above aim to improve people's lives by helping them cope with anticipated improvidence—imprudent behavior that is not virtuously and reasonably aimed at securing benefits for others (Heath 2009). Such nonvirtuous imprudence might be impulsive or principled, the latter exemplified by the "righteous dope fiend" whose considered conviction is that the life of a hard-drug addict is choice-worthy, admirable, not to be regretted. To reiterate, any egalitarian will be suspicious of even mildly paternalistic policy, since each individual will have access to lots of private information that bears on what would be best for her. But an RE view might be expected to take a stronger stand against it on the basis that it is respectful to persons to provide them with fair shares of opportunity for successful pursuit of their own chosen way of life, whether or not they choose to use those opportunities prudently.

NSD also encourages women to fully participate in the labor market and to occupy paid and profitable roles in market exchange. NSD encourages men and women in their romantic relationships (same sex or opposite sex) to secure egalitarian sharing of their burdens and benefits, including paid employment, housework, and child-rearing. NSD places a heavy thumb and perhaps an elbow on the scales, favoring broadly egalitarian family relationships. In this respect and maybe others, NSD is nonneutral on the good, pursuing policies justifiable if at all only by appeal to controversial judgments about some ways of life being better than others for those following them, and seeking to promote people following these controversial (but arguably, based on evidence and argument) better ways of life.

## NSD and Long-Term Growth and Prosperity

It might seem obvious that if in each year you equalize people's income by taxing high earners and transferring the money to low earners, you lessen the incentives of both high and low earners to be economically productive. Over time economic production decreases; the pie to be distributed gets ever smaller. In the long run we're all worse off, and our descendants will be worse off than they would be if we had refrained from equalizing. But what seems obvious is probably incorrect, in the case of NSD. Acknowledging that conclusive evidence on the causal impact of social spending on economic growth is not to be had, such evidence as we have does not support the claim that over the long history of their generous welfare states, equalizing as the Nordics do it tends overall to lessen economic growth and prosperity (Lindert 2021; Jensen 2021; Kenworthy 2019; but see for example Acemoglu et al. 2017). This upbeat assessment allows that some parts of the generous welfare state package may be growth-reducing: unemployment benefits do seem to dampen employment and growth. Since it's likely that the economic incentives making the pie smaller are in play, they must be outweighed by other features of Nordic policies. We find these countervailing features both in how NSD governments tax their citizens to gain funds for public spending and in how the collected funds are spent.

A preliminary comment: the problem that threatens to afflict societies that indulge in generous redistribution gets called "equity versus efficiency," but from a WE standpoint, the problem is a conflict between maximizing equality-weighted well-being in the short run and in the long run, and this is no true conflict at all. WE requires us to treat all people as equally important for purposes of deciding on actions and policies whether they are living now, or near to the present, or in the distant future. (Of course, as our capacity to calculate the expectable effects of policies that might be enacted now on the further future, that further future gradually drops out of consideration.) If equalizing now expectably resulted in lowering total equality-weighted well-being of persons over the long run, we egalitarians should stop equalizing.

On the side of taxation, compared to rich countries with less generous pro-poor welfare state policies, the Nordic countries tend to favor taxes that induce lower deadweight losses. The Nordics rely more on taxes on consumption than taxes on wealth and income. Insofar as taxes do fall directly on income, they are proportional, not progressive—the rate of tax one pays does not increase as one's income rises. Also, income taxes take the form of payroll taxes, easy to collect and hard to evade, and consumption taxes mostly are broad taxes applying evenly to all consumption and take the form of value-added taxes (VATs), which are also easy to collect and hard to evade. Also, the exception to broad taxes on all consumption tends to be "sin" taxes that target activities such as use of alcohol, tobacco, and gasoline that impose negative externality costs on people other than the users. A consumption tax is a tax on one's income minus one's savings. This hurts the poor, who find it harder to save than do wealthier citizens. But the encouragement to save is growth-promoting.

On the side of government expenditure, NSD governments have done well at redistributing in ways that invest in productivity, jobs, and economic growth. To start, it is well established that investing in the education of children of poor parents increases their economic contributions when they become adults, and so increases future economic productivity and prosperity (Heckman 2006). The Nordics do a good job of this, compared to non-Nordic states. But even setting aside funding high-quality schools, generous parental leave following childbirth, affordable preschool care for toddlers, and affordable day care for school-age children, and other characteristic Nordic forms of social spending help growth, both by their impact on children and by facilitating mothers' careers (Lindert 2019, 2021; Kenworthy 2011, 2019). Also, mandatory health insurance and universal healthcare provided by government agency in the Nordics improves longevity more than is achieved in countries where private markets play the dominant role in these sectors.

The Nordic welfare state policies do well at providing young adults with a good start in life via education, training for jobs, and a competitive market economy. A sluggish market environment weighed down by excessive labor and product regulation worsens the availability of job opportunities for youths entering the job market. In Norway, Sweden, and Denmark, the proportion of those aged twenty to twenty-four classified as NEETS (not in education, employment, or training) has hovered around 10 percent for males and 8 percent for females, compared to corresponding rates of 14 percent of males and 16 percent of females in the US and 33 percent and 32 percent in Italy. A faltering start in engagement in the productive economy when young is associated with lower lifetime earnings and less steady employment.

Here we are moving beyond looking at effects of social spending and looking at the wider environment that youths encounter. But the message is that Nordic institutions taken together lean toward equality between young and old rather than showing a pronounced tilt toward benefits for the old, in this way giving a boost to economic growth. Another indicator of pro-growth policy is social mobility—how strongly the education and social status of parents are correlated with those of their children. In the Nordics, for children of parents who have not completed secondary education, social mobility upward is good, though downward mobility of less talented children of parents who have completed tertiary education, which we should also see if social mobility is good, is less impressive (Jensen 2021; Esping-Andersen and Cimentada 2018).

## Is Valuing Equality a Mistake?

The Danish political scientist Carsten Jensen has observed that "The Nordic nations are among the most equal on Earth" and that "If you are a fan of equality, there is much to like about the Nordics" (Jensen 2021, 7). But is it a mistake to care about equality and hold (1) that it is morally valuable for its own sake, or (2) that it is somehow a good means to support values we should care about?

Philosopher Harry Frankfurt has delivered a resounding "No!" to part 1 of this question. He affirmed (1987) that how one person's economic condition compares to another's does not in itself matter morally or prudentially; so a fortiori whether one person's condition compares to another's in the particular way of being equal does not in itself matter. He further opined that what does genuinely matter is whether one has enough money for one's purposes, given one's desires. Many others have observed that equality of condition across people could be brought about just as well by making better-offs worse off, with no gain in the condition of anyone. As the political theorist Douglas Rae (1981) commented, equality is indifferent between vineyards and graveyards. If leveling down in this way does not improve the overall situation in any respect, it seems that equality cannot be in itself valuable. Frankfurt later (2015) widened his claim: it is not just monetary equality that is per se valueless, but equality in any condition one might care about—overall resources, opportunities, well-being/welfare, whatever. This to my mind is a plausible claim (Arneson 2022, 14–15, 54).

There may be less to this issue than meets the eye. Suppose we agree that equality in itself does not matter. (If it subjectively feels to you as though it mattered, and you come to care about it, you are making a mistake.) How one person's condition compares to that of another does not in itself matter. This leaves it open that, on the dimension of well-being/

welfare, bringing about a benefit (avoiding a loss) of a given size for someone is impersonally more valuable, makes the world better, the worse off the person would otherwise have been in absolute terms. This is the priority view (Parfit 1991). Of course, one could flatly deny this claim, too, but that would be a hard position to defend. You have one delicious ice cream cone, which you could keep for yourself or instead give to Dolores, who is leading a terrible life, very low in welfare. We could develop variants of this example in which Dolores is heading toward a life that is improved, less and less terrible, scoring higher in terms of an absolute quality-of-life or welfare standard. Or we could imagine that Dolores's life is even more hellish. In these variations, Dolores would get exactly the same welfare boost from the ice cream, however well or badly in welfare terms her life will otherwise go. No further consequences flow from your choice, for Dolores or anyone else. Surely you have greater reason to give the ice cream cone to Dolores, the worse off in absolute terms she would otherwise be. Even if in the example Dolores would get somewhat less enjoyment and benefit from your ice cream, as we imagine her life otherwise being absolutely worse, there can be more reason overall to give the ice cream to the Dolores whose life is absolutely worse.

However, accepting priority, and valuing both how large the benefit one might gain for self or others is and how well off or badly off in well-being the potential beneficiary would otherwise be without this benefit, one is accepting the Pigou-Dalton claim: a transfer of welfare from a better-off to a worse-off person, without reducing the welfare that is transferred, without changing the worse-off status of the recipient, and without affecting anyone else's welfare, is always an improvement (stated in Adler 2012, 114–15, 339). The new status quo is morally better than the preceding one. Just by arithmetic, the shift described has to be making the world better. The absolute noncomparative claim implies a comparative claim: better to help the worse-off than the better-off, all else equal.

This discussion has slid from a claim about the impersonal value of outcomes to a claim about what one ought to do, what outcome one should strive to reach. The second claim does not follow from the first. This gap is filled by positing that that each of us is bound by a moral duty of beneficence, to improve the world by impersonal standards to some degree. When one acts, one always has some moral reason to make the resulting state of affairs morally better, not worse. How much reason? And how much priority attaches to helping the worse off? As always, we have to think about a lot of diverse examples, trying to settle both on judgments about particular cases and judgments about general rules that explain and justify the particular judgments, and looking for agreement with others or a good account of why those who disagree are wrong. And we expect, whatever provisional views we arrive at are liable to shift in the future with further evidence and reflection.

That's priority. Go back now to equality. An extreme egalitarian holds that the more equal people's condition is in some outcome, the better the outcome is, all things considered. A moderate egalitarian does not agree that equality rules the roost in this way. Instead she holds that the greater the aggregate of individual well-being summed across persons in some outcome, the better it is, and the more equal the distribution of welfare across persons in some outcome, the better it is. The overall impersonal value of an outcome or state of affairs depends on how these two components of value should be balanced against one another. The economist Marc Fleurbaey (2015) has demonstrated that for any prioritarian standard for evaluating outcomes, there will be some moderate egalitarian standard that yields the same implications for choice in any decision problem we might face, so long as each possible choice is certain to give rise to a particular outcome. This result does not render priority versus equality a nonissue; it can yield conflicting implications for deciding between risky choices. However, the Fleurbaey result highlights the idea that since both priority and moderate equality views are committed to Pigou-Dalton, they both merit being characterized as egalitarian in a broad sense. I am happy myself to state that WE tells us we ought to maximize priority-weighted or alternatively equality-weighted well-being summed across persons. The upshot is that the Frankfurt objection to equality should not stampede us into rejecting egalitarianism.

However, we are not yet out of the woods. Supposing that equalizing welfare is desirable, following Pigou-Dalton, does not automatically give us reason to embrace equalizing income and wealth. After all, there is no one-to-one correlation between shifts in money income and shifts in well-being. With a small professor's income, Arneson may drink beer and live well, whereas with a movie star's income, he would use cocaine or heroin and live far less well. And more importantly, in many situations, the real well-being gains we get from further increases in income decline as our income level rises. And priority adds that their moral value declines more. Nonetheless, on the whole and on the average, surely we should expect people to be better off in real terms, flourishing and not just getting by, as they get more cash—even if people do not always make and act on sensible judgments about how to spend it, and even if, unfortunately, some people are terribly imprudent. So increasing people's income tends to boost their lifetime well-being, and by priority, boosting the well-being of those who are otherwise heading for less lifetime well-being matters morally more.

Finally, even if the types of equality that NSD sustains were not intrinsically morally valuable, good in themselves, they might for all that be instrumentally valuable in ways we should prize. Consider what gets called "relative poverty." This does not actually refer to destitution or poverty, having to make do on little money. It's inequality in post-tax post-transfer income. The Nordics unquestionably lessen this, not only by taxing and transferring pre-tax pre-transfer income, but by compressing the distribution of the latter, via having education and family life that prepare individuals for adult work, having a competitive market economy that does not lean heavily on business regulation and sustains high employment, and by having collectivist wage-setting practices. Also, arguably, the particular ways the Nordics tax and transfer also set these countries apart from low-tax countries such as Australia and the United States and from Southern European welfare states. By whatever means, the Nordic countries stand out for sustaining low relative poverty. Within a country, this is measured by the Gini coefficient (a measure of what magnitude of transfer would be required to render everyone's disposable income the same), or by the ratio of the disposable income of those at the 90th percentile to those at the 50th and of those at the 50th to those at the 10th, or by the proportion of households with disposable income less than one half of the disposable income of the household that is at the center of the income distribution. Why suppose this reasonably matters to anyone?

I have accepted that how your income compares to that of other people does not in itself matter morally. But how your income compares to that of others might matter, not in itself, but by virtue of further goods and bads it tends to bring about. Relative poverty also gets called "social exclusion." If you believe that it matters, you probably believe it generates instrumental bads, especially for those at the bottom, but maybe for those who are relatively rich as well, via distracting snobbery and such. If relative poverty in a country is high, a lot of its members are unable fully to participate in the ordinary life of the society; they are outsiders. Paul Krugman (2024) has commented that with high relative poverty, a society doesn't feel like a place in which most people live "in more or less the same material universe." Sensing this might well tend to lower the relatively poor's self-esteem and capacity to effectively pursue valuable projects one cares about, resulting in lower genuine well-being. (Of course, those who are relatively wealthy, and especially very wealthy, might get a boost from being on top, but if all you care about is being better off in money than others, compressing the distribution of income in a capitalist market economy would still leave a relative ranking of people from best off in disposable earnings to worst off.)

The upshot of this discussion is that even if how one person's condition compares to that of another never in itself matters at all morally, (a) how well or badly off one is in absolute well-being terms still plausibly matters morally in itself, affecting the moral value of securing an additional well-being gain for a person, and (b) having less money than others, being relatively poor, can be instrumentally bad, give rise to various bads (and goods, maybe) that in turn have an impact on people's lifetime well-being.

## The Global Justice Objection to Nordic Social Democracy

Up to this point, this essay has mainly assessed and praised Nordic social democracy considered as a set of arrangements that affect the inhabitants of the rich countries that have been following this path for several decades. If we ask, for example, what impact Swedish social democracy has had on the lives of Swedes, the answer is that it has delivered a high level of social justice for all, by egalitarian standards. In particular, Nordic social democracy outperforms the less generous welfare state programs of the United States and the United Kingdom and the more socially conservative welfare state arrangements of continental and especially Southern Europe. Countries in the latter group, including Italy (and one could toss in Asian countries such as Japan and South Korea), have so far done far less than the Scandinavian countries to promote the full freedom of women to participate fully in society on equal terms with men.

What happens to the assessment of Nordic social democracy if we widen our focus and consider its global impact? From the broadly egalitarian perspective that this essay has suggested we should all endorse, things immediately look very different. If we seek political and social arrangements that boost prosperity and well-being for those whose condition is below average, giving greater priority to the worse off all over the earth, Nordic social democracy operating in rich countries like Sweden and Denmark looks to be redistribution from the very rich to the somewhat less rich—not a big deal at all, morally speaking. The people with low disposable income in rich countries, whom we rich-country inhabitants ordinarily would identify as the poor, are in global terms in the top half of the income distribution. From a global egalitarian standpoint, they should be making sacrifices to help the global poor. Emphasizing the duty of rich Swedes to help poor Swedes misunderstands what our priorities should be: all Swedes (all of the globally well-off) should be working to bring about better lives for impoverished people in poor countries in Africa, East Asia, Central America, and elsewhere.

It gets worse. Some theorists have urged that allowing and enforcing much greater freedom to migrate from country to country than current nation states permit would be a uniquely feasible and effective way to promote prosperity and well-being worldwide and reduce or eliminate global poverty. Crudely put, in poor countries people are poor because where they currently live, their labor can only be deployed on scant and low-quality capital. If I were impoverished in Somalia and could move to say, Chicago, and seek employment there, I would either be able to work more productively on better capital, or at least work in a job whose wage is higher than I can now get due to generally higher productivity there. (A haircut costs more in Chicago than in Somalia.) With completely open borders, it has been estimated that in the neighborhood of a third of the world's population would relocate, leading to massive economic gain. The gains would largely accrue initially to those who move to places where their incomes will increase, but those who choose to remain in place in poor countries might well benefit from less crowding and competition for resources after the movers have departed. Also, we know that those who move to richer countries to gain higher income tend massively to transmit some of it back to family members in their country of origin, further reducing world poverty. You might suspect that the gains of those who would migrate to rich countries in this scenario would come at the expense of the present inhabitants of these rich countries, now forced to compete against newcomers. But studies by economists suggest that for the most part immigrants would contribute economically in ways that complement rather than substitute for the skills and labor of the rich-country citizens, leading to gains all around, or at most small losses for a few. One economist has stated that closing borders as countries now do is foregoing huge gains—leaving "trillion dollar bills just lying on the pavement" (Clemens 2011).

However, there appears to be a conflict between preserving or instituting the generous welfare state policies of Nordic social democracy in rich countries and fulfilling global justice duties by opening the doors—if not fully, at least wider than they are at present—to temporary or permanent migrants from poor countries. One problem is that at least in the short run, a massive influx of extremely poor migrants greatly increases the cost of generous welfare state programs and hence reduces the voters' willingness to pay for them. This problem could be avoided if rich countries admitted migrants only as guest workers lacking citizenship and rights to the welfare state benefits that citizens enjoy, but then social democratic equality among the country's inhabitants disappears. Either way, goodbye to Nordic social democracy as we know it.

A second, perhaps more decisive problem is that generous welfare states arise and persist in countries with culturally and ethnically homogeneous populations. In these countries the "we" who pay most taxes identify with the "them" who are recipients and see them as part of "us." In countries with heterogeneous populations, not so much. We might wish this were not the case, but it seems to be the reality. The United States, with its history of slavery and continuing hostility of whites toward blacks, along with stimulating but rancorous ethnic diversity, is a glaring illustration. Economists Alberto Alesina and Edward Glaeser report that about 50 percent of the difference in generosity toward the poor between Europe and United States is racially based. They state, "A large literature has documented racial and ethnic antipathies, and a smaller literature has compellingly linked these feelings with hostility to welfare" (2004, 133–34).

Glen Weyl (2018) provocatively poses the challenge for global egalitarians who celebrate generous welfare state policies in rich countries by asking, which countries in the world do most on a per capita basis to reduce global poverty? The answer is that the oil-rich Gulf Coast Council countries of the Middle East do the most. They take in huge numbers of guest workers from poor countries on a revolving door basis to do much of the labor, freeing their own well-off citizens from having to do much of it. The meager pay the guest workers get exceeds what they could expect in their home countries, and much of this pay is transmitted back to impoverished relatives back home. No generous welfare state benefits flow to the guest workers. On a per capita basis, authoritarian and repressive regimes like Kuwait do more to alleviate global poverty than Scandinavian social democracies.

The challenge, simply put:

1. Global justice requires maximizing equality-weighted well-being of all people, not just one's fellow countrymen.
2. To maximize the equality-weighted well-being of all people, not just one's fellow countrymen, requires a major opening of

national borders, permitting many people from all across the earth to resettle in rich countries.

3. A major opening of national borders permitting many people from across the earth to resettle in rich countries is incompatible with the initiation and continuation of Nordic (generous) social democratic policies in rich countries.
4. Conformity with what global justice requires is incompatible with the initiation and continuation of Nordic (generous) social democratic policies in rich countries.

This argument looks to be valid, so if we accept 1, 2, and 3, we must embrace the conclusion 4, and the euthanasia of Nordic social democracy.

Let's consider whether there are grounds for rejecting one or more of premises 1–3 and defending the continuation (and strengthening) of Nordic social democracy. Premise 1 might be contested on various grounds. One is that people have special-tie duties to the members of their own political society, which take priority, to some extent, over their duties of beneficence pressing them to help needy people everywhere across the globe.

Another is that if justice has an egalitarian character, what equality demands of us is to regard and treat those we interact with as equals. We should relate as equals to all. In matters of governance, we relate as equals by practicing a true democracy in which all have equal opportunity to influence political decision-making. On the face of it, relational egalitarian justice, even if it has wide global scope of application, can be satisfied without compressing the world's distribution of wealth across countries and peoples. Establishing and sustaining political democracy in a nation-state does not require great wealth. With true democracy in each country of the world, global relational egalitarian justice might be satisfied even though there remains huge inequality of wealth between economically better-off and worse-off countries.

But neither of these gambits looks promising. If we ought to be welfarist egalitarians, then widening the scope of egalitarian concern requires boosting prosperity in poor countries and compressing the worldwide distribution of wealth and income. And widening the scope of egalitarian concern appears to be mandatory once you think about it. If I could choose either to help a poor child in Africa live ten extra good years to age forty or instead help an already well-off person in my own country live an extra ten good years to age ninety, the former option is morally superior. Regarding duties to fellow countrymen, one might hold that they exist but have lesser priority than global justice duties, when the two sets of duties pull in different directions. Help your fellow countrymen only with resources you have left after fulfilling higher-priority global justice duties (Caney 2011).

Also, one might accept that we can have significant special-tie personal obligations, to friends and family and colleagues, with whom we personally interact, without accepting that we can have similar special ties (and accompanying obligations) to those with whom we have anonymous impersonal relationships, such as fellow members of our own ethnic group or fellow citizens of our nation state (Arneson 2016).

This claim requires clarification. In a sense we have special-tie obligations that may be impersonal and anonymous to those with whom we have ordinary trading relations. If I make a contract, I should keep it. But family and friend relationships and special-tie obligations stemming from them can arise without voluntary choices to form such relationships, and special-tie relationships and obligations stemming from ethnic and nation-state membership are claimed to arise similarly in the absence of voluntary commitment. These group memberships are also claimed to be similar to friendship and family ties in persisting as long as the relationship persists and giving rise to significant and somewhat open-ended demands. I am suggesting that these features are not plausibly associated with anonymous, impersonal relationships.

We should be extreme cosmopolitans, regarding ourselves first and foremost as citizens of the world. (This position allows that national patriotic sentiments and patriotic duties might in some circumstances be good means to extreme cosmopolitan goals.)

The upshot is that we should accept premise 1. But in an ecumenical spirit, I note that if people have significant obligations to fellow members of their nation-state that take some priority over duties to humanity—people everywhere, and future people as well—that will weaken the objection to Nordic social democracy based on global justice.

In contrast, premise 2 screams for rejection. First, open borders, or anything close to that, would be a huge disruptive transformation that might not deliver anything close to the huge benefit its advocates anticipate. Its economic consequences are unknown (Hanson 2009). Some increase in migration into rich countries from present levels might well be beneficial, but how much increase? Moreover, even if much more open borders would be beneficial if accepted, popular resistance in rich countries might well lead to backlash and bad consequences overshadowing and eventually destroying these economic benefits.

Even more important, for rich countries and their inhabitants, global justice duties are duties not to harm, and beyond that, involve beneficence directed at poor-country inhabitants. There will almost always be several alternative ways to satisfy any beneficence duties (Wellman 2008, 126–27). So even if opening borders to increased migration would be a very effective way to fulfill one's global justice duties, there will in actual and likely circumstances be others. Sweden could contribute to aid programs in Somalia, or provide expert advice or technological knowledge, or donate or loan capital, or send troops to restore good order in the face of civil war. In particular, insofar as people are poor because their access to capital is scant and hence their labor is unproductive, this problem could be solved either by moving people to where the capital is or by moving capital to where the people are.

Furthermore, there is a plus to rich people who are living under NSD seeking to fulfill their global justice duties by moving, or better, donating, capital to people in poor countries rather than by facilitating large increases in in-migration of people from poor countries. In the migration scenario, the costs to NSD citizens, via collapse or erosion of generous welfare state practices, will be borne preponderantly by the rich-country poor. In the capital transfer alternative scenario, the costs are mainly borne by rich-country taxpayers, with more taxes and higher rates of taxation falling more on rich-country wealthier persons. The second scenario is more fair. Also, we should acknowledge, the idea of open borders is utopian. Rich-country voters will not vote for it, and in wealthy nondemocracies, dictators will not impose it. For any feasible degree of global justice fulfillment on the part of rich countries attained by opening borders to large-scale migration, there will be a more fair, equally feasible degree of global justice fulfillment attained by capital transfer from rich to poor countries. Rather than deny that rich countries in current times are bound by very demanding global justice duties, we should favor shifting a good part of the burden of fulfilling that burden to the shoulders of the rich.

This line of thought will attract objections. An obvious one is that significant donation of capital (or the equivalent) from Scandinavian countries to the global poor would itself conflict with the maintenance of generous NSD policies. The response is that we should distinguish between generous and ample NSD policies. With less tax money available to fund those policies, there will be some penny-pinching, but this is compatible with maintaining a generous egalitarian and pro-poor tilt. Another worry is that the capital transfer being envisaged would clearly dampen economic growth in NSD countries, but this effect should be offset by rising growth rates in poor-country recipients of this aid. And if economic development policies are successful, they need not be sustained for an indefinitely long time.

A more serious worry is that the history of economic aid from rich to poor countries over past decades decisively shows that simple transfer of money from rich to poor countries is not a recipe for generating sustained economic takeoff in struggling countries (Alesina and Dollar 2000; Easterly 2001; Deaton 2013, ch. 7; also Deaton 2023). If the institutions and culture in the receiving country are not adequate to absorb the gift, the gift will do no good and may do harm.

In reply, foreign aid handed out by wealthy countries since World War II has largely been carried out to serve big-power rivalries, not to improve the world. The experiment of seriously trying to lift struggling poor countries into prosperity has not yet been tried. Naysaying its prospects would be premature. (For an argument supporting the idea that many of the global poor are caught in poverty traps from which they can permanently extricate themselves with the aid of a sufficient transfer of assets, see Balboni et al. 2022.) Also, given that institutions and culture certainly do matter, what that shows is that effective aid must be directed in ways that facilitate economic growth and poverty elimination by facilitating complementary institutional and cultural change. In some situations, for some stretches of time, the best judgment is that nothing can be done for now in some places where conditions are deplorable. Handing money to an entrenched dictator who gives no sign of willingness to put good policies in place would not help. For progress, all that is needed is that among the poor countries, some of them can be helped effectively here and now.

If premise 2 is false, what is there to say about 3? It's speculative, and debatable. No law of physics absolutely rules out the possibility that ethnically and culturally heterogeneous groups of people might live together amicably, with wide social trust and solidarity, yielding a stable voting majority for generous welfare state policies. However, if 2 is false, the argument that leads to the pessimistic conclusion about the compatibility of fulfilling global justice, construed as having wide scope of application, and initiating and maintaining Nordic social democracy, falls to the ground.

To return to the question: does compressing the distribution of income and life prospects among the global rich pale to insignificance by comparison with compressing it across the entire global population? There are reasons to support a "No" answer. Recall the prioritarian view that getting a benefit to a person is morally more valuable, the worse off the person would otherwise be in lifetime well-being. Assuming that very roughly those with higher income will tend to have overall better lives, a transfer of a benefit without loss from the very best-off to someone at the very bottom of the world distribution will be morally more valuable than transferring the benefit to someone above the very bottom of the distribution, but a transfer from the best-off to someone in the middle of the distribution still brings about significant moral gain (how much depends on what weight attaches to priority for the worse-off). The welfarist egalitarian gains that Nordic social democracy sustains are not, morally speaking, small potatoes.

It should not be assumed without question that the higher one's disposable income is, the better one's life is. Relative poverty (social exclusion), not being able to participate fully in the life of one's community, plays some role. From another angle, with an eye on US citizens with no more than a high school education, the economist Angus Deaton points out that by several indicators, including life expectancy, their quality of life has deteriorated in recent years (Deaton 2023). He floats the conjecture that by sensible fine-grained assessment of their overall conditions of life, many of them are appropriately classified as below the top half of global inhabitants. Even if his conjecture holds for Americans, and not for citizens of Scandinavian welfare states, who exhibit many fewer signs of troubled lives than members of the group Deaton is characterizing, if only generous welfare state policies or some equivalent factor keeps the working class of rich countries from being aptly classified as part of the broad global poor, this would signal that the collapse of NSD institutions where they persist would register, by proper global justice accounting, as a big deal.

## REFERENCES

Acemoglu, D., J. Robinson, and T. Verdier. 2017. "Asymmetric Growth and Institutions in an Interdependent World." *Journal of Political Economy* 125: 1245–1305.

Adler, M. 2012. *Well-Being and Fair Distribution: Beyond Cost-Benefit Analysis*. Oxford: Oxford University Press, 2012.

Alesina, A., and D. Dollar. 2000. "Who Gives Foreign Aid to Whom and Why." *Journal of Economic Growth* 5: 33–53.

Alesina, A., and E. Glaeser. 2004. *Fighting Poverty in the U.S. and Europe: A World of Difference*. Oxford: Oxford University Press.

Anderson, E. 1999. "What Is the Point of Equality?" *Ethics* 109: 287–337.
Arneson, R. 2016. "Extreme Cosmopolitanisms Defended." *Critical Review of International Social and Political Philosophy* 19: 555–73.
Arneson, R. 2022. *Prioritarianism.* Cambridge: Cambridge University Press.
Balboni, C., O. Bandiera, R. Burgess, M. Ghatak, and A. Heil. 2022. "Why Do People Stay Poor?" *Quarterly Journal of Economics* 137 (2): 785–844.
Brennan, J. 2012. *What Everyone Needs to Know about Libertarianism.* Oxford: Oxford University Press.
Caney, S. 2011. "Humanity, Associations, and Global Justice: In Defence of Humanity-Centered Cosmopolitan Egalitarianism." *The Monist* 94: 506–34.
Clemens, M. 2011. "Economics and Immigration: Trillion Dollar Bills on the Sidewalk?" *Journal of Economic Perspectives* 25: 83–106.
Cohen, G. 2009. *Why Not Socialism?* Princeton: Princeton University Press.
Deaton, A. 2013. *The Great Escape: Health, Wealth, and the Origins of Inequality.* Princeton: Princeton University Press.
Deaton, A. 2023. *Economics in America: An Immigrant Economist Explores the Land of Inequality.* Princeton: Princeton University Press.
Easterly, W. 2001. *The Elusive Quest for Growth: Economists' Adventures and Misadventures in the Tropics.* Cambridge, MA: MIT Press.
Esping-Andersen, G., and J. Cimentada. 2018. "Ability and Mobility: The Relative Influence of Skills and Social Origin on Social Mobility." *Social Science Research* 5: 13–31.
Fleurbaey, M. 2015. "Equality versus Priority: How Relevant Is the Distinction?" *Economics and Philosophy* 31: 203–17.
Frankfurt, H. 1987. "Equality as a Moral Ideal." *Ethics* 98: 21–43.
Frankfurt, H. 2015. *On Inequality.* Princeton: Princeton University Press.
Hanson, G. 2009. "The Economic Consequences of the International Migration of Labor." *Annual Review of Economics* 1: 179–207.
Heath, J. 2009. *Economics without Illusions.* New York: Broadway Books.
Heckman, J. 2006. "Skill Formation and the Economics of Investing in Disadvantaged Children." *Science* 312: 1900–1902.
Jensen, C. 2021. *Equality in the Nordic World.* Aarhus: Aarhus University Press; Madison: University of Wisconsin Press.
Jensen, C., and K. van Kersbergen. 2017. *The Politics of Inequality.* New York: Palgrave.
Kenworthy, L. 2011. *Progress for the Poor.* Oxford: Oxford University Press.
Kenworthy, L. 2019. *Social Democratic Capitalism.* Oxford: Oxford University Press.
Kenworthy, L. 2022. *Would Socialism Be Better?* Oxford: Oxford University Press.
Kolodny, N. 2023. *The Pecking Order: Social Hierarchy as a Philosophical Problem.* Cambridge, MA: Harvard University Press.
Krugman, P. 2024. "Can Biden Revive the Fortunes of American Workers." *New York Times*, May 3, Opinion/A20.
Levitsky, S., and L. Way. 2002. "The Rise of Competitive Authoritarianism." *Journal of Democracy* 13: 51–65.
Lindert, P. 2019. *Welfare States.* Cambridge: Cambridge University Press.

Lindert, P. 2021. *Making Social Spending Work*. Cambridge: Cambridge University Press.
Lippert-Rasmussen, K. 2018. *Relational Egalitarianism: Living as Equals*. Cambridge: Cambridge University Press.
Miller, R. 2018a. "Learning from Libertarianism: Thanks from an Unrepentant Social Democrat." In *The Routledge Handbook of Libertarianism*, ed. J. Brennan, B. van der Vossen, and D. Schmidtz, 3–21. New York: Routledge.
Miller, R. 2018b. "Is Capitalism Corrupt?" *Social Philosophy and Policy* 35: 31–53.
Miller, R. 2019. "Social Democracy and Free Enterprise." *Journal of Social Philosophy* 50: 597–619.
Nozick, R. 1974. *Anarchy, State, and Utopia*. New York: Basic Books.
Parfit, D. 1991. "Equality or Priority?" *The Lindley Lectures*. Lawrence: University of Kansas Press.
Rae, D., D. Yates, and others. 1981. *Inequalities*. Cambridge, MA: Harvard University Press.
Rawls, J. 1999. *A Theory of Justice*, rev. ed. Cambridge, MA: Harvard University Press.
Sejersted, F. 2011. *The Age of Social Democracy: Norway and Sweden in the Twentieth Century*, trans. R. Daly, ed. M. Adams. Princeton: Princeton University Press.
Wellman, C. 2008. "Immigration and Freedom of Association." *Ethics* 119 (1): 109–41.
Weyl, G. 2018. "The Openness-Equality Trade-off in Global Redistribution." *Economic Journal* 128: F1–F36.

CHAPTER 7

# Reparations for the Mega-Rich

Mollie Gerver

On a dry summer morning in 1992 a young woman named Kiden was sitting on her front patio in southern Sudan. Militias on horseback rode into town and confiscated her land because she was a member of the Bari tribe. She later sold tea on the side of the road for over a decade, moved abroad to work in the hotel industry, and saved over $40,000, which she invested to make considerably more money. She eventually re-obtained the land she lost twenty years prior.[1]

The year that Kiden won her land back, Ellen Pao was working 14,000 kilometers away in California at the venture capitalist firm Kleiner Perkins. Pao had joined Kleiner Perkins seven years prior, hired because of her degrees in engineering and business; she eventually led the company's expansion into China. She earned over half a million dollars annually throughout the 2000s, but was consistently overlooked for promotion. In 2013 she unsuccessfully sued Kleiner Perkins for $16 million in earnings lost from gender-based discrimination.[2]

Kiden and Pao had very different experiences. Kiden was seeking land lost from ethnic cleansing, while Pao was seeking money she never gained due to sexism. Kiden was returning to her childhood home and was successful, while Pao was seeking compensation and was unsuccessful. Though their experiences differed, they had one thing in common: both were wealthy individuals claiming rights to assets lost from discrimination.

It is not clear that either woman had a right to all assets she sought. Neither was wronged more than other victims of discrimination. Kiden was not wronged more than other Bari citizens who never owned land prior to fleeing southern Sudan. Pao was not wronged more than other workers who faced sexism but did not receive the salary she earned. If Kiden and Pao were not wronged more than others, perhaps they had no right to seek more assets than others. Moreover, in obtaining more assets than others, they accrued wealth beyond what they needed, while others—including other victims of discrimination—were left in poverty. If the very wealthy do not have a right to additional wealth, perhaps Kiden and Pao did not have a right to the assets they sought. Yet this might seem unfair: even the wealthy should not be harmed by wrongful discrimination. They would be harmed if they were unable to access assets lost from discrimination.

This puzzle is not merely academic. In the history of restitution, some states have denied wealthy refugees access to lost assets because these refugees did not need these assets, while others did.[3] We might imagine a similar policy for discrimination lawsuits, limiting the money a given claimant could obtain and redistributing the rest to those in greater need. Had Pao won $16 million under such a policy, this money could potentially be taxed at 100% and redistributed to those living in destitution. This would seem justified in one sense—it would ensure no one owned assets they had no right to own—but unfair in another: Pao would be making less money than her male counterparts because she was a woman.

In the next section, I first present this novel puzzle. I demonstrate that it runs deep, and cannot be easily dismissed by appealing to two traditional arguments raised in support of compensation for harm in general.

In section 2 I present two solutions to this puzzle that do not rely on traditional arguments in support of compensation in general. The first solution begins with the premise that, though the wealthy may have no right to the wealth they lost from discrimination, they have a right to not lose wealth in a wrongful manner. Similar to a criminal who has no right to the goods she steals, but a right to not be stopped through violent police action, the wealthy have no right to the wealth they own, but do have a right to not lose this wealth through discrimination.

The second solution appeals to the way poor minority members are disadvantaged when their wealthy counterparts suffer harmful discrimination. They are disadvantaged because, when wealthy minority members are discriminated against because of their minority identity, the expected return on investments made by poor minority members is reduced: the most they can make is less than the most members of the majority can make. This creates one justification for countering discrimination against wealthy minority members. I call this the "Investment Argument." While the Investment Argument is promising when poor minority members have money they can invest, this Investment Argument has little relevance when poor minority members have few or no dollars to invest. In such cases, the justification for returning all assets to the wealthy is considerably weakened. In section 3 I respond to objections.

Before I begin, a number of clarifications are in order. Throughout the chapter I focus on cases where policies promoting distribution conflict with policies countering discrimination.[4] I focus particularly on compensation and restitution, the policies most at risk of conflicting with principles of distributive justice: when Pao sought lost earnings and Kiden sought her land, the assets they sought enriched them and not others.

For simplicity, I refer to compensation and restitution as "reparations," as both are intended to repair the loss arising from discrimination by providing assets equal to those lost from discrimination.[5] Importantly, I put aside reparations that serve only as a symbol of apology for discrimination, or to compensate for psychological harm.[6] If reparations were only apologies or compensation for psychological harm, those who lost fewer assets could receive the same reparations as those who lost more. If a janitor was denied a promotion due to discrimination and lost out on $1000 a year, he would be owed the same compensation for psychological harm as Pao and Kiden, assuming the psychological harm was equal. That is not what occurs: those who lose more wealth from discrimination receive more money than those who lose less. Worryingly, those who lose more wealth from discrimination tend to be wealthier already, and so less in need of the money they receive. My goal is to consider why this might be justified, given duties of distributive justice.

When discussing duties of distributive justice, I refer to duties to promote a distribution of goods between the wealthy and poor that is of a particular pattern. A government policy that granted assets to wealthy minority members, rather than distributing these assets to the poor, might disrupt such a pattern. Though there is disagreement over what a minimally just pattern entails, there is agreement across a range of scholars that the very wealthy have no right to additional assets that could be redistributed to those who lack a minimally decent life.[7] My aim is to consider whether, if one accepts this minimal principle, one ought to support mechanisms for countering discrimination that conflict with this principle.

## 1. The Puzzle

There are two potential reasons one might counter discrimination via reparations. Both reasons seem to conflict with principles of distributive justice, giving rise the puzzle I present.

### *1.1. Harm*

One reason we might wish to counter discrimination is to counter the harm from discrimination. According to a commonly held view, those who are harmed from wrongdoing ought to be compensated for this harm. If a wealthy individual is punched in the stomach, and as a result is forced to give up her money, she loses wealth in a manner that is wrong. She is therefore owed compensation for this wrong in the form of the assets she lost.[8] Similarly, if a wealthy individual is wrongly discriminated against, and as a result loses assets, she loses wealth in a manner that is wrong. She is therefore owed reparations to counteract the harms from this wrong.[9]

But even if a person has been wronged, and is harmed as a result, they are not owed reparations for the harm of losing assets they had no right to own. If I steal your laptop, and someone takes the laptop from me via physical assault, I have been wronged from the assault and harmed from this wrong—I lost the laptop—but I should not be given the laptop back. The laptop should instead be returned to the rightful owner. A similar claim could be raised regarding Kiden and Pao. If the very wealthy have no right to additional wealth that could be given to others in need, then Kiden had no right to her former land and Pao had no right to $16 million.

Some might reject this objection, claiming that we can ensure a fair distribution of goods while also providing reparations for discrimination; it is just a matter of taxing the reparations of the wealthy and issuing similar taxes for those who never faced discrimination.[10] For example, if the South Sudanese government established Kiden's wealth at $1.5 million without her land, and the land was worth an additional $1 million, it could tax her returned land at 100 percent, and those worth $2.5 million would be taxed at $1 million. This would ensure that she was provided reparations in one sense, without either obtaining assets she had no right to own, or facing a disadvantage compared to other ethnic groups. Similarly, if Pao had won $16 million, the state could tax 100 percent of it, and if male executives made $16 million more than they had a right to, it could then tax this $16 million at 100 percent as well. Pao would not obtain assets to which she had no right, and would not be financially worse off from discrimination.

While such a solution may be ideal, it may be difficult to implement in practice. It may be difficult for the government to effectively tax all South Sudanese of comparable wealth at the same rate, but relatively easier to "tax" Kiden by not returning her land. It may be difficult for the US government to effectively tax all executives of comparable wealth at the same rate, given the tax loopholes utilized by wealthy executives, but easy to tax Pao had she been awarded money in a lawsuit. In such cases, we are left with the same puzzle: though both women were disadvantaged because of discrimination, if they had no right to the assets lost from this discrimination, it is not clear if the government would be permitted to provide them assets they lost.

Perhaps the best version of the harm-based reason to provide reparations for discrimination is that it incentivizes individuals to combat discrimination. Pao was incentivized to sue her former employer, thus giving her employer a reason to stop discrimination, because she knew there was a chance of gaining tens of millions of dollars in compensation. Kiden was incentivized to seek compensation or restitution of her land, giving the government a reason to stop discriminatory land distribution, because she knew she would be able to keep the land she re-obtained. Even if neither had a moral right to the assets they lost from discrimination, it was good that they had a chance to gain such assets to help prevent discrimination in the future.

This explanation, however, would not justify the return of assets lost from discrimination. It would merely justify providing money to incentivize lawsuits, and this money may be worth more or less than the assets lost from discrimination. Pao may have been incentivized to sue her employer if she would receive not $16 million, but $10 million, or $50 million. If the money necessary to incentivize lawsuits is less or more than the assets lost, it cannot provide a justification for reparations of the precise assets lost.

A similar version of the harm-based account faces a similar objection. According to some, if a wrongdoer pays reparations for the harm arising from the wrong, she can more easily express her acknowledgement of the wrong, which can lead to forgiveness from victims, strengthening trust between the wrongdoer and victims.[11] This explanation explains why reparations are owed, but it does not explain why the reparations should be equal to the loss arising from the wrong. In many cases a victim will begin to trust a perpetrator, or feel the wrong has been acknowledged, if reparations are less or more than the monetary loss incurred. If victims have a right to the precise loss incurred, a good theory will explain why.

### *1.2. Rule of Law*

In general, the law requires that individuals only lose assets in particular ways; they cannot be stolen, taken through violence, or arbitrarily confiscated. Sometimes such laws have value because they protect moral rights, but they can have value even if they do not. One reason they can have value is that they are passed through democratic institutions: if there are noninstrumental values in following laws that reflect the will of the people, a law that calls for the return of assets lost ought to be respected if passed by a democratic body. Similarly, if a law calls for the return of assets lost from wrongful discrimination, it ought to be respected.

One limitation of this argument is that it is irrelevant when laws are not governed via democracy, as when Kiden lost her land in 1980s Sudan. More importantly, this reasoning does not explain why democratic institutions should themselves pass legislation supporting reparations for wealthy victims of discrimination. If extreme inequality is wrong, perhaps democratic institutions should refrain from laws that return assets to the wealthy, including wealthy victims of discrimination.

A more promising argument relating to the rule of law concerns not the value of democracy, but the value of plans. Humans often plan their lives with the assumption that a given law will persist, or at least that it ought to persist. For example, if a farmer presumes that laws governing property will remain stable, and the land she toils on will remain in her possession, this allows her to plan for the harvest. She would struggle to plan for the harvest if she did not know whether the land she toiled on now would be hers tomorrow. Being able to plan one's life has value. It has value partly because it enables autonomy, giving individuals control over their lives, and partly because it creates utilitarian benefits, helping economies function. It also contributes to the development of a routine, making various tasks easier to perform.[12] It is easier for a farmer to harvest her crops if she plans to wake up every day at 5 a.m., prepare breakfast at 5:15, rev up the reaper engine at 6:00, take a break at 12:00, and so forth. If she can be fairly certain that the land will remain in her possession, because the law says it will, her daily routines will be easier to follow, becoming a habit with time, and requiring far less willpower to pursue.

If the rule of law has value because it promotes planning, then if a person suddenly finds themself unable to plan because their life has been altered, something morally undesirable has occurred.[13] This person has a right to compensation or restitution to continue their plans.[14] When Kiden made her life plans in Juba in the early 1990s, she made these plans based on the reasonable expectation that the rule of law would be upheld, and that her land would remain in her possession. She had a right to her land to once again continue her life plans. When Pao made her life plans in California in the 2000s, she made these plans based on the reasonable expectation that she would be promoted before her colleagues if she were more successful at generating a profit.

Importantly, even if Pao knew she would face sexism, she had good reason to believe sexism ought to be tackled, and so made life plans with the expectation that it would be tackled. When one makes plans based on the state of affairs that ought to exist, one gains similar value in being able to follow through with these plans: following through allows one to live a life with greater stability, ease, and perhaps certain utilitarian benefits.

The above argument has a number of limitations, which others before me have noted: it is not relevant when individuals cannot continue plans because the institutions of society have been so devastatingly destroyed that their assets will not help them return to plans they left behind.[15] Moreover, the plan-based argument is only relevant when victims are given swift reparations for their loss, allowing them continue the plans they created prior to the disruption.[16] Kiden received her land back over twenty years after fleeing, and Pao could not access swift compensation, because it can take years to prove gender-based discrimination.

More importantly, the claim gives rise to the same puzzle: it seems to conflict with certain principles of distributive justice. It seems unjust for wealthy and poor individuals to have dramatically unequal access to plans they can realize, especially if poor individuals lack access to plans that can ensure a minimally decent life. We can correct for this injustice by redistributing assets to the poor, rather than giving assets back to the wealthy. This might interrupt the wealthy's life plans, but it is not clear that they had a right to plans that depended on vast wealth. To see the force of this claim, return again to the stolen laptop. If I pursue my life plans around a laptop I stole, and I am violently attacked by an assailant who steals "my" laptop, I have no right to get this laptop back, even though getting it would help me realize my life plans. If we take seriously the idea that the wealthy often have no right to the vast assets they lost, just as I have no right to the laptop I lost, then the inability to plan seems like a poor justification for providing assets lost.[17]

We could stop here, concluding that many victims of discrimination have no right to compensation or restitution of assets lost. A number of scholars reach this conclusion in cases like Kiden's when discussing displaced populations,[18] but it is relevant for far more cases, including those like Pao. If justice demands that the wealthy not obtain wealth lost when others lack basic necessities, perhaps reparations for wealthy victims of discrimination should be rejected.

## 2. Demeaning Treatment and the Investment Argument

We can avoid this conclusion by focusing on the nature of discrimination itself. I first argue that discrimination is wrong when it demeans minority members, and one can be wrongly demeaned even when losing an asset to which one had no right, creating a reason to return such assets. Still, the concern for promoting distributive justice lingers. We might feel that, if the poor do not benefit at all from such reparations, their interests outweigh the interests of the wealthy. I argue that reparations to wealthy victims of discrimination do help poor minority members in one important way: they help them avoid demeaning discrimination by ensuring that each dollar they invest has an expected return equal to that of each dollar held by members of the majority. As mentioned earlier, I call this the Investment Argument.

### *2.1. Preventing Demeaning Treatment*

Discrimination is often wrong because it is demeaning. It is demeaning because victims are treated in a differential manner due to their ethnicity or gender, and this fails to recognize them as having their own unique attributes, instead viewing them merely as members of a group. For example, if an individual is arrested because of her ethnicity, this treats her as merely a member of a given ethnic group, not as an individual with her own unique claims and attributes. Such discrimination is particularly demeaning because she is denigrated to a lower social status when arrested, disadvantaging her compared to others.[19]

If discrimination is wrong when it demeans minorities, and particularly when it disadvantages them compared to others, then we can wrongly discriminate against individuals by denying them assets to which they have no right. For example, if a prosecutor only arrests wealthy thieves of an undesired ethnic minority, she demeans them by targeting them for their ethnicity, and wrongs them by confiscating their stolen goods. She wrongs them even if they have no right to these stolen goods. She therefore has reason to either arrest majority members at the same rate, or if this is not possible, to return stolen goods to minority thieves. She has this reason even if the thieves have no right to these stolen goods.

This response—returning assets to individuals who have no right to these assets—has precedence in criminal law. Imagine that a prosecutor barges into Bob's home with no evidence that he had committed any crime, and she uses physical violence against him, forcing him to reveal a laptop he had stolen, and finding evidence that he stole this laptop. She bags the laptop, brings it to the police station, and stands before a judge several months later, using evidence she had obtained through violent means. If her only evidence was obtained through violence, the evidence would likely be inadmissible, and in many jurisdictions she would fail to obtain a conviction.[20] After the trial, she would be forced to return to Bob the laptop he had stolen. This is true even though everyone, including the judge, knows that the laptop is not rightfully Bob's.

This is relevant for Kiden and Pao. It may be true that the current South Sudanese government could transfer Kiden's land to impoverished individuals, but just as a judge should not rely on inadmissible evidence to return stolen goods to their rightful owners, the government ought not rely on racist confiscation to give land to poor individuals. Racist confiscation is wrong because it demeans the victims of confiscation, even if victims had no right to the land at all. Kiden was demeaned when land was taken because of her Bari identity; she was treated as merely a member of a tribe rather than an individual, even if she had no right to this land. Similarly, Pao was demeaned when denied a promotion because she was a woman, losing out on money merely because of her gender, even if she had no right to this money. Were she to have won a lawsuit, and were the state to have redistributed the award to those in need, the state would be utilizing demeaning discrimination to redistribute to those in need, creating a weighty reason to not do so.

This argument has some weight: it provides one reason to provide reparations. However, it has less weight when the agent engaging in discrimination is distinct from the agent providing reparations. When a prosecutor returns stolen goods obtained through discrimination or violence, she is returning goods she herself obtained through discrimination or violence. In contrast, when a state returns property lost from discrimination, it is often returning goods another agent took through discrimination. It was the former Sudanese government that had paid militias to confiscate Kiden's land, rather than the state of South Sudan, established only in 2011. If the new state is a separate agent from the one that wrongfully took her land, then it would not itself be actively discriminating when redistributing her land to others: it would merely be utilizing the discrimination of another agent to help those in greater need. Even if doing so is wrong, it seems less wrong than actively engaging in discrimination.

This is especially true if those obtaining assets from the wealthy face the same level of discrimination as the wealthy, if not more. In California, many low-income women face discrimination that prevents them from being hired or promoted.[21] They would benefit from obtaining the reparations that Pao sought. In South Sudan, a large number of low-income Bari citizens face regular discrimination in attempting to access jobs,[22] and they would benefit from the land that Kiden re-obtained.

In other words, even if the demeaning nature of discrimination provides one reason to give reparations to the wealthy, this reason can seem weak given the needs of the poor. If this is true, then the case for providing reparations to the wealthy can be strengthened by demonstrating that they help the poor.

### 2.2. The Investment Argument

The Investment Argument begins with the premise that the money we have is materially more valuable if its expected return is higher. For example, a dollar I invest in a firm that is sure to profit is more valuable than a dollar that I do not invest at all, instead keeping under my mattress.

Nearly every person's dollars are, in this way, worth a slightly different amount. The dollars in my wallet are worth less than the dollars in my aunt's wallet if my aunt cares about investing in profitable businesses, and the dollars in my sister's wallet are worth more than the dollars in my aunt's wallet if my sister invests her money in job training that garners an even higher income.

One reason a dollar may be more profitable for one person than another is that one person is legally permitted to invest this dollar, while the other is not. If I cannot legally invest my money in profitable firms, but my neighbor can, the dollar I hold is worth less than the dollar my neighbor holds.

Another reason a dollar may be worth less is that, even if I do manage to invest the money in a profitable firm, I know the government will not protect my profits from being stolen by others. If I know that my profits can be stolen and never returned, while my neighbor's profits will be protected, then the dollars I hold are worth less than my neighbor's.

This has implications for poor minority members likely to face discrimination. Each poor minority member knows that, if she invests in education, land, or a business, the expected return on investment is lower than the expected return of poor majority members, all else being equal. Her expected return could be lower because she is barred outright from investing money in education, land, or a business, while a majority member is not. Her expected return could also be lower if she is less likely to be promoted to the top echelons of a given industry. If the most money she is likely to gain is lower than the most a majority-member is likely to gain, then the average predicted return she can obtain may be lower than the average predicted return of a majority member. She therefore holds dollars whose expected average return is lower than the dollars of a poor majority member.

The reason this type of discrimination is unjust is for the reasons raised in the previous section: it disadvantages minority members in a way that relegates them to a lower status, treating them as members of a group rather than as individuals; their money is worth less because of their group membership. This is demeaning, and to counteract this demeaning treatment, governments should adopt certain polices. One potential policy is to try and eradicate discrimination in general. The South Sudanese government could ensure that all individuals do not lose their land because of discrimination, and the US government could ensure that no individuals face gender-based discrimination.

In reality, such a policy is unlikely to be effective in the near future. Given that discrimination will probably continue, the government has reason to at least ensure that poor minorities' dollars are not worth less due to discrimination they will probably face. This is possible by promising poor citizens that if they grow wealthy and are denied even more money due to discrimination, they will be compensated for this denial. Under such a policy, if poor individuals grow wealthy from their investment, and then lose out on further wealth because of discrimination, they can obtain the assets they lost from discrimination. The government would be providing reparations not merely to protect wealthy victims from demeaning discrimination at the expense of poor individuals. It would be providing reparations so that poor minorities have assurance that, if they grow wealthy, they will not be disadvantaged from discrimination, ensuring that the dollars they hold now have equal expected return to the dollars held by the majority.

Consider this logic in the case of Pao. When Pao was a younger woman in the late 1990s, the dollars she held were of lesser value compared to the dollars of men of comparable socioeconomic status, because the most she could probably make was less than the most that men could probably make. The US government had good reason to assure her that, if she invested money in education, and found herself overlooked for promotion because of her gender, she would obtain compensation for the money lost from the discrimination she faced. Only then would her investments as a nonwealthy person have equal expected return to the expected return of men's investments, such that her dollars would have similar value to the dollars of men.

A similar logic is at play for property taken in a discriminatory manner. As a young Bari woman living in 1990s Sudan, Kiden's land would have been worth less in her hands if, in the future, it would be confiscated and then denied to her as a result of her wealth in 2012. She would be disadvantaged if wealthy majority members who never had their land confiscated could keep land in their possession while she could not get her land back. Similarly, low-income Bari residents today have an interest in living in a country where even the wealthy can obtain reparations for land confiscated in a discriminatory manner. This is because, while wealthy Bari residents receiving reparations would disadvantage poor Bari residents in one way, because land would not be distributed to them, it would advantage them in another, increasing the value of the assets they already hold. The South Sudanese government has good reason to assure poor citizens that, if they invest in their land, and their land is taken because of their ethnicity, they can get this land back. Only then will their investments not yield lower expected returns due to discrimination, ensuring that land held now does not have lower value due to discrimination.

Note that this theory is not derived from the general right of all individuals to equal opportunities. We might think, for example, that if poor minorities can expect to face discrimination, they lack opportunities equal to those of their majority peers, and justice requires equal opportunities. My argument is not committed to the claim that justice demands equal opportunities. It is merely committed to the claim that poor minorities should not be demeaned because of their minority status, and they are demeaned if the dollars they hold are of less value due to the discrimination they may face. They can avoid this demeaning devaluing of their dollars if they are promised reparations for assets lost from discrimination they face. And because it is the poor who are protected, we needn't claim that reparations are justified to protect wealthy minorities alone. It is precisely because of the effects on the poor that reparations for the wealthy are especially justified.

The above argument is similarly not committed to the claim that reparations are justified to increase the expected return of dollars held by all poor individuals. There may be no intrinsic value in poor individuals having dollars with higher expected return; we might care only about poor individuals having more actual dollars. The Investment Argument instead claims that, even if having dollars with greater return is not intrinsically valuable, there is value in poor minority members not being denied greater returns because of their minority status. More generally, claiming that there is no intrinsic value in individuals having X is compatible with the claim that there is value in minorities not being denied X because of their minority status. For example, claiming there is no intrinsic value in individuals sitting in Classroom A rather than B is compatible with the claim that minorities ought not to be deprived of the ability to sit in Classroom A because of their minority status. Such segregation would be wrong not because sitting in Classroom A has greater value, but because there is something wrong in assigning students to Classroom B because they are members of a minority.

The above also explains why, even if a given minority member will remain poor throughout her whole life, and so would not gain from a policy where the wealthy can access reparations, she is still wrongly discriminated against if her current dollars have a lower expected return. It could be comparable to being given a lower-payout lottery ticket: imagine that Ashula is given a lottery ticket with a one in a billion chance of winning $1 million, but Stephen is given a lottery ticket with the same chance of winning $2 million. Both are unlikely to win, but if Ashula is given her ticket because she has darker skin than Stephen, she would be wronged even if neither has a winning ticket. This would be especially true if Ashula is consistently given lower-payoff lottery tickets throughout her life compared to Stephen, constantly reminding her of her lower perceived worth. When a poor minority member will probably face discrimination if she grows wealthy, she is essentially handed lower-payoff lottery tickets throughout her life. Every dollar she invests in education, a business, or another venture is less likely to yield as much money as the money obtained by majority members, and this is demeaning even if she remains poor regardless. This provides one reason to provide reparations if she grows wealthy, even if she will not grow wealthy.

There is a related reason to provide reparations to wealthy victims of discrimination. Even when a poor minority member is unlikely to grow wealthy, and so would not financially benefit from a policy where the wealthy access reparations, she may still one day give birth to a child who will grow wealthy, or her child may give birth to a child who will grow wealthy. If the poor might later have children or grandchildren who grow wealthy, and their children will be unable to access reparations for discrimination, then their children or grandchildren will be disadvantaged because of discrimination. Assuming that current individuals have an interest in their offspring not facing disadvantage, then current poor minority members will be unfairly disadvantaged compared to the majority if, should their children or grandchildren grow wealthy and face discrimination, they will be unable to access reparations.

The Investment Argument similarly justifies reparations to wealthy minority members born into wealth. While such wealthy individuals never experienced poverty, and so never experienced poverty with dollars worth less, those currently experiencing poverty might one day grow wealthy, giving birth to children born into wealth. They would have dollars worth less than those of the majority if their future children could not gain reparations for discrimination if born into wealth.[23]

The above provides one good reason to give reparations to the wealthy. If the wealthy and poor both have a right to not be demeaned via discrimination, and reparations to the wealthy mitigate demeaning discrimination against the poor, this is a reason to give reparations to the wealthy.

Though this provides one reason, this reason is not always decisive. Because it is merely one strong reason to provide reparations, it can be outweighed by stronger competing considerations. One competing consideration is related to the other interests of the poor. Though poor minority members would have dollars with greater expected return if reparations were given to the wealthy, they would have more actual dollars if governments replaced reparations with redistribution. Low-income Bari individuals could have more dollars if the South Sudanese government gave them Kiden's land, and low-income women could have more dollars if the state of California gave them Pao's lawsuit winnings. There would then be a question of which sort of value—the number of dollars, or their expected return—was more important. In cases where the poor lack the most basic needs, we ought to prioritize the number of dollars rather than their expected return, and institute redistribution rather than reparations to the wealthy. This is because, if individuals are so poor that they lack money to invest, it matters less that any money they invest would have a higher expected return. Moreover, the value of ensuring very basic necessities seems greater than the value of ensuring that poor minority members have money with expected return equal to the expected return of money held by majority members.

It remains the case that, when poor minority members are not quite so poor, and do hold some assets, there may be a decisive reason to provide reparations to the wealthy. This is because, even though poor minority members would be advantaged in one way if reparations were redistributed to them, they would be simultaneously disadvantaged in that their dollars would have lower return compared to those of majority members. It is generally wrong to provide a disadvantage to a minority in one domain, even if they are given an advantage in another. For example, imagine if minority applicants were admitted to a university without the need for an interview, giving them an advantage, while also requiring that only they have high grades on an entrance examination, giving them a disadvantage. The differential treatment would be wrong even if the advantage of not needing an interview made up for the disadvantage of needing higher grades, such that all minority members had the same chance of admission as majority members.[24] They would be wronged because the differential treatment would be demeaning, treating them as members of a group as opposed to individuals. The same logic is at play with reparations: if differential treatment is wrong, there is one good reason to allow Pao to keep at least some of her $16 million and Kiden to keep at least some of her land. This will help ensure that the advantages and disadvantages held by poor majority and minority members are on par.

There is a second competing consideration to that arising from the Investment Argument. Sometimes the interests of poor individuals likely to face discrimination must be weighed against the interests of poor individuals likely to face other disadvantages.

Consider, for example, poor individuals without skills valued in the market. Such individuals are likely to have lower salaries compared to poor individuals with skills valued in the market. They therefore hold dollars with lower expected return compared to dollars held by poor individuals with skills. Many may feel this is unjust, at least when individuals lack skills because they were denied quality education. If this is unjust, it makes sense to sometimes redistribute from those with skills to those without. If Pao and Kiden were successful partly because of their skills, there is reason to redistribute reparations they received to those who have little money because of their fewer skills. However, note that even in such cases it is not clear this reason is decisive. That is because, in redistributing reparations in this way, skilled but poor minority members' dollars would have lower expected return than skilled but poor majority members' dollars. This is because the skilled but poor minority members can expect to make less money compared to skilled but poor majority members, given that they are more likely to suffer discrimination and have reparations redistributed if they ever grow wealthy. If so, there is a kind of dilemma: either poor minorities are protected from discrimination by ensuring that their dollars do not have lower expected return from discrimination, or poor unskilled individuals are protected from inequality by ensuring that their dollars do not have lower expected return from lack of skills.

I do not have a solution to this dilemma, but a compromise could be reached. Some of Kiden and Pao's reparations could be taxed and redistributed to all below a given income bracket, allowing Kiden and Pao to keep the rest. Regardless of whether one adopts such a compromise, it remains the case that any reparations Kiden and Pao can keep are justified by appealing not only to the interests of Kiden and Pao, but to the interests of poor minority members as well.

## 3. Objections

There are, broadly speaking, three potential objections against the Investment Argument.

### *3.1. The Poor Have No Right to Unjust Gains*

One objection is that, if poor minorities are less likely to grow very wealthy because of discrimination, but growing very wealthy is unjust, we ought not promise the poor reparations if they grow wealthy and face discrimination. To see the force of this claim, imagine that minorities were more likely to have property they steal stolen by others, and so were less likely to grow wealthy from theft. We would not want to promise a minority member that, if she steals a laptop from David, and David's laptop is stolen from her, the police will return the laptop to her rather than David. It is true she is worse off because she cannot grow as wealthy as majority thieves, but we would not want to assure access to any laptop she steals, assuming she has no right to the laptop she steals.

One response to this objection is to reject the claim that individuals like the thief have no right to the assets they steal. If the thief has a right to not face discrimination, and can only avoid discrimination by being given back the laptop she stole, she has a derivative right to the laptop. Of course, this right might not be decisive: there may be competing rights, such as the right of David to have his laptop. It remains the case that there is one reason for the thief to access the laptop, and this can be explained by appealing to the wrong of discrimination.

More importantly, even if the above thief lacks any right to the laptop she steals, there is good reason to believe that Kiden and Pao do have a right to the assets they lost. This is because the initial puzzle I presented, unlike the case of the thief, presumed that Kiden and Pao have no right to their wealth solely because the poor needed more resources. If the concern is that the poor need more resources, this concern is weakened if the poor's resources become more valuable when wealthy minorities access reparations. This argument is not relevant for the case of the thief, assuming she acts wrongly not because of others' needs. She may act wrongly because theft can cause a disruption in societal order, or she may act wrongly because individuals have a right to keep a portion of the assets they created or received, and theft undermines this right. Regardless of why and whether theft is wrong, if the thief acts wrongly for reasons unrelated to the resources of the poor, then the argument I present remains inapplicable to her, even if it is applicable to Kiden and Pao.

### *3.2. When Discrimination Ends*

There is a second objection. Some might claim that the Investment Argument is inapplicable when minorities no longer face discrimination. If female venture capitalists and Bari Juba residents no longer faced discrimination, then poor women and poor Bari residents would no longer hold dollars yielding a lower return due to this discrimination. If so, there would be one less justification for providing reparations to wealthy victims of discrimination in the past.

Even when discrimination has ended, there is still reason to support a policy of providing reparations. If all are aware that reparations for discrimination will be provided even if discrimination ends, all individuals could be confident that their dollars will not have lower expected return because of discrimination. For example, imagine that a low-income woman in 2019 will grow wealthy in 2020, and will also probably experience discrimination in being promoted further that year. If it takes her until 2045 to prove discrimination took place, and no reparations for discrimination will be provided if discrimination ends in 2045, then in 2019 her money has lower expected value compared to a man's: she knows that she will probably face discrimination that a man does not face, and will not receive reparations if she only files a lawsuit when discrimination is no longer prevalent.

In other words, for poor minority members to be confident that their money does not have lower expected return due to discrimination, they must be confident that reparations will be provided even if discrimination ceases once reparations are sought.

### *3.3. Advantage Alongside Disadvantage*

The final objection is that the Investment Argument is inapplicable when poor individuals are likely to face discrimination and advantage simultaneously. For example, there is some evidence that Asian Americans are more likely to be hired in tech firms, but less likely to be promoted to managerial positions in tech firms, due to stereotypes that Asians are not skilled managers.[25] If a given Asian American experiences unfair advantages alongside discrimination, the expected return on her investment in education will be the same as the return of those unlikely to face either advantage or discrimination. If this is true, then promising a given Asian American reparations if she grows wealthy and faces discrimination cannot be justified by appealing to the lower expected return of the dollars she holds while still poor.

Even if there is evidence that a minority group faces both advantages and discrimination, such that their dollars do not have lower expected return from discrimination, a related Investment Argument still justifies reparations. If individuals are more likely to be hired, but less likely to be promoted, then their dollars are worth more in one sense—they are more likely to yield employment—but less in another sense—they are less likely to yield great wealth. They therefore face both an advantage and a disadvantage. As noted in the previous section, it is wrong to arbitrarily disadvantage a minority in one domain even if you advantage them in another. It is wrong to admit minority applicants to a university only if they have higher grades than others, even if they were also advantaged because they are not required to sit through an interview. The differential treatment is demeaning, even if an advantage means they are not worse off, all things considered. To avoid this differential treatment in job hiring, land use, and other economic domains, the government should ensure that anyone facing discrimination in the future will be given reparations for this discrimination. Assuming that this will counteract the disadvantages any one group obtains, the demeaning nature of discrimination can be prevented.

A similar objection, and similar response, arise when all individuals in society face discrimination, but in different sectors. Imagine that Group A is discriminated against in sector X, Group B in sector Y, and Group C in sector Z, such that Group A has unfair advantages in sectors Y and Z, Group B in sectors X and Z, and Group C in sectors X and Y.[26] Such is the case if Bari citizens are more likely to be sold land compared to Nuer and Dinka citizens, but less likely to be hired for employment compared to Nuer and Dinka citizens.[27] In such a scenario, it may be that all individuals who are poor hold dollars with equal expected return, because all can expect to face the same level of discrimination and advantage. We therefore cannot claim that the wealthy should be given reparations to ensure that poor minorities do not hold money with lower return compared to poor majority members.

We can respond to this objection by again appealing to the way dollars hold different values. If dollars held by poor Bari citizens have a higher expected return when invested in land, and a lower expected return when invested in job training, and if one can be wrongly discriminated against when disadvantaged in one domain and advantaged in another, then poor Bari citizens can be wrongly discriminated against. This wrong can be countered with reparations to Bari citizens who face discrimination in any given domain. Similarly, if poor Dinka citizens hold dollars that have higher expected return when invested in job training and lower return when invested in land, and so are advantaged in one domain and disadvantaged in another, they are wronged. The harm from this wrong can be avoided by providing reparations to all Dinka citizens who face discrimination in any given domain.

## 4. Conclusion

When Kiden was forced to give up her land, she lost land due to discrimination. When Ellen Pao was overlooked for promotion, she failed to obtain money due to discrimination. We might suppose that Kiden and Pao had a right to the wealth they lost, but in obtaining this wealth they obtained far more than they needed. We might think their wealth ought to have been redistributed to those with far less, including poor individuals who were themselves victims of wrongful discrimination.

I considered and rejected two potential arguments against this claim, both focusing on the interests of wealthy minority members. I then presented an alternative argument focusing on the interests of the poor: poor individuals likely to face discrimination if they grow wealthy hold assets with lower expected return compared to those unlikely to face discrimination. If they are wronged when holding assets with lower expected return due to discrimination, we ought to counter this discrimination. We can do so by promising poor individuals that, if they ever face discrimination in the future, they will receive restitution or compensation equal to the assets lost from this discrimination. Only then will the assets they hold now not hold lower value from discrimination faced later.

The above theory, it is worth emphasizing, is limited to cases involving discrimination. It provides no justification for reparations to counter other wrongs, such as theft or physical assault. While providing reparations to wealthy victims of theft or assault would help the poor in one way—their expected return on investments would increase if investments were protected from violence and assault—the amount of money they held would decrease compared to a world where the government redistributed reparations to the poor. There is no reason to believe the first policy is preferable to the other, and the Investment Argument provides no reason to suppose it is. This is because the Investment Argument focuses on helping poor minority members avoid demeaning treatment, and they are demeaned if they hold dollars of different value due to the discrimination they are likely to face. It is not clear if anyone is demeaned in a world where the wealthy cannot access reparations for assault or theft. If reparations for these other wrongs are justified, another theory must explain why.

NOTES

1. Personal interview, Juba, 26 December 2012.

2. Ellen Pao v. Kleiner Perkins Caufield and Byers LLC, Complaint from Ellen Pao, available at https://s3.amazonaws.com/s3.documentcloud.org/documents/1672582/pao-complaint.pdf

3. Heller and Serkin 1999, 1402; Lehrman 1953.

4. By "discrimination" I mean the wrongful differential treatment of women and particular religious and ethnic groups.

5. I put aside reparations intended, not to be equal to assets lost, but equal to assets required to live a decent life, or equal to the assets necessary for communities to be autonomous (Kymlika 1995, 220; Kutz 2004, 283). An example of the latter

would the Kenyan government providing the Kikuyu tribe with limited land in the 1960s, far less land than the Kikuyu lost during colonialism, but enough for them to create a semiautonomous community (Rutten 1997). Such reparations were more akin to redistribution, and needn't entail the return of the precise assets lost.

6. Waldron 1992, 6–7; Kutz 2004, 279–80.

7. For theories that imply or explicitly support this minimal criteria, see Arneson 1989, 77–93; Cohen 1989, 906–44; Dworkin 1981a and 1981b; Frankfurt 2000, 87–103; Nussbaum 1990, 203–52; Shields 2016; and Segall 2013.

8. Gau 1991; Klimchuk 2003, 50; Kurtz 2004, 300; Nozick 1974, 152–53; Perry 2000, 269; Thomson 1986, 149.

9. Of course, the wrong she experiences does not disappear with the reparations—perhaps the wrongness of discrimination is not reducible to its harms—but she at least avoids the harms arising from the wrong. For arguments in support of the claim that discrimination is not only wrong when causing harm, see Eidelson 2013, 205; Gerver 2018b; Hellman 2008, 27–35; Lu 2005, 154; Rawls 1999, 155–56, 386; Parr and Slavny 2015, 100–114.

10. Anderson (1991) makes a related argument in support of providing compensation for wealthy individuals in general.

11. De Greiff 2008, 466; Lu 2017, 243.

12. Goodin 1991, 153–57; Nine 2018.

13. Stilz 2011, 582–87; Stilz 2013, 336–41; Nine 2018.

14. Or, more specifically, they have a right to compensation to continue plans based on a reasonable expectation that the status quo would continue, or at least ought to continue (Goodin 1991, 153–57; Waldron 1992, 18; Perry 2000.) It is not enough, as Goodin notes, to claim that an individual has a right to reparations to continue plans formed with reasonable expectations, because one can reasonably expect to be wronged. If a farmer expects to have her land taken because of her ethnicity, we cannot claim the theft disrupted her reasonable expectations, as she expected her land to be taken. In such cases the farmer would be wronged because she had reason to believe the status quo—access to her land—ought to not be disrupted due to discrimination.

15. Kalmanovitz 2010.

16. Goodin 1991; Waldron 1992, 18–19; Kutz 2004, 295.

17. I am not claiming here that the poor's rights to redistribution can take priority over the wealthy's right to reparations. I am claiming that the wealthy have no rights to reparations if they lost wealth to which they have no right. For claims similar to the former, see Klimchuk 2003, 63; Kutz 2004, 295–96.

18. Elster 1992; Kalmanovitz 2010; Kutz 2004, 301–2; Lu 2005, 155–59; Stilz 2013, 353–54; Waldron 1992, 24–28.

19. Some view the wrong of discrimination as demeaning particular groups. Others view the wrong of discrimination as making particular groups worse off, whether by demeaning them, excluding them, denying them equal opportunities, or materially harming them. Both sets of theories would accept that it is wrong to disadvantage groups in a manner that demeans them. See Collins 2003, 25; Eidelson 2013, 205; Hellman 2008; Khaitan 2012, 2015; Lippert-Rasmussen 2013, 175; and Segall 2012.

20. For a discussion on inadmissible evidence, see Ho 2008, chs. 5 and 6.

21. Interview with Abdalla, Juba, 19 March 2012.

22. Ross Dunham 2017.

23. It is worth emphasizing that this argument concerning the intergenerational effects of discrimination is relevant even if one is opposed to inheritance more generally. In the world we live in, there is no 100 percent inheritance tax, and parents can expect to give money to their children if they have money on their death. Given this fact, poor minorities face a disadvantage, in that the money they have now has lower expected return because, if their children are born into the wealth, the most their children will make from their inheritance is less than the money wealthy majority children can make with their inheritance. They are therefore victims of wrongful discrimination, even if members of both the majority and minority have no right to inheritance. To counter this discrimination, parents must be promised that any children they have born wealthy will access reparations from any discrimination they face.

24. Others have noted that discrimination can be wrong even if no agent is harmed, raising similar examples of individuals who are not, all things considered, disadvantaged from discrimination. See Slavny and Parr 2015, 100–114; Gerver 2018a; Hellman 2008, 27–35; Eidelson 2013, 205.

25. Lee and Zhou 2015; Woo 2000; Gee, Denise, and Wong 2015.

26. This possibility is especially relevant in the context of gender-based discrimination. See Lippert-Rassmusen 2013, 21 and 94–95; Gheaus 2012, 9–10.

27. For an overview of the advantages Bari citizens hold in the domain of land, and various discriminatory practices against different ethnic groups and subgroups, see Badiey 2014, ch. 5, and Gerver 2018b.

## REFERENCES

Anderson, Elizabeth. 1991. "Compensatory Justice." In *Nomos XXXIII*, ed. John Chapman. New York: NYU Press.

Arneson, Richard. 1989. "Equality and Equal Opportunity for Welfare." *Philosophical Studies* 56 (1): 77–93.

Badiey, Naseem. 2014. *The State of Post-Conflict Reconstruction: Land, Urban Development and State-Building in Juba, Southern Sudan*. Rochester, NY: Boydell and Brewer.

Cohen, G. A. 1989. "On the Currency of Egalitarian Justice." *Ethics* 99 (1989): 906–44.

Collins, Hugh. 2003. "Discrimination, Equality, and Social Inclusion." *Modern Law Review* 66 (1): 16–43.

De Greiff, Pablo. 2008. *The Handbook of Reparations*. Oxford: Oxford University Press.

Dunham, Catherine Ross. 2017. "Third Generation Discrimination: The Ripple Effects of Gender Bias in the Workplace." *Akron Law Review* 51 (1): 55–98.

Dworkin, Ronald. 1981a. "What Is Equality? Part I: Equality of Welfare." *Philosophy and Public Affairs* 10 (3): 185–246.

Dworkin, Ronald. 1981b. "What Is Equality? Part 2: Equality of Resources." *Philosophy and Public Affairs* 10 (4): 283–345.

Eidelson, Benjamin. 2013. "Treating People as Individuals." In *Philosophical Founda-*

*tions of Discrimination Law*, ed. Deborah Hellman and Sophia Moreau. Oxford: Oxford University Press.
Elster, Jon. 1992. "On Doing What We Can: An Argument Against Post-Communist Restitution and Retribution." *East European Constitutional Review* 1 (2): 15.
Frankfurt, Harry. 2000. "The Moral Irrelevance of Equality." *Public Affairs Quarterly* 14:87–103.
Gaus, Gerald F. 1991. "Compensation and Equality." In *Nomos XXXIII*, ed. John Chapman. New York: NYU Press.
Gee, Buck, Denise Peck, and Janet Wong. 2015. "Hidden in Plain Sight: Asian American Leaders in Silicon Valley." Ascend: Pan Asian Leaders 2015, accessed 25 November 2017. https://c.ymcdn.com/sites/ascendleadership.site-ym.com/resource/resmgr/Research/HiddenInPlainSight_Paper_042.pdf
Gerver, Mollie. 2018a. "Paying Minorities to Leave." *Politics, Philosophy & Economics* 17 (1): 3–22.
Gerver, Mollie. 2018b. *The Ethics and Practice of Refugee Repatriation*. Edinburgh: Edinburgh University Press.
Gheaus, Anca. 2012. "Gender Justice." *Journal of Ethics and Social Philosophy* 6 (1): 1–24.
Goodin, Robert. 1991. "Compensation and Redistribution." In *Nomos XXXIII*, ed. John Chapman, 143–77. New York: NYU Press.
Harman, Elisabeth. 2004. "Can We Harm and Benefit in Creating?" *Philosophical Perspectives* 18: 89–113.
Heller, Michael, and Christopher Serkin. 1999. "Revaluing Restitution: From the Talmud to Postsocialism." *Michigan Law Review* 97 (6): 1385–1412.
Hellman, Deborah. 2008. *When Is Discrimination Wrong?* Cambridge, MA: Harvard University Press.
Ho, H. L. 2008. *A Philosophy of Evidence Law: Justice in the Search for Truth*. Oxford: Oxford University Press.
Jackson, Frank. 1997. "What Effects?" In *Reading Parfit*, ed. Jonathan Dancy. Blackwell Wiley.
Kalmanovitz, Pablo. 2010. "Corrective Justice vs. Social Justice in the aftermath of War." In *Distributive Justice in Transitions*, ed. Morten Bergsmo, César Rodríguez Garavito, Pablo Kalmanovitz, and Maria Paula Saffon. Oslo: Torkel Opsahl Publisher, International Peace Research Institute.
Khaitan, Tarunabh. 2012. "Dignity as an Expressive Norm: Neither Vacuous nor a Panacea." *Oxford Journal of Legal Studies* 32 (1): 1–19.
Khaitan, Tarunabh. 2015. *A Theory of Discrimination Law*. Oxford: Oxford University Press.
Klimchuk, Dennis. 2003. "Autonomy of Corrective Justice." *Oxford Journal of Legal Studies* 23 (1): 49–64.
Kutz, Christopher. 2004. "Justice in Reparations: The Cost of Memory and the Value of Talk." *Philosophy and Public Affairs* 32 (3): 277–312.
Kymlicka, Will. 1995. *Multicultural Citizenship: A Liberal Theory of Minority Rights*. Oxford: Oxford University Press.
Lee, Jennifer, and Min Zhou. 2015. *The Asian American Paradox*. New York: Russell Sage Foundation.

Lehrman, Hal. 1953. "The New Germany and Her Remaining Jews: Reporters Notebook." *Commentary* (December 1), accessed 18 April 2017. https://www.commentarymagazine.com/articles/the-new-germany-and-her-remaining-jewsa-reporters-notebook

Lewis, David. 2000. "Causation as Influence." *Journal of Philosophy* 97 (4): 182–97.

Lippert-Rassmusen, Kasper. 2013. *Born Free and Equal? A Philosophical Inquiry into the Nature of Discrimination*. Oxford: Oxford University Press.

Lu, Catherine. 2005. "Delivering the Goods and the Good." In *Calling Power to Account: Law, Reparations, and the Chinese Canadian Head Tax Case*, ed. David Cyzenhaus and Mayo Moran, 147–64. Toronto: Toronto University Press.

Lu, Catherine. 2017. *Justice and Reconciliation in World Politics*. Cambridge: Cambridge University Press.

McDermott, Michael. 2002. "Influence vs. Sufficiency." *Journal of Philosophy* 99 (2): 84–101.

Nine, Cara. 2018. "The Wrong of Displacement: The Home as Extended Mind." *Journal of Political Philosophy* 26 (2): 240–57.

Nozick, Robert. 1974. *Anarchy, State and Utopia*. Oxford: Blackwell.

Nussbaum, Martha. 1990. "Aristotelian Social Democracy." In *Liberalism and the Good*, ed. R. B. Douglas, Gerald M. Mara, and Henry Richardson, 203–52. New York: Routledge.

Perry, Stephen. 2000. "On the Relationship Between Corrective and Distributive Justice." In *Oxford Essays in Jurisprudence*, ed. J. Horder. Oxford: Oxford University Press.

Rawls, John. 1999. *A Theory of Justice*, rev. ed. Cambridge, MA: Harvard University Press.

Robert, Rodney C. 2006. "The Counterfactual Conception of Compensation." *Metaphilosophy* 37 (3–4): 414–28.

Rutten, Marcel. 1997. "Land Reform in Africa: Lessons from Kenya." In *The Diversity of Development: Essays in Honor of Jan Kleinpenning*, ed. A. L. Naerssen, M. M. E. M. Rutten, and A. Zoomers. Assen: Van Gorcum.

Segall, Shlomi. 2013. *Equality and Opportunity*. Oxford: Oxford University Press.

Shields, Liam. 2016. *Just Enough: Sufficiency as a Demand of Justice*. Edinburgh: Edinburgh University Press.

Shiffrin, Seana. 1999. "Wrongful Life, Procreative Responsibility, and the Significance of Harm." *Legal Theory* 5: 17–148.

Slavny, Adam, and Tom Parr. 2015. "Harmless Discrimination." *Legal Theory* 21 (2): 100–114.

Stilz, Anna. 2011. "Nations, States, and Territory." *Ethics* 121 (3): 572–601.

Stilz, Anna. 2013. "Occupancy Rights and the Wrong of Removal." *Philosophy and Public Affairs* 41 (4): 324–56.

Thomson, Judith. 1986. "Preferential Hiring." In *Rights, Restitution, and Risk*, ed. William Parent. Cambridge, MA: Harvard University Press.

Waldron, Jeremy. 1992. "Superseding Historic Injustice." *Ethics* 103 (1): 4–28.

Woo, Deborah. 2000. *Glass Ceilings and Asian Americans*. Walnut Creek, CA: AltaMira Press.

CHAPTER 8

# How to Conceive a Pluralistic Metric of Justice?

## *The Example of Sen's and Nussbaum's Conception of Capability*

Ortrud Leßmann

### 1. Introduction

Amartya Sen and Martha Nussbaum are the two main advocates of the capability or capabilities approach (CA). They agree on some essential aims and claims of the CA, yet it is widely acknowledged that their versions of the CA differ in some crucial respects. This is reflected partly in their respective preference for using the singular (Sen) or the plural (Nussbaum) of capability. Nussbaum (2011, 18) gives the plurality of dimensions of well-being as the reason why she prefers the plural. I argue in this chapter that it is indeed the underlying idea of plurality incorporated in their different conceptions of capability that is at the heart of the differences between Sen's and Nussbaum's respective versions of the approach: though both agree on the plurality—and incommensurability—of values involved, they differ in dealing with this plurality. While Sen looks at "bundles of functionings" and "capability sets," Nussbaum argues for taking the "capabilities" as separate components and warns against trading them off. She focuses on providing a list of the values involved, whereas Sen is opposed to setting up a list, and in particular to "completing" a list.

While this chapter is mainly concerned with tracing and highlighting the differences between Sen's and Nussbaum's conceptions of capability, I hold that these differences reveal them to be accessing the issue of pluralistic metrics of justice[1] from different angles. They approach the conception with different disciplinary backgrounds and different aims, namely evaluation (Sen) versus political conception (Nussbaum). These differences in aims can be found in discussions of other theories of justice as well. My aim is to show that even a political conception of justice such as Nussbaum's has to distinguish between aggregative evaluation and trading-off values and therefore has to be able to look at the complete picture by saying more about the structure of the metric.

This chapter is organized as follows: after briefly presenting Sen's and Nussbaum's conceptions of capability and other core terms of their respective approaches, I discuss in depth the underlying ideas of plurality and how they impact the evaluative exercise. Though both argue for changing the "metrics" of justice, their proposals differ greatly with regard to relating incommensurable values to each other. The well-known debate about listing dimensions has distracted attention from this problem and is only briefly taken up. In conclusion I argue that the differences in their conceptions of capability can be used to exemplify a more general problem with regard to pluralistic metrics of justice that has mostly been ignored so far.

## 2. The Two Capability Conceptions of Sen and Nussbaum

This section briefly introduces the conceptions of capability by Sen and Nussbaum.

### *2.1. Sen's Conception of Capability*

Though Sen (1980) first spoke of "capabilities," it is the notion of "functionings" that is crucial for Sen's version of the CA and forms the basis for understanding his conception of capability. Sen claims that well-being is best seen in terms of functionings, i.e., "beings and doings." Thereby he positions his approach between resourcist approaches—in particular Rawls's theory of justice as fairness—on the one hand and Utilitarianism on the other: he regards the command over resources as a prerequisite for exercising certain functionings and assigning a utility value as a way of evaluating the achieved functionings (fig. 8.1).

For instance, without a bike one cannot exercise the functioning "riding a bike" (Sen 1985, 10). However, there are people who cannot ride a bicycle, even if they have one, either because of physical limitations (such as being too small for the bicycle in question) or because they simply have not

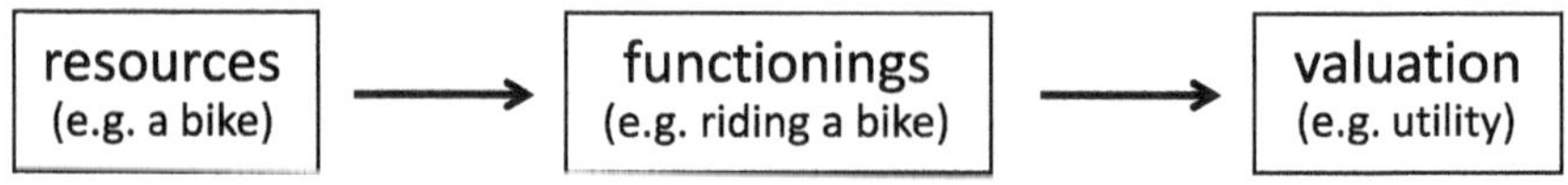


Fig. 8.1. Resources, functionings, and utility

learned how to ride a bike. Thus, functionings come about as a result of the combination of resources on the one hand and individual features on the other hand. Sen (1985, 11) has called these individual features "utilization functions." Later on he referred to the "conversion of resources . . . into freedoms" (Sen 1992, 33), which led Kuklys (2005) and Robeyns (2005) to introduce the term "conversion factors" that is now widely used (see fig. 8.2). Kuklys and Robeyns distinguish personal (e.g., physical features), social (e.g., social norms and institutional arrangements), and environmental (e.g., climate and geography) conversion factors.

Sen gives a lot of examples for functionings, ranging "from such elementary things as being adequately nourished, being in good health, avoiding escapable morbidity and premature mortality, etc., to more complex achievements such as being happy, having self-respect, taking part in the life of the community and so on" (Sen 1992, 39). And he states that "[t]he various 'doings' and 'beings' a person achieves are thus potentially all relevant to the evaluation of that person's living standard" (Sen, Muellbauer, and Hawthorn 1987, 29). Thus, a valuation function has to take this multitude of functionings into account. Sen views utility functions as one example how such an evaluation may be done. He points out, however, that "*valuing* a life and measuring the *happiness* generated in that life are two different exercises" (Sen 1985, 12). Hence, while resources are mere prerequisites of well-being, and utility (as an indicator of happiness) may be seen as a valuation function regarding well-being, "functionings are *constitutive* of a person's being, and an evaluation of well-being has to take the form of an assessment of these constituent elements" (Sen 1992, 39).

Sen's conception of capability can be derived in three steps. The first is the switch of the evaluative variables away from resources and utility to functionings in the sense just described. The second important step is to acknowledge the multidimensionality of life. It is always a *bundle* or combination of functionings that describes a life situation and has to be evaluated. The introduction of freedom of choice into the model is the third and most important step. Sen imagines that the individual can choose among various ways of leading a life, i.e., among various bundles of functionings:

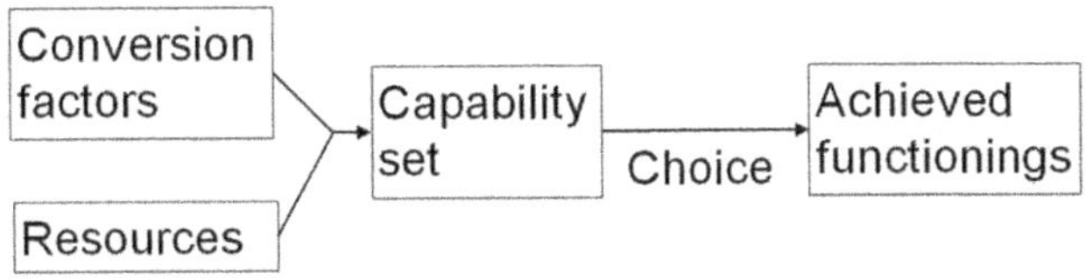


Fig. 8.2. Resources and conversion factors determine the capability set (Sen). (*Source:* Author's own drawing following Robeyns 2005, 98.)

"A person's 'capability' refers to the alternative combinations of functionings that are feasible for her to achieve" (Sen 1999, 75). Note that this is not about choosing a set of functionings. Selecting relevant functionings is rather a prerequisite for defining the capability set that offers a choice among bundles or combinations of functionings; for example, if I choose to do a tour on my bicycle on Saturday afternoon, I will miss whatever is on TV that afternoon and I cannot read a book that afternoon or answer the phone either. *Thus, there are always trade-offs involved: whenever I choose to do or be something I choose at the same time not to do or be something else.* This may seem trivial at first glance, but think of states such as "being healthy" that afford a lot of small decisions in favor of healthy food and activities.

As Sen points out, capability is a freedom type of notion. It reflects the freedom of choice a person has to choose a life she "has reason to value" (Sen 1999, 74). Sen uses the notion of "achieved functionings" to refer to achievements. In his book *Development as Freedom*, Sen (1999) has used the notions of "substantive freedom" and "capability" interchangeably. He clearly states that capability models freedom in terms of an opportunity set from which the person has to choose but one option, one bundle of functionings. Unfortunately he sometimes also refers to "capabilities" in the plural, thus blurring the understanding of capability as the set of available options.[2] Nevertheless, capability in Sen refers to the freedom to choose among several options that consist of feasible combinations of functionings.

### 2.2. Nussbaum's Conception of Capability

Nussbaum first refers to Sen's notion of "capability" in her paper "Aristotle on Political Distribution" (1988). She introduces the CA as a "contemporary relative" of Aristotle's theory of distribution and seconds Sen's criticism that resources and goods are means to freedom of choice but bear no intrinsic value. She embraces Sen's approach of focusing on the "functionings towards which these goods are useful" (Nussbaum 1988, 153), but adds that it is necessary to "have an account" of those functionings in order to "estimate the worth of distributable goods." She then moves from using the notion of "functioning" to that of "capability to function" on the grounds that the CA aims to make "people able to live and act in certain concrete ways" and "capable of choosing to act in these ways, not simply to push them into so acting" (Nussbaum 1988, 153). It is in order to acknowledge the "value of choice" that "we will define our goal in terms of capabilities, not actual functioning" (1988, 153). She holds this view till today (2000, 87; 2006, 79; 2011, 24).

Crucial to Nussbaum's conception of capability is the idea of levels of capability (fig. 8.3): "basic capability" is "the innate equipment of individuals that is the necessary basis for developing the more advanced capabilities, and a ground for moral concern" (Nussbaum 2000, 84). An example of this is the capability of a newborn baby to see and hear, and the capability for speech and language in a rudimentary way as well. "Internal capability" is given "if and only if the person is so organized at [time] *t* that, should the appropriate circumstances present themselves, the person can choose an A action" (Nussbaum 1988, 160). They are "traits of intellect and character and body" (Nussbaum 1988, 160), "trained or developed traits and abilities, developed, in most cases, in interaction with the social, economic, familial, and political environment" (Nussbaum 2011, 21).

Still a person "may be prevented from functioning in accordance with it" (Nussbaum 2000, 84) if the appropriate circumstances do not present themselves. The notion of "combined capabilities" accounts for this in denoting the combination of internal capabilities with suitable external conditions. "Combined capability"[3] is given "if and only if at [time] *t* the person [has the internal capability] of A and there are no circumstances present that impede or prevent the exercise of A" (Nussbaum 1988, 164). Nussbaum (2000, 85) gives the following example: "Citizens of repressive nondemocratic regimes have the internal but not the combined capability to exercise thought and speech in accordance with their consciences." Of course, the capability to think and express one's views is discouraged in repressive nondemocratic states. Nussbaum points to the necessity of encouraging and developing certain skills in order to exercise these capabilities. She states that "[t]he distinction between internal and combined capabilities is not a sharp one, because developing an internal capability usually requires favorable external conditions" (Nussbaum 2000, 85; 2011, 23). Yet it seems that combined capabilities point to the fact that external

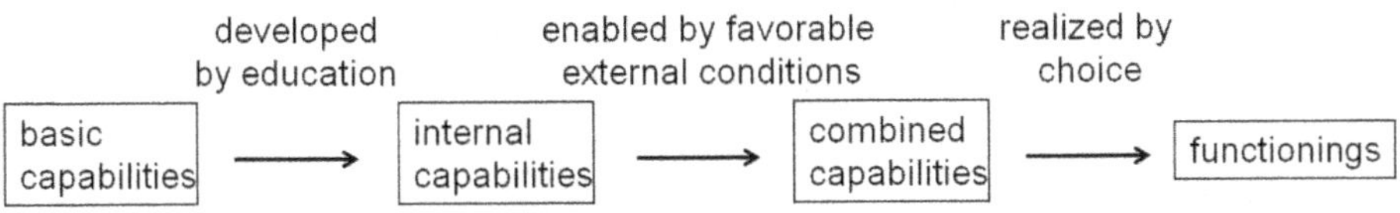


Fig. 8.3. Development of capabilities (Nussbaum)

conditions at a given point in time tend to constrain the exercise of capabilities while they may enhance the development of internal capabilities in the course of time.

Nussbaum thus advocates defining political goals in terms of combined capabilities; i.e., according to her, a society should strive to produce internal capabilities and give people the external conditions to exercise them. Still, capability is (only) the ability and opportunity to function, whereas "functioning is an active realization of one or more capabilities" (Nussbaum 2011, 24–25).

As mentioned earlier, Nussbaum further holds that "if this view is to have sufficient content" (Nussbaum 1988, 174), it is necessary to provide an account of those "functions [that] are particularly central in human life, in the sense that their presence or absence is typically understood to be a mark of the presence or absence of human life" (Nussbaum 2000, 71–72). Her list is, however, not a list of functions or functionings, but one of "capabilities as central requirements of a life with dignity" (Nussbaum 2006, 75).

Nussbaum has used different methods to justify the content of her list (on these changes and for a critique see Alkire 2002, 38–45; Jaggar 2006; Clark 2013), arriving at the conviction that the list "could, over time, become the basis for an 'overlapping consensus'" (Nussbaum 2011, 79; 2000, 76; 2006, 70). The use of the Rawlsian term "overlapping consensus" reflects a shift in Nussbaum's work from seeing the CA mainly as a contemporary ally of Aristotelian ideas to highlighting that "contractarian theories, especially in their moralized Kantian form [such as Rawls's], are close allies of the capabilities approach" (Nussbaum 2006, 95). While Nussbaum set up the list in the first, Aristotelian period, she has in fact maintained the list with minor changes in the second, Rawlsian period (since 2000),[4] although she has always emphasized that it is "open-ended and subject to ongoing revision and rethinking." The current list is given in the appendix to this chapter.

Crocker (1995, 163) characterized Nussbaum's view of capabilities as "internal powers." In contrast, he says about Sen's view that "for Sen, capabilities are not powers of the person that might or might not be realized in different situations. They are, rather, options (sets of compossible options) for actions." This remark points to the difference in the logical structure of their capability concepts that is the main concern of this paper.

## 3. Pluralism and the Issue of Metrics

Sen and Nussbaum agree that life is "inescapably plural"[5] and hence a plurality of dimensions has to be considered in theories of justice. They agree on some of the reasons for this, as is laid out in section 3.1. In particular they both point to the incommensurability of values as the main reason for plurality, but they draw different conclusions from this. While Sen explicitly aims at comparing bundles of these incommensurable dimensions, Nussbaum argues for treating them separately. Her "metric of justice" hence differs profoundly from Sen's (section 3.2). Now one may argue that for her purpose—providing a political conception—it is more important to select dimensions than to relate the dimensions to each other. Section 3.3 considers this argument.

### *3.1. Incommensurability and Multidimensionality*

Both Sen and Nussbaum defend the pluralistic character of the approach. Sen (1999, 76–77) argues that "[t]he capability approach is inescapably pluralist," and Nussbaum (2000, 81) speaks of the "irreducible plurality of the list."

Sen gives three reasons for the plurality of the approach: (1) the plurality of functionings (or the multidimensionality of the functioning space), (2) the coexistence of the evaluative perspectives of functioning achievements and capability as freedom, and (3) the possibility of further concerns relevant for evaluative purposes, including agency and procedural concerns. The first point states that functionings cannot be reduced to one dimension or aggregated and converted into one measure. At the same time, we have to keep in mind that Sen (1987, 29) views the list of relevant functionings as "possibly infinite" and does not recommend any predetermined version of a list. He allows, therefore, defining a list according to the evaluative purpose at hand (Sen 1996, 116). The second point refers to Sen's distinction between well-being achievements and well-being freedom. The concepts of (functioning) achievements and capability sets (as opportunity sets) compete with each other and complement each other at the same time. Sen (2002, 607) suggests combining information on both in what he calls "comprehensive" outcomes—in contrast to "culmination outcomes," which only comprise the achievements (consequences). The third point hints at evaluative criteria such as "rules and procedure" (Sen 1999, 77). Information on this can also be included in the concept of "comprehensive outcomes," but Sen (2005, 156) holds that the concept of capability does not fully include information on such considerations, while he claims at the same time that they "must also be accommodated in normative social choice theory."

In summary, by emphasizing the importance of freedom of choice, Sen clearly allows for plurality within the approach, and by inviting the inclusion of other considerations, such as processes and rules, he pushes plurality far beyond questions of weighting. As Robeyns (2011, ch. 3.3; 2016; 2017) explicates, there can be more than one "capability theory of justice," which may induce competition among capability theories.

As said, Nussbaum (2011, 108–10) also defends the pluralistic character of the approach. Specifically, she hints at six ways she has "integrated a sensitivity to cultural pluralism" into her view: (1) her list is open-ended and open to debate and change; (2) the list is deliberately abstract and leaves the task of specification to the nations that want to implement it; (3) the list is a "partial moral conception," introduced for political purposes only; (4) the elements of the list are capabilities, not functionings, thus leaving room for freedom of choice; (5) the list includes "major liberties that protect pluralism," such as freedom of speech, freedom of association, and freedom of conscience; and finally, (6) "a strong separation between issues of justification and issues of implementation" precludes the imposition of the list on other nations by force.

Comparing their arguments, Nussbaum agrees with Sen on the first point—the multidimensionality of the list entails plurality: "The irreducible plurality of the list limits the trade-offs that it will be reasonable to make, and thus limits the applicability of quantitative cost-benefit analysis" (Nussbaum 2000, 81). With regard to Sen's second point (the distinction between freedom and achievement), Nussbaum (2000, 14) thinks that these ideas can "be captured as aspects of the capability/function distinction." I will argue that this indicates a fundamental difference between Sen's conception of capability and hers. I discuss below the differences between Nussbaum's understanding of capabilities and functionings and Sen's conception and use of the terms. With respect to Sen's third point of including further concerns such as processes, Nussbaum (2011, 95) agrees with him that the CA is an outcome-oriented approach, but goes further in stating that it "seeks political procedures . . . that will achieve that result [the preferred outcome] as nearly as possible" (Nussbaum 2006, 82), giving outcomes priority over processes. In (5) and (6) of the last paragraph she further mentions procedural rules, namely political liberties and noninterference (negative liberty). Yet by including liberties in her list, she puts them next to outcomes, and it is unclear how these guiding principles for processes of political deliberation figure in the CA: as outcomes or rules.

As pointed out, both Sen and Nussbaum see the main reason for plurality in the multidimensionality of the CA. Stating that the approach is irreducibly plural means that both agree on the incommensurability of these dimensions. Sen (2009, 240) gives the following definition of (in-)commensurability: "Two distinct objects can be taken to be commensurable if they are measurable in common units (like two glasses of milk). Noncommensurability is present when several dimensions of value are irreducible to one another." The assumption of commensurability is an important argument in Sen's and Nussbaum's critique of utilitarianism (that evaluates states of affairs in the common unit of utility). This is as far as their agreement goes. While Sen (2004a, 45; 2009, 241) states "The presence of noncommensurable rewards only indicates that choice decisions will not be trivial (reducible just to counting what is 'more' to what is 'less'), but it does not at all indicate that it is impossible—or even that it must be particularly difficult." Nussbaum (2011, 59) confirms the "incommensurability of all the important opportunities or capabilities," but warns against trading off values and suggests instead looking at the components of her list separately. Let me investigate this issue in more detail.

Sen (1985, 19) aims at an approach that allows interpersonal comparisons of well-being (Beitz 1986, 290). The impossibility of interpersonal comparisons in terms of utility is a major motivation for Sen to develop the CA: "An approach that cannot easily accommodate interpersonal comparisons is seriously handicapped in substantiating the notion of well-being." He argues that "functionings can lend themselves to easier interpersonal comparison than comparisons of utilities (or happiness, pleasures or desires)," although he is well aware that "interpersonal comparisons of *overall* advantages also require 'aggregation' over heterogeneous components" (Sen 1999, 76).[6] He suggests approaching the goal of comparing overall advantages by specifying which functionings shall be taken into consideration, since "the very identification of the set of value-objects, with positive weights, itself precipitates a 'dominance ranking' (x is at least as high as y if it yields at least as much of each of the valued objects)" (Sen 1993, 32). This dominance ranking only leads to a partial ordering, i.e., there are some situations that cannot be ranked vis-à-vis each other. However, Sen (1992, 46–49) is quite optimistic to extend the ordering step by step through introducing and narrowing a weighting scheme based on the intersection of rankings. The basic idea is that we may not be able to reach an agreement on the exact weights that should be applied in an aggregation function, but we should be able to agree on a range of weights that may be narrowed further. Note that this procedure complies with the incommensurability of values: the dimensions are measured separately in different measurement units. Only the full specification of weights amounts to a kind of commensuration of values.

Nussbaum has a different goal in mind and deals with these issues in a less technical way—and thus it is not always clear how her arguments relate to Sen's. She argues that "[a]ny decent political plan . . . would seek to promote a range of diverse and incommensurable goods" (Nussbaum 2011, 127)[7] and explicates: "It is the whole set of such entitlements, suitably defined, that is held to be required by justice, and no entitlement can substitute for any other" (Nussbaum 2006, 85). "One should not suppose, for example, that the absence of the political liberties would be made up for by tremendous economic growth" (Nussbaum 2000, 81). This is not only important on the aggregate level, but has to be ensured for each and every citizen (Nussbaum 2011, 127). As long as no weighting is introduced, Sen's dominance ranking complies with Nussbaum's refusal to substitute one good for another.

### *3.2. Evaluative Space and Metric*

As shown above, the irreducible plurality of the CA is important for both Sen and Nussbaum. They agree in rejecting utilitarian and resourcist approaches. They both argue that functionings and capabilities are better suited to answer the question "Equality of what?" (Sen 1980) than these alternative approaches. In Sen's (1993, 50) view, "the capability approach is concerned with showing the cogency of a particular *space* for the evaluation of individual opportunities and successes." Nussbaum (2000, 12) "wholeheartedly [agrees] with Sen's claims about the capability space," but misses the point that Sen does not refer to "the capability space" but rather to the "functioning space." This may seem as a minor difference, but in fact it hints at crucial differences in their understanding of the issue of evaluation.

For Sen (1992, 20) "[t]his problem of the choice of the 'evaluative space' (that is, the selection of the relevant focal variables) is crucial to analysing inequality." Sen's use of the word "space" is, however, ambiguous: on the one hand he uses it in a figurative manner, indicating what variables are important for the evaluation of well-being. In this sense the "functioning space" can be distinguished from the "utility space" or the "space of primary goods." On the other hand, Sen interweaves this use of the term with a technical and mathematical meaning[8] indicating which variables form the dimensions of a multidimensional space (in the mathematical sense as illustrated in figure 8.4) that serves as the basis for evaluating well-being.[9] This is the reason why he refers to the "functioning space" and not the "capability space":

> We should first note that capabilities are defined derivatively from functionings. In the space of functionings any point, representing an *n*-tuple of functionings, reflects a combination of the person's doings and beings, relevant to the exercise. The capability is a set of such functioning *n*-tuples, representing the various alternative combinations of beings and doings any one (combination) of which the person can choose. Capability is thus defined in the space of functionings. If a functioning achievement (in the form of an *n*-tuple of functionings) is a *point* in that space, capability is a *set* of such points (representing the alternative functioning *n*-tuples from which one *n*-tuple can be chosen). (Sen 1993, 38; 2009, 236)

Thus, functionings are the value-objects defining the evaluative space and serve as dimensions of the evaluative space.[10] Having chosen functionings as the focal variables (and selected the relevant ones, e.g., being healthy, being literate, and moving around in figure 8.4), the next step is to introduce weights for the functionings (Sen 1992, 44–49). In a third step, Sen (1992, 49–53) asks on which concept to focus: functionings or capability. He points out "that there is no difference *as far as the space is concerned* between focusing on functionings *or* on capabilities" (Sen 1992, 50).

Value is thus attached first to the functioning-achievements since functionings are the value-objects (that have to be selected for the exercise at hand). Second, value is attached to being able to choose from a set of

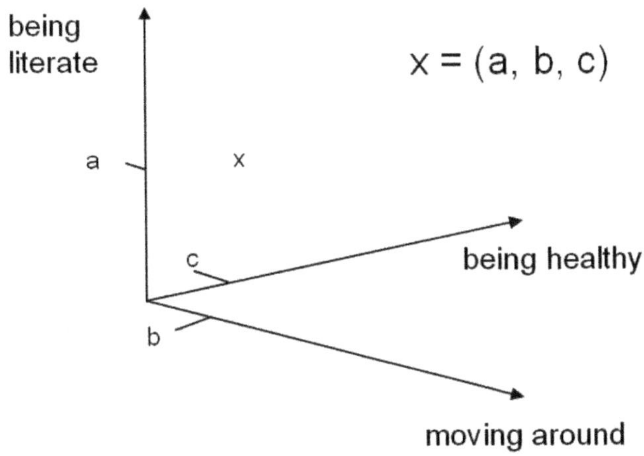


Fig. 8.4. An illustration of the functioning space in Sen with an *n*-tuple of three functionings

options because of "the intrinsic value of freedom" (Sen 1988, 293). Putting the focus of analysis on freedom demands to look at the capability of a person rather than on her actual achievement in terms of functionings. On several occasions Sen (1992, 112; 1993, 38–40; 1999, 148) has recommended taking the concept of capability—and not actual achievements—as a policy goal. He does so because in his view the intrinsic value of freedom contributes to well-being achievement (Sen 1993, 39). At the same time, Sen hints at difficulties of assessing capability sets: "[T]he capability set is not directly observable, and has to be constructed on the basis of presumptions" (Sen 1992, 52). Thus, assessing capability sets will usually start with information on achieved functionings, but needs to go beyond this to estimate which functioning bundles would have been feasible for the individual, too (Sen 1999, 131).

The concept of capability suggested by Sen has, however, a straightforward mathematical interpretation: it is defined as a subset in the multidimensional space of functionings (chosen as value-objects from the possibly infinite list of functionings, see section 3.3). Each element of the capability set is, consequently, a multidimensional bundle or *n*-tuple of functionings.

In contrast to Sen, Nussbaum does not refer to an "evaluative space." She is less concerned with the task of evaluation and interpersonal comparisons (or measurement for that matter). Her objective is to lay down normative guidelines for political purposes. Yet, as pointed out before, she

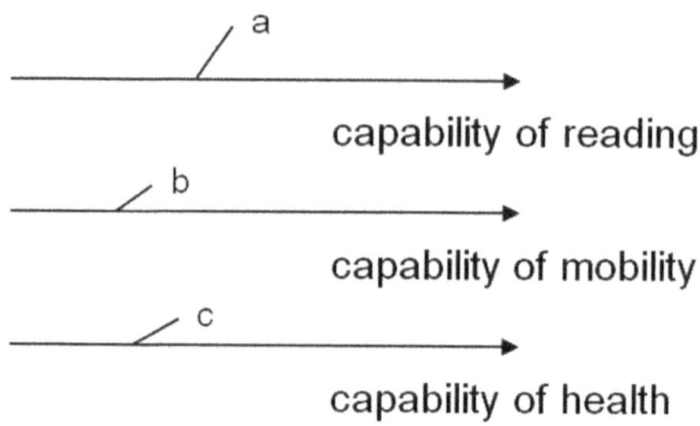


Fig. 8.5. Capabilities and functionings in Nussbaum

agrees with Sen on the disadvantages of other metrics of justice, and proposes her "central functional capabilities" (Nussbaum 2000, 78) as value-objects. The first difference to note is, thus, a difference in phrasing: Sen views functionings as the value-objects whereas Nussbaum advocates capabilities. As Nussbaum (2000, 85) points out, the list "is a list of combined capabilities" (see section 2.2), i.e., each item is a combination of an internal ability with external circumstances that allow a person to function in this way and to choose the extent of goodness she wants to achieve in this capability. Nussbaum (2000, 88) thus pays respect "for people and their choices": (a) The goals are really feasible for the individual. (b) The individual is left free to function as he or she pleases.

The opportunity to choose a life one values and wants to live has some value of its own (Nussbaum 1988, 153). In her view, combined capabilities equal Sen's idea of "substantive freedoms" or capability (Nussbaum 2011, 21). I would like to challenge this view, since she looks at each capability separately (fig. 8.5). The dimensions do not form a "space" in the mathematical sense. Hence, the term "capability set" has no apparent meaning in Nussbaum's approach. She does not consider bundles of possible achievements, but focuses on individual dimensions. While she acknowledges the interdependence and mutual influence of capabilities, she forbids trade-offs between dimensions and does not offer a model of evaluation that involves the interplay of dimensions with each other.

She further argues for the introduction of thresholds and restricts her discussion of substitution and trade-offs to the threshold level: "The approach does not invite, and positively forbids, trade-offs and balancing when we are dealing with the threshold level of each of these requirements" (Nussbaum 2006, 85), cf. her discussion of tragic choices in (2000, 81; 2011, 37). If clear threshold levels for all dimensions were determined, they would define an implicit weighting scheme valid only at the threshold level. Nussbaum does not aim at interpersonal comparisons beyond this and never considers combinations of achievements (she merely acknowledges that "the items on the list are related to one another in many complex ways"; Nussbaum 2000, 81).

In summary, though Sen and Nussbaum both reject other metrics of justice, though they agree on the importance of freedom of choice and on demanding that policy be directed toward capability, not functioning achievements, there is a fundamental difference in their use of the words and hence conceptions: Sen views "capability" as a derivative concept and defines it as a subset in the functionings space consisting of bundles or *n*-tuples of functionings. "Functioning" here labels the dimensions of that space and does not indicate necessarily the achieved level of functionings. Freedom of choice relates to feasible combinations (*n*-tuples) of functionings. Opposed to that, Nussbaum labels the dimensions of evaluation "capabilities," whereas she indicates the level of achievement in a dimension (and nothing else) by "functioning." Freedom of choice then relates to the feasible levels of excellence in a function or capability.

### *3.3. Listing Dimensions and Different Aims*

As stated above, Nussbaum insisted on the importance of listing the relevant dimensions for "completing the approach" in her very first contribution on the CA (Nussbaum 1988, 176). She has thus started a debate with Sen that is still ongoing. Their diverging views on whether or not to list capabilities (or functionings) are well known.[11] In my view, the debate has overstated some differences. In particular, Sen does not generally object to listing functionings (or capabilities), but does object to "fixing . . . a cemented list of capabilities" (Sen 2004b, 78). He has, in fact, given many examples and stated that the list "is, of course, an enormous—possibly infinite—list, since a person's activities and states can be seen in so many different ways (and can also be persistently subdivided)" (Sen, Muellbauer, and Hawthorn 1987, 29).

While Sen's remark about the possible infinity of the list sheds some doubt on the fundamental question of whether Nussbaum's aim to complete the approach by listing dimensions is feasible, the difference between their examples lies mainly in the level of specification and has to do with the difference in their aims. For a political conception,[12] it seems advisable to leave the task of specification for those who adopt the conception, whereas an evaluative analysis has to specify the dimensions in such a way that they can be measured empirically. (It may, however, be a good exercise for Nussbaum to undergo the painstaking task of specifying dimensions for testing the analytical cogency of the items.) Does the purpose of a political conception also justify Nussbaum's radical prohibition of trade-offs between dimensions?

Nussbaum (2006, 310) is careful to emphasize that her approach is concerned with the ability of each person to reach the threshold level and leaves the approach deliberately incomplete with regard to justice beyond the threshold level. At the same time, she explains that capability, not actual achievement, has to be taken as the goal of a political conception. In consequence the threshold levels have to be defined in terms of capability and not actual achievement, and this is where I see a problem: the state may be able to guarantee each capability separately, and yet achieving all threshold levels in combination may be impossible. To illustrate, imagine a hotel advertising its rooms.[13] The advertisement mentions that the rooms are "comfortable and spacious," have "a splendid view over the ocean," and are "close to the restaurant." All the statements are true, but there is no single room offering all: space *and* a splendid view *and* proximity to the restaurant.

Nussbaum (2006, 175) touches on this problem when she states that "it may not be possible for a nation to secure them [plural and diverse ends] up to the threshold level, but then it becomes a purely practical question what to do next." However, she does not take into account that the goals are defined as "capabilities, not actual functioning" (1988, 153). By looking at the dimensions separately, the situation may be the same as in the example of the hotel: the threshold level of each capability is guaranteed by the state and feasible but may become unfeasible in combination with the other capabilities. In contrast to this, Sen directly looks at feasible *combinations* of functionings and thus avoids this problem. His model is further not restricted to the threshold levels.

## 4. Discussion and Conclusion

This paper traces differences in Sen's and Nussbaum's respective conceptions of capability in order to question the requirements for pluralistic metrics of justice. Many debates on such metrics concentrate on the question of selecting (or listing) relevant values while disregarding the relationship between these values. The two tasks are interrelated in the sense that the more dimensions have to be considered, the more complex is the relationship among them. Conversely, the specification of relations may lead to commensuration and thus to the deletion of a value from the list—for example, if two values overlap heavily and hence cannot be sufficiently distinguished from each other.

Philosophical debates further discuss various "principles" or "patterns of justice" such as equality, priority, and sufficiency. While this question is also related to the issue of relationships between values or dimensions focused on in this paper, it is not the same either, since the principles can be applied to a one-dimensional metric, too. Often the discussion of the principles is simplified by referring to the one-dimensional case even if a pluralistic metric is endorsed (e.g., Meyer and Roser 2009).

Against this background I show how Sen and Nussbaum differ in conceiving the metric of justice endorsed by the capability approach, although both agree on changing the metric toward functionings and capabilities as well as on the plurality of incommensurable values involved: first, they draw different conclusions from the incommensurability of values. Sen suggests complying with incommensurability by using different measures for the various dimensions. He further pictures the various dimensions in a multidimensional space in the mathematical sense, i.e., he looks at *bundles* of functionings. His search for interpersonal comparisons of well-being is a search for methods of aggregate evaluation of such bundles. In contrast to that, Nussbaum argues for viewing the components of her list as separate in order to comply with incommensurability. She thus refrains from an aggregate assessment of capabilities. Yet she acknowledges that interdependencies between dimensions need to be considered, e.g., in setting a threshold. In this context she judges that "this is hardly to make trade-offs in an unacceptable sense" (Nussbaum 2006, 175). In any case, both Sen and Nussbaum know that a plurality of values will at first result in incomplete orderings. This does not worry either of them.

Second, Nussbaum emphasizes the importance of setting up a list, while Sen disputes this. Rather than tracing the debate on the list another time, I have asked whether their different approaches can be explained by their diverging aims. While granting that the provision of a political conception aimed at by Nussbaum is less demanding in terms of specification than the evaluation and interpersonal comparison of well-being Sen is looking for, I have argued that it is nevertheless important to consider if the political goals can be achieved *in combination*. This holds in particular if the goals are defined as freedoms.

Freedom has some procedural features, although the CA is seen by both Sen and Nussbaum as outcome-oriented. However, Sen draws a sharp distinction between processes and outcomes and claims that the CA has not much to offer concerning procedural justice, whereas Nussbaum includes procedural elements such as political liberties in her list. It is unclear whether Sen refers in his statement on procedural justice also to the principles of justice mentioned above. These can be seen as procedural in the sense that they define rules that govern the choice between outcomes. Sen has never said clearly if he endorses one of the principles (equality, sufficiency, or priority), and if so as applied to functioning or capability, although he has introduced the notion of capabilities in his article "Equality of What?" (1980). Nussbaum (2006, 291–95) suggests that justice demands equality with regard to some capabilities while sufficiency with regard to others.[14] This is an issue for further investigation.

## APPENDIX

Nussbaum's list of central functional capabilities as given in Nussbaum 2000 (78) and 2011 (33–34) respectively:

1. *Life*. Being able to live to the end of human life of normal length; not dying prematurely, or before one's life is so reduced as to be not worth living.
2. *Bodily Health*. Being able to have good health, including reproductive health; to be adequately nourished; to have adequate shelter.
3. *Bodily Integrity*. Being able to move freely from place to place; to be secure against violent assault, including sexual assault and domestic violence; having opportunities for sexual satisfaction and for choice in matters of reproduction.
4. *Senses, Imagination, and Thought*. Being able to use the senses, to imagine, think, and reason—and to do these things in a "truly human" way, a way informed and cultivated by an adequate education, including, but by no means limited to, literacy and basic mathematical and scientific training. Being able to use imagination and thought in connection with experiencing and producing works and events of one's own choice, religious, literary, musical, and so forth. Being able to use one's mind in ways protected by guarantees of freedom of expression with respect to both political and artistic speech, and freedom of religious exercise. Being able to have pleasurable experiences, and to avoid non-necessary [2011: nonbeneficial] pain.

5. *Emotions*. Being able to have attachments to things and people outside ourselves; to love those who love and care for us, to grieve at their absence; in general, to love, to grieve, to experience longing, gratitude, and justified anger. Not having one's emotional development blighted by fear and anxiety. . . .
6. *Practical Reason*. Being able to form a conception of the good and to engage in critical reflection about the planning of one's life. . . .
7. *Affiliation*. A. Being able to live with and towards others, to recognise and show concern for other human beings, to engage in various forms of social interaction; to be able to imagine the situation of another [the following is missing in 2011] and have compassion for that situation; to have the capability for both justice and friendship.

   B. Having the social bases of self-respect and non-humiliation; being able to be treated as a dignified being whose worth is equal to that of others. This entails protection against discrimination [2011: provisions of non-discrimination] on the basis of race, sex, religion, caste, ethnicity, or national origin.
8. *Other Species*. Being able to live with concern for and in relation to animals, plants, and the world of nature.
9. *Play*. Being able to laugh, to play, to enjoy recreational activities.
10. *Control over One's Environment*. A. Political. Being able to participate effectively in political choices that govern one's life; having the right of political participation, protections of free speech and association.

    B. Material. Being able to hold property (both land and movable goods) [2011 adds: and having property rights on an equal basis with others]; having the right to seek employment on an equal basis with others; having the freedom from unwarranted search and seizure. [2011 adds: In work, being able to work as a human being, exercising practical reason and entering into meaningful relationships of mutual recognition with other workers.]

ACKNOWLEDGMENT

First ideas on how to carve out the distinction between Sen's and Nussbaum's version of the capabilities approach (CA) go back to my doctoral thesis. Since then, the paper has evolved in several steps. In the course of this journey, I benefited a lot from comments from and discussions with many colleagues and would like to extend special thanks to Udo Ebert, Manfred Holler, Matthew Braham, Geoff Hinchliffe, Jürgen Volkert, Jean-Michel Bonvin, Antoinette Baujard, and Henry Richardson.

NOTES

1. To my knowledge this term was introduced by Cohen (1989) along with the alternative term "currency of justice."

2. In oral communication (during a symposium on his "The Idea of Justice" in Rotterdam on 1 July 2010), Amartya Sen once conceded that it is a linguistic mistake to use the plural "capabilities," but that he uses the term to facilitate communication.

3. Nussbaum (1988, 164) introduced this concept, calling it "external capability." This notion was criticized by Crocker (1995) and Gasper (1997, 261) as misleading since it stands for the extent to which an internal capability can be exercised given external conditions. As a consequence, Nussbaum (2000, 84) changed it to "combined capability," indicating the combination of internal capabilities with external conditions.

4. Clark (2013, 175) also holds that the list stayed essentially the same since the very beginning.

5. Sen uses this phrase several times (Sen 1999, 76–77; 2009, 233).

6. If not stated otherwise, the emphasis is in the original.

7. She states the incommensurability of the items on her list, but to my knowledge she has never provided any arguments about why specific items of her list are not commensurable, such as "life itself" and "bodily health." In operationalizing the list, it is often difficult to unambiguously assign indicators to the elements of her list (Brandolini and D'Alessio 2009) so that the incommensurability of some items can be questioned.

8. Qizilbash (2006, 22) notes this ambiguity as well.

9. He discusses the meaning of "space" in the context of the informational content of the various approaches (Sen 1992, 43).

10. Sen (1996, 118–19) states, "functioning is only a *dimension*."

11. See Nussbaum (1988, 2000, 2003, 2011) and Sen (1993, 2004b, 2005; Sen et al. 2003) as well as the comments of Crocker (1992, 1995), Qizilbash (1996), Gasper (1997, 2003), Agarwal, Humphries, and Robeyns (2003), Robeyns (2003, 2005), and Alkire (2008) on the debate.

12. Nussbaum (2011, 89–93) has elaborated on this by referring to Rawls's conception of "political liberalism." However, this paper does not directly pertain to her concept of political liberalism, and a detailed discussion goes beyond the scope of this paper.

13. I am grateful to Bernhard Babic for this illustration.

14. Both their approaches have been assessed as being sufficientarian, see Kaufman (2006).

REFERENCES

Agarwal, Bina, Jane Humphries, and Ingrid Robeyns. 2003. "Exploring the Challenges of Amartya Sen's Work and Ideas: An Introduction." *Feminist Economics* 9 (2–3): 3–12. https://doi.org/10.1080/1354570032000099039

Alkire, Sabina. 2002. *Valuing Freedoms: Sen's Capability Approach and Poverty Reduction*. Oxford: Oxford University Press.

Alkire, Sabina. 2008. "Using the Capability Approach: Prospective and Evaluative Analyses." In *The Capability Approach: Concepts, Measures and Applications*, ed. Flavio Comim, Mozaffar Qizilbash, and Sabina Alkire, 26–50. Cambridge: Cambridge University Press.

Beitz, Charles R. 1986. Review: *Resources, Values and Development*, by Amartya Sen (Cambridge, MA: Harvard University Press, 1984). *Economics and Philosophy* 2 (2): 282. https://doi.org/10.1017/S147806150000267X

Brandolini, Andrea, and Giovanni D'Alessio. 2009. "Measuring Well-Being in the Functioning Space." In *Debating Global Society: Reach and Limits of the Capability Approach*, ed. Enrica Chiappero Martinetti, 91–156. Milan: Fondazione Giangiacomo Feltrinelli.

Clark, David Alexander. 2013. "Creating Capabilities, Lists and Thresholds: Whose Voices, Intuitions and Value Judgements Count?" *Journal of Human Development and Capabilities* 14 (1): 172–84. https://doi.org/10.1080/19452829.2013.762181

Cohen, Gerald A. 1989. "On the Currency of Egalitarian Justice." *Ethics*, 906–44.

Crocker, David A. 1992. "Functioning and Capability: The Foundations of Sen's and Nussbaum's Development Ethic." *Political Theory* 20 (4): 584–612.

Crocker, David. 1995. "Functioning and Capability: The Foundation of Sen's and Nussbaum's Development Ethic, Part 2." In *Women, Culture, and Development*, ed. Martha Nussbaum and Jonathan Glover, 153–98. New York: Oxford University Press.

Gasper, Des. 1997. "Sen's Capability Approach and Nussbaum's Capabilities Ethic." *Journal of International Development* 9 (2): 281–302. https://doi.org/10.1002/(SICI)1099-1328(199703)9:2<281::AID-JID438>3.0.CO;2-K

Gasper, Des. 2003. *Nussbaum's Capabilities Approach in Perspective: Purposes, Methods and Sources for an Ethics of Human Development*. Available at www.iss.nl

Jaggar, Alison M. 2006. "Reasoning About Well-Being: Nussbaum's Methods of Justifying the Capabilities." *Journal of Political Philosophy* 14 (3): 301–22.

Kaufman, Alexander, ed. 2006. *Capabilities Equality: Basic Issues and Problems*. London: Routledge.

Kuklys, Wiebke. 2005. *Amartya Sen's Capability Approach: Theoretical Insights and Empirical Applications*. Berlin: Springer.

Meyer, Lukas, and Dominic Roser. 2009. "Enough for the Future." In *Intergenerational Justice*, ed. Axel Gosseries and Lukas Meyer, 219–48. Oxford: Oxford University Press.

Nussbaum, Martha. 1988. "Nature, Function, and Capability: Aristotle on Political Distribution." In *Oxford Studies in Ancient Philosophy*, Supplementary Volume. Oxford: Oxford University Press.

Nussbaum, Martha. 2000. *Women and Human Development: The Capabilities Approach*. The John Robert Seeley Lectures. Cambridge: Cambridge University Press.

Nussbaum, Martha. 2003. "Capabilities as Fundamental Entitlements: Sen and Social Justice." *Feminist Economics* 9 (2–3): 33–59. https://doi.org/10.1080/1354570022000077926

Nussbaum, Martha. 2006. *Frontiers of Justice: Disability, Nationality, Species Membership*. Cambridge, MA: Belknap Press of Harvard University Press.

Nussbaum, Martha. 2011. *Creating Capabilities: The Human Development Approach*. Cambridge, MA: Belknap Press of Harvard University Press.
Qizilbash, Mozaffar. 1996. "Capabilities, Well-being and Human Development: A Survey." *Journal of Development Studies* 33 (2): 143–62. https://doi.org/10.1080/00220389608422460
Qizilbash, Mozaffar. 2006. "Capability, Happiness and Adaptation in Sen and J. S. Mill." *Utilitas* 18 (1): 20–32. https://doi.org/10.1017/S0953820805001809
Robeyns, Ingrid. 2003. "Sen's Capability Approach and Gender Inequality: Selecting Relevant Capabilities." *Feminist Economics* 9 (2–3): 61–92. https://doi.org/10.1080/1354570022000078024
Robeyns, Ingrid. 2005. "The Capability Approach: A Theoretical Survey." *Journal of Human Development* 6 (1): 93–117.
Robeyns, Ingrid. 2011. "The Capability Approach." *Stanford Encyclopedia of Philosophy*. http://plato.stanford.edu/entries/capability-approach/
Robeyns, Ingrid. 2016. "Capabilitarianism." *Journal of Human Development and Capabilities* 17 (3): 397–414. https://doi.org/10.1080/19452829.2016.1145631
Robeyns, Ingrid. 2017. *Wellbeing, Freedom and Social Justice: The Capability Approach Re-Examined*. Cambridge, UK: Open Book Publishers.
Sen, Amartya. 1980. "Equality of What?" In *The Tanner Lectures on Human Value*, ed. Sterling M. McMurrin, 195–220. Salt Lake City: University of Utah Press.
Sen, Amartya. 1985. *Commodities and Capabilities*. New York: Oxford University Press.
Sen, Amartya. 1988. "Freedom of Choice." *European Economic Review* 32 (2–3): 269–94. https://doi.org/10.1016/0014-2921(88)90173-0
Sen, Amartya. 1992. *Inequality Reexamined*. New York: Oxford University Press.
Sen, Amartya. 1993. "Capability and Well-Being." In *The Quality of Life*, ed. Martha Nussbaum and Amartya Sen, 30–53. Oxford: Oxford University Press.
Sen, Amartya. 1996. "Freedom, Capabilities and Public Action: A Response." *Notizie Di Politeia* 12 (43/44): 107–25.
Sen, Amartya. 1999. *Development as Freedom*. New York: Oxford University Press.
Sen, Amartya. 2002. *Rationality and Freedom*. Cambridge, MA: Belknap Press.
Sen, Amartya. 2004a. "Incompleteness and Reasoned Choice." *Synthese* 140 (1/2): 43–59. https://doi.org/10.1023/B:SYNT.0000029940.51537.b3
Sen, Amartya. 2004b. "Capabilities, Lists, and Public Reason: Continuing the Conversation." *Feminist Economics* 10 (3): 77–80. https://doi.org/10.1080/1354570042000315163
Sen, Amartya. 2005. "Human Rights and Capabilities." *Journal of Human Development* 6 (2): 151–66. https://doi.org/10.1080/14649880500120491
Sen, Amartya. 2009. *The Idea of Justice*. London: Allen Lane.
Sen, Amartya, Bina Agarwal, Jane Humphries, and Ingrid Robeyns. 2003. "Continuing the Conversation." *Feminist Economics* 9 (2–3): 319–32. https://doi.org/10.1080/1354570032000089788
Sen, Amartya, John Muellbauer, and Geoffrey Hawthorn. 1987. *The Standard of Living*. Cambridge: Cambridge University Press.

CHAPTER 9

# Liberal Democratic Foreign Policy, International Toleration, and Welfare State Capitalism

David A. Reidy

## I. Introduction

In Part I of *The Law of Peoples*, John Rawls articulates and defends eight principles to which liberal democratic peoples' foreign policies and conceptions of international justice must adhere.[1] At the core of these principles is the idea that, as peaceful bodies politic possessed of endogenously realized and sustained corporate moral personality, liberal democratic peoples are to recognize, respect, and engage one another as independent free equals. Liberal democratic peoples realize and sustain their corporate moral personality through their political and legal institutions and the activities of citizens and officials therein. Here moral personality is constituted as it is for individuals, by the presence of two developed capacities: first, rationally to determine and advance one's good, and second, reasonably to propose and honor mutually acceptable terms of interaction with others similarly disposed. Among liberal democratic peoples, Rawls includes all peoples reliably constitutionally committed to legitimate democratic politics publicly oriented by any one of a family of generically liberal but differentially reasonable public political conceptions of justice. It follows that, facing one another as independent free equals, liberal democratic peoples will in their foreign policies and conceptions of international justice neither condition their recognition and respect of, or engagement with, others on fidelity to, nor aim in their international interactions at coercing others into, any particular generically liberal political conception of justice. Each is to leave others free to determine for itself which is the most reasonable generically liberal public political conception of justice. Rawls further argues that the so-called "democratic peace thesis" provides some reason for thinking that liberal democratic peoples faithful to foreign policies and conceptions of international justice that adhere to his eight principles will remain, in the absence of any global Leviathan or comparable exogenous force, peaceful in their relations to one another.

In Part II, Rawls then turns to the question of whether, as a matter of their principled foreign policies and conceptions of international justice, peaceful liberal democratic peoples should ever recognize, respect, and engage with, also as independent free equals, bodies politic neither liberal nor democratic but nevertheless similarly endogenously possessed of corporate moral personality. He conjectures that there may be cases in which they should. He frames his case for this conjecture around a fictional well-ordered and "decent" Islamic constitutional republic, "Kazanistan." He offers several reasons to support his conjecture, not least that the citizens of "Kazanistan" are endogenously secured conditions adequate to their liberalizing and democratizing their body politic through their own political agency. Still, many readers have doubted that liberal democratic peoples should, as a matter of their principled foreign policies and conceptions of international justice, recognize, respect, or engage with, as independent free equals, bodies politic neither liberal nor democratic, even if as corporate bodies they possess the capacities essential to moral personality. And all have agreed that Rawls fails to develop any reasons—say by showing that the democratic peace thesis extends to polities like "Kazanistan"—for thinking that a "Kazanistan" will, in the absence of a global Leviathan or similar exogenous force, remain peaceful in its relations with liberal democratic peoples (or, for that matter, with other well-ordered and "decent," but neither liberal nor democratic polities, like it).

Some of the reasons Rawls offers to support his conjecture regarding "Kazanistan" lead naturally to the further question of whether, as part of their principled foreign policies and conceptions of international justice, liberal democratic peoples should also recognize, respect, and engage with, as independent free equals, bodies politic not only neither liberal nor democratic but also lacking corporate moral personality, even though possessing resources adequate to its endogenously realizing and sustaining corporate moral personality. Such polities he characterizes as "benevolent absolutisms." Here Rawls argues that liberal democratic peoples' principled foreign policies and conceptions of international justice should condition their recognition and respect for, and engagement with, other bodies politic, as independent free equals, on their possessing endogenously realized and sustained corporate moral personality. So liberal democratic peoples should not treat "benevolent absolutisms" as they treat "Kazanistan." Yet, Rawls suggests that liberal democratic peoples have no right to interfere in the domestic affairs of "benevolent absolutisms," and that the members of a "benevolent absolutism" have a right to defend themselves against unwanted coercive international intervention. The main reason for this appears to be that the members of a "benevolent absolutism" are endogenously secured conditions adequate developing and exercising their moral personality to the point of their investing their body politic, through their own agency, with reliably enduring corporate moral personality. This, Rawls appears to think, is sufficient to deny liberal democracies any right to interfere in their affairs and to afford their members a right to defend themselves against unwanted coercive international intervention.

Much ink has already been spilled over Rawls's position regarding a principled liberal foreign policy toward "Kazanistan" and the "benevolent absolutism." I am on record defending his position that liberal democratic peoples ought in their international relations to recognize, respect, and engage with the former as a free equal, and ought not interfere with the latter, assuming of course that each is internationally peaceful. In this essay I engage a question closely related to the foregoing but not much discussed either by Rawls or his readers: what should liberal democratic peoples' foreign policies and conceptions of international justice require of them (and of "Kazanistan") in their relations with welfare capitalist states? This is a tricky question. Welfare capitalist states cut across Rawls's ideal theory taxonomy of bodies politic: liberal democratic peoples, "decent" well-ordered peoples, and "benevolent absolutisms." And even if their foreign policies and conceptions of international justice were to align with Rawls's eight principles, there are good reasons to doubt that they would remain peaceful in their international relations, whether with liberal democratic peoples, "Kazanistan," or "benevolent absolutisms." Historically, welfare capitalist states seem naturally to drift toward becoming a kind of internationally disruptive "outlaw state."

In his work on domestic institutions and relations between citizens, Rawls consistently defended markets and the price system, and he was not opposed in principle to private ownership in the means of production. But he consistently rejected capitalism, both the laissez-faire and welfare state varieties, both domestic and global. The general tendency of capitalism, even welfare state capitalism, as a public political self-understanding is, in Rawls's view, dispiriting and deracinating. Thus, we should not be surprised if welfare capitalist states pose problems for *The Law of Peoples*, despite Rawls's lack of attention to them there.

## II. *The Law of Peoples*

In *The Law of Peoples* Rawls undertakes to complete his revised argument, as set out in *Political Liberalism*, for the claim that it is neither unreasonable nor unrealistic for any determinate human population to endeavor to realize and sustain itself as a just and stable constitutional liberal democracy.[2] In *A Theory of Justice* he centered his argument around a specific conception of justice that he dubbed "justice as fairness."[3] He argued that it was reasonable and realistic to think that under favorable conditions all intelligent persons of good will could, indeed would, publicly recognize and adopt it as more reasonable than available alternatives, and also that if institutionally embodied it would draw those subject to it into a more or less comprehensive shared worldview and self-understanding in terms of which each would publicly recognize that the sense of justice they all shared was fully congruent with (even if not reducible to) their rational nature and so their good in the most basic sense. This would be sufficient to stabilize their cooperation without the introduction of a Leviathan or similar exogenous force.

Over time, Rawls began to doubt whether in any free society, and so in any society institutionally embodying "justice as fairness," any such (more or less) comprehensive shared worldview and self-understanding could ever arise and persist (without impermissible oppression). This led him to doubt whether it was reasonable and realistic to suppose that under favorable conditions all intelligent persons of good will would publicly recognize and adopt "justice as fairness" as more reasonable than available alternatives. Some, perhaps many, such persons, sure; but all? Surely those drawn to different (more or less) comprehensive worldviews and self-understandings would eventually find themselves differentially ranking the reasonableness of candidate various liberal and democratic conceptions of justice.

So, Rawls recast his argument in *Political Liberalism*. Doing so involved making many changes. He recast justice as fairness as a *public political* conception of justice. It was publicly addressed to, and concerned only political and legal relations between, citizens as such. It was publicly articulated and defended in public political terms that could stand alone as common ground between citizens, apart from their diverse comprehensive worldviews and self-understandings. It was but one member of a wider family of reasonable, or at least not unreasonable, generically liberal and democratic, and so at least minimally egalitarian, public political conceptions of justice. Each member of this family would affirm, first, a familiar list of basic liberties (including political liberties), along with their priority over other political values such as economic efficiency or the perfection of some determinate national character, and second, formal nondiscrimination within the division of labor along with some measures aimed at constraining inequalities of opportunity, and a basic social minimum adequate to ensuring that all citizens have a meaningful opportunity to exercise their basic liberties. But each member of the family would then build on these common commitments in its own way. Unanimity over which was most reasonable was unlikely and would in any case never persist. At best, an enduring majority might support a particular conception as most reasonable. But even if this conception was institutionally realized and sustained over time, citizens would never publicly share one and the same view of whether and how their acquired sense of justice aligned with their rational nature or good as specified by their diverse comprehensive worldviews and self-understandings. Nevertheless, they might still converge in an overlapping consensus over various generically liberal, democratic, and egalitarian political values of great weight, not least those of political legitimacy and civic friendship, that they could together realize and sustain only by confining their political and law-making activity to the space—of reasonable political disagreement—bounded by the family of reasonable generically liberal public political conceptions of justice. And this may be adequate to stabilizing their political and legal cooperation without the introduction of a Leviathan or similar exogenous force.

Thus, in *Political Liberalism*, Rawls concluded (barring certain highly unfavorable but not inevitable conditions) that it was still reasonable and realistic to suppose that any determinate human population that was already situated historically within a broadly liberal, democratic, and egalitarian tradition could realize and sustain itself as a stable legitimate constitutional liberal democracy capable of perfecting itself as just through its own efforts. But, as in *Theory*, Rawls reached this conclusion only under the simplifying assumptions that, first, he was addressing populations that already shared a certain tradition, and second, international relations were either non-existent or irrelevant. In *The Law of Peoples*, he lifts the latter assumption.

*The Law of Peoples* aims to show that it is neither unreasonable nor unrealistic to suppose that any number of distinct populations, each adequately connected to a broadly liberal, democratic, and egalitarian tradition, could realize and sustain themselves as diverse and independent constitutional liberal democracies peacefully and reasonably interacting with one another internationally. This requires articulating and defending principles of foreign policy and international justice that diverse constitutional liberal democracies could publicly recognize and adopt as a shared reasonable and realistic framework for orienting their relations one to another, including in any international shared political institutional and law-making activity they might together undertake. As in *Political Liberalism*, Rawls sets to the side questions regarding the *most reasonable* foreign policy or conception of international justice for relations between diverse independent liberal democratic peoples. Not because he has no view of the matter, but rather because he thinks it is unrealistic to think that in the absence of oppression, diverse and independent liberal democratic peoples will ever agree on the matter. Instead, as in *Political Liberalism*, he focuses on the conditions or criteria satisfied by the various members of a family of *sufficiently* reasonable foreign policies or public political conceptions of international justice. These conditions or criteria he sets out in the form of eight principles. Beyond these, liberal democratic peoples will inevitably arrive at different views of which foreign policies and public political conceptions of international justice are most reasonable. Elements of these they may incorporate into international law and give institutional embodiment through shared international political and law-making activity, whether treaty-making, custom, or otherwise, that they all accept as legitimate. But they will accept as legitimate only international political and law-making activity that accords with the eight principles.

Many readers have objected to the fact that, at least as explained by Rawls, these eight principles express very little that is distinctively liberal or democratic. For example, while they include a commitment to human rights, these rights are mostly limited to basic needs (food, water, essential health care) and those covered by Articles 3–18 of the Universal Declaration of Human Rights (along with the conventions on Genocide and Apartheid). Those covered by later articles of the UDHR or by many subsequent human rights documents are not basic human rights or human rights "proper." As "human rights," these are predicated on voluntary undertakings in international political and law-making activity. Some may express distinctively liberal democratic aspirations. Of course, Rawls expresses no objection to "human rights" thus understood. His point is only that the human rights that liberal democracies *must* include in their foreign policies and conceptions of international justice, prior to and apart from any voluntary undertakings in international political and law-making activity, are those related to basic needs or covered by Articles 3–18 (along with the previously mentioned conventions). Many readers object that, especially from the point of view of liberal democratic peoples, this is an impoverished conception of human rights.

Rawls also makes it clear that while liberal democracies must include in their diverse foreign policies and conceptions of international justice a commitment to ensuring one another reliable access to resources needed for each endogenously to sustain itself as a body politic with corporate moral personality (e.g., a mutual insurance scheme to address severe disasters), they need not include any particular constraints on material inequalities between them, or even any general principle of international distributive justice (beyond the presumed mutual advantage implied by free and fair trade). Of course, Rawls allows that diverse liberal democratic peoples may commit to such constraints or principles through legitimate international political and law-making activity. His point is only that their foreign policies and conceptions of international justice are not unreasonable or unrealistic merely because they do not. Of course, diverse liberal democratic peoples are unlikely unanimously to converge in legitimate international political and law-making activity on which constraint or principle is most reasonable.[4]

Many readers have found it difficult to understand why liberal democratic peoples concerned to identify the principles of a reasonable and realistic foreign policy and conception of international justice would not settle on principles the content of which was more robustly liberal and democratic. A large part of the answer here is that, as in *Political Liberalism*, Rawls is assuming that both within and between liberal democratic peoples, reasonable disagreement, not only in (more or less) comprehensive worldviews and self-understandings, but also in political judgments of relative reasonableness, is a permanent fact, ineliminable without coercive oppression. This means that among liberal democratic peoples, realized institutions and political traditions will vary considerably. Thus it would be unreasonable and unrealistic to suppose that liberal democratic peoples would not themselves be and remain significantly diverse. Some may never regard others as more than just barely liberal or democratic. Rawls's hope for a peaceful world within which liberal democracies are free to perfect themselves in their own ways thus turns identifying not the most reasonable and realistic foreign policy or conception of international justice but rather on the criteria satisfied by all sufficiently reasonable and realistic such policies and conceptions, and so by any international political and law-making activity certifiable as at least legitimate from a liberal democratic point of view.

In *The Law of Peoples*, Rawls further puzzled readers by then taking up the question of what a principled liberal democratic foreign policy and conception of international justice should require with respect to relations between liberal democracies and other bodies politic neither liberal nor democratic, but nevertheless ready and willing to honor in their international relations with liberal democracies the same criteria governing legitimate international coercion to which liberal democratic peoples properly hold one another. He considers two cases. The first is that of the well-ordered decent constitutional republic possessed of corporate moral personality. He offers as a fictional case "Kazanistan." The second is that of the "benevolent absolutism." Though peaceful and almost fully compliant with the eight principles of the law of peoples and with basic human rights, it fails fully to honor basic human rights in the area of political participation, and so as a consequence lacks corporate moral personality.

"Kazanistan" is an internationally peaceful Islamic theocratic constitutional republic. Though neither liberal nor democratic, its domestic order is "decent" and "well-ordered." It possesses the institutionally realized capacities essential to corporate moral personality. It accepts and is prepared to honor in its relations to liberal democratic peoples the same principles of foreign policy and international justice (commitments to basic human rights, to ensuring that all determinate populations have access to resources adequate to their realizing and sustaining corporate moral personality, and so on) that liberal democratic peoples require of one another (prior to and apart from any voluntary undertakings in shared international political and law-making activity). It is thus ready and able to join liberal democratic peoples in legitimate international political institution-building and law-making activity. Rawls conjectures that, on balance, liberal democratic peoples have good and sufficient reasons to extend to "Kazanistan" the same principled recognition, respect, and engagement that they extend to one another. They should tolerate "Kazanistan," not in a begrudging fashion or for merely pragmatic reasons. Rather, they should recognize, respect, and engage "Kazanistan" as they do one another, as full members in good standing in an international society of independent free and equal peoples.

Unlike "Kazanistan," the "benevolent absolutism" is not "well-ordered." Its form is that of unilateral or managerial coordination rather than well-ordered cooperation, of rule *by* law rather than rule *of* law. It lacks the institutionally realized capacities essential to corporate moral personality. Yet nothing stands in the way of it, through the agency of its members, endogenously realizing and sustaining corporate moral personality. Its members have all they need to effect a transition from rule by law to rule of law, and from their being population of subjects benevolently coordinated from the outside to a people constituted as such from within through "decent" and "well-ordered" cooperation. Thus, Rawls concludes that while liberal democratic peoples have good reasons to withhold from benevolent absolutisms full recognition, respect, and engagement as independent free equals within their international relations, including international political institution-building and law-making activity, they have no right to interfere in the domestic affairs of benevolent absolutisms, and the members of benevolent absolutisms have a right to defend themselves against unwanted interference.

## III. The Grounds of Liberal Democratic Toleration

At the center of political liberalism is the idea that it is unrealistic to expect that all, or even most, persons born and raised within an independent and enduring constitutional liberal democracy, even one that is faithful to Rawls's own principles of justice as fairness, will settle in reflective equilibrium into self-understandings and a worldview (more or less) comprehensively liberal and democratic and firmly situated within what Rawls, in Part III of *Theory*, characterized as the third stage of moral development, the morality of principle. Within a morality of principle, persons understand themselves, and so adopt (more or less) comprehensive worldviews that express their status as rational and reasonable persons and so free equals. But under conditions of freedom, there will be in every generation some, perhaps many, who inevitably settle in reflective equilibrium into self-understandings and worldviews that are neither comprehensively liberal or democratic nor firmly situated within a morality of principle. Some, perhaps many, will settle into self-understandings and worldviews that are traditional and religious, and aligned with what in Part III of *Theory* Rawls characterized as the second stage of moral development, the morality of association. Within a morality of association, persons understand themselves, and so adopt (more or less) comprehensive worldviews that express their status as rational persons responsible to specific roles or group memberships, sometimes hierarchically arranged, within a common-good cooperative undertaking. Persons drawn to such self-understandings and worldviews may be ready and willing politically and legally to cooperate with others as free and equal citizens on liberal and democratic terms, perhaps even the terms of justice as fairness. But they will not understand or experience so doing as congruent with their own rational nature or good as persons in the same way as do persons who are drawn to self-understandings and worldviews more or less comprehensively liberal and democratic and aligned with a morality of principle.

Further, within any free society the inevitable diversity of self-understandings and worldviews, and realized stages of moral development, will lead politically and legally reasonable citizens to different judgments in reflective equilibrium regarding the most reasonable conception of justice to orient their shared political and legal activity. Some may settle on justice as fairness. But others may settle on other public political and generically liberal and democratic conceptions of justice.

Given these inevitabilities, in any generation those who have settled in reflective equilibrium into self-understandings and a worldview that is (more or less) comprehensively liberal and democratic and securely associated with a morality of principle, and who as such have perhaps judged justice as fairness to be the most reasonable of the family of generically liberal and democratic and egalitarian principles of justice—say someone like Rawls himself or someone like the kind of person who in *Theory* he unrealistically supposed everyone living in a liberal democracy would become—face a difficult choice. On the one hand, they might allow that in principle it would be permissible for them to capture and use public political power to try through one or another coercive intervention, even if only various sorts of incentives, to bring about the further intellectual and moral development of their compatriots, hoping to bring the vast bulk of them closer to their own more comprehensively liberal and democratic self-understandings and worldview, to a morality of principle, and to justice as fairness as the most reasonable conception of justice. Of course, they would know that what is permissible in principle might be practically foolish. And since any undertaking coercively to draw everyone closer to their comprehensively liberal and democratic self-understandings and worldview, morality of principle, and determinate sense of justice would have to be sustained across generations, practical considerations might warrant substantial toleration and non-intervention. But even if no such undertaking is ventured, its mere permissibility, in principle, would entail a public political culture within which those who did not share self-understandings and a worldview more or less comprehensively liberal and democratic, aligned with a morality of principle and a sense of justice oriented by justice as fairness, would know that from their fellow citizens (more "enlightened" by their own lights) they would never enjoy more than a begrudging or pragmatic toleration. Their alienation from or hostility to shared *political and legal* activity would seem all but inevitable. Certainly, civic friendship, rooted as it is in mutual recognition, respect, and engagement in shared political and law-making activity would be substantially compromised. Indeed, those merely pragmatically tolerated would probably internalize a psychologically and sociologically dangerous sense of wounded pride. There are, then, costs to withholding principled toleration from those whose self-understandings and worldviews are not comprehensively liberal and democratic or associated with a morality of principle and so whose sense of justice is not specifically oriented by justice as fairness, but who are nevertheless prepared as citizens to honor generically liberal public political principles in shared political and law-making activity. For Rawls, these costs are rather substantial.

Now, in *The Law of Peoples*, Rawls carries this pattern of thinking forward to the context of international relations. As corporate agents, liberal democratic peoples are rational and reasonable and so face one another in international relations as free equals. By contrast to their individual members, their moral capacities are endogenously realized and sustained, and so they are independent of one another in a way that natural human beings as the members of or citizens within a polity are not. Without one another, natural human beings cannot even meet their basic needs, much less realize and sustain their moral capacities.[5] Liberal democratic peoples can. Thus, liberal democratic peoples do not face one another internationally as free equals in the same way that their citizens domestically face one another as free equals. The former are possessed of an independence that the latter lacks. But this difference aside, facing one another as free equals, liberal democratic peoples will, like their citizens, recognize that it is neither reasonable nor realistic to require of one another, as a condition of shared political and law-making activity, participation in a shared, wide, and general reflective equilibrium that ranges across determinate self-understandings, (more or less) comprehensive worldviews, and specific conceptions of justice between them. Indeed, given the relatively more substantial independence of peoples as compared to individual natural human persons, the former may display more path dependent diversity than the latter. In any event, liberal democratic peoples will inevitably face one another as diverse. Some will no doubt judge others less than fully just, perhaps even barely liberal or democratic. Some may reject the self-understandings and (more or less) comprehensive worldviews of others. Some may see the public political culture of others as straddling the distinction between a morality of association and a morality of principle. Thus, prior to and apart from the possibility of a "Kazanistan" or "benevolent absolutism," the most fully developed and robustly liberal and democratic of liberal democratic peoples will already face a circumstance and choice analogous to that faced in the domestic context by the sort of citizen Rawls contemplated in Part III of *Theory*. Perhaps like Rawls himself, this citizen's self-understanding and worldview was fully aligned with a (more or less) comprehensive liberal democratic morality of principle. But as Rawls recognized in *Political Liberalism* this citizen would inevitably face others ready and willing politically and legally to engage with her as a free equal but unready and unwilling to adopt her self-understanding, worldview, and (more or less) comprehensive liberal democratic morality of principle. Thus, as in *Political Liberalism*, so too in *The Law of Peoples:* the possibility of free equals engaging in and sustaining shared cooperative political and law-making activity stable in the right way turns on an overlapping consensus on the more permissive deontic notion of legitimacy rather than a single reflective equilibrium centered on the more restrictive notion of justice.

Of course, within *Political Liberalism*, while substantial, the diversity of self-understandings, worldviews, and so on of individual citizens able politically and legally to engage one another as free equals is circumscribed by their shared history and institutions. This limiting condition is absent in *The Law of Peoples*. And so the diversity, not only between liberal democratic peoples, but between all peoples able politically and legally to engage one another as free equals, may be more substantial. Indeed, some peoples so able (e.g., "Kazanistan") may lack not only liberal democratic institutions, but a history of liberal democratic tradition. Others (e.g., a "benevolent absolutism") may lack the rule of law or a history of constitutional republican tradition, yet neither threaten liberal democratic peoples and their reasonable international relations nor unreasonably prevent their own members from realizing themselves as a rule of law constitutional republic with corporate moral personality. As noted above, Rawls argues that on balance liberal democratic peoples should recognize, respect, and engage the former (e.g., "Kazanistan") as a free equal, and should not interfere with the latter (the members of which have a right to defend themselves against unwanted interference). I have suggested that central to Rawls's reasoning is that a polity need not be liberal and democratic, indeed need not even have corporate moral personality, for its members to have all that they need to realize and sustain themselves through their own agency as a liberal democratic people. But this requires some further explanation. So too does the implication that the reasonableness of a body politic within international relations is significantly independent of the reasonableness of its domestic institutions and the internal relations between its members.

## IV. Moral Personality: Individual and Corporate

The domestic order of an independent and enduring *just* liberal democracy is thoroughly or fully reasonable. On a continuous basis it reliably provides all its members with the institutional conditions necessary and sufficient to their fully adequately *developing and exercising* their basic moral capacities as free and equal citizens at the third stage of moral development, within a morality of principle, across all domains of shared activity. The domestic order of an independent and enduring *legitimate but not yet just* liberal democracy is not thoroughly or fully reasonable in this sense. But surely it is still reasonable, and more reasonable than many alternatives (or not simply unreasonable), even if it is not thoroughly or fully reasonable. While it may not provide all its members with the institutional conditions necessary and sufficient to their *fully adequately exercising* their developed basic moral capacities as free and equal citizens at the third stage of moral development, within a morality of principle, across all domains of shared activity, it does provide them with the institutional conditions necessary and sufficient to their fully adequately *developing* these capacities and to *meaningfully exercising* them to some significant degree, including in shared political and law-making activity. Indeed, what drives citizens in a legitimate but not yet just liberal democracy to struggle together for justice is their desire for institutions reliably able to sustain a more fully adequate exercise of their developed moral capacities. This struggle they are able to undertake because their basic social structure is adequate to the development of their moral capacities as free equals and to some significant meaningful use these capacities in political and law-making activity. Of course, in a legitimate but not yet just liberal democracy their exercise of these capacities in political and law-making activity may sometimes have to take the form of sustained public political dissent or civil disobedience.

The domestic order of a legitimate but not yet just liberal democracy will necessarily satisfy more than basic needs and Articles 3–18 of the *Universal Declaration of Human Rights* (along with the conventions on Genocide and Apartheid). Later articles, say regarding democratic political participation, liberal nondiscrimination, or certain elements of basic justice it may only partially and incompletely satisfy. But it will certainly satisfy more than what the law of peoples requires of it, which is, of course, why many readers object that the law of peoples is too weak.

Now consider a domestic order, say that of a "Kazanistan," that is, from the point of view of citizens as free equals, neither legitimate nor generically liberal and democratic. At best it may be in trivial compliance with some, and perhaps in noncompliance with many if not all, of these later articles. Still institutionally it secures for all those subject to it both basic needs and Articles 3–18 of the *Universal Declaration of Human Rights* (and the two mentioned conventions). And while it may not treat its members as free and equal citizens, it treats them all as citizens; as fully responsible members of a common cooperative undertaking, none are merely the subjects of others. This surely marks a significant or threshold crossing achievement. Further, such a polity might, despite being neither liberal nor democratic, even generically, institutionally realize the moral capacities essential to its having corporate moral personality. Of course, its domestic order may not afford its members the institutional conditions adequate to their meaningfully exercising their basic moral capacities as free and equal citizens in many domains of shared activity, including political and law-making activity. This raises the question: Why think its domestic order is a reasonable means, even if only barely, of its realizing, sustaining, and exercising its corporate moral personality? Surely liberal democratic peoples should not tolerate "Kazanistan" as Rawls suggests if its domestic order is a fully unreasonable means to its realizing, sutaining, and exercising its corporate moral personality.

Well, first, securing basic needs and complying with Articles 3–18 (and the conventions of genocide and Apartheid) may be sufficient for the domestic order of a corporate body politic reliably to secure for all its members institutional conditions necessary and sufficient to their *fully developing* (even if *not fully exercising*) their moral capacities as rational and reasonable free equals within a morality of principle. A body politic need not be liberal or democratic to secure for all its members the institutional conditions necessary and sufficient to their so *developing* their moral capacities. And it need not be liberal or democratic to afford all its members meaningful opportunities to *exercise* their fully developed moral capacities in at least some domains outside of political and law-making activity. Finally, it need not be liberal or democratic to afford all its members at least some opportunity to exercise some of their moral capacities in political and law-making activity. Of course, it will have to secure various conditions of family life, allow diverse associations and activities within civil society, and guarantee all at least some forms of political participation. But none of this requires liberal democracy.

Second, corporate moral personality does not depend on political and law-making activity being liberal and democratic. To be sure, it requires political and law-making activity to be inclusive, reason-giving, and oriented toward the common good. But this may be institutionally secured through deliberative hierarchies within which citizens participate in various ways as rational and responsible to differential roles or groups at the second stage of moral development, within a morality of association. Just as churches, universities, teams, and other common good associations may realize and sustain corporate moral personality without organizing themselves as liberal democracies, so too with bodies politic. Of course, within any polity that secures basic needs and Articles 3–18 (and the conventions on genocide and Apartheid), many if not all citizens will develop their moral capacities as rational and reasonable free equals and so eventually press within some or all of their common good associations, including their polity, for liberalization and democratization. But this is about the perfection, not the realization, of the various corporate moral personalities of which they are a part.

Putting the foregoing two points together: a body politic need not be liberal or democratic to secure for its members institutions adequate to their fully developing and in limited spheres exercising (outside of political and law-making activity) their moral capacities as rational and reasonable free equals within a morality of principle; it need not be liberal or democratic to afford its members institutions adequate to their meaningfully exercising their moral capacities at least as rational and responsible citizens in political and law-making activity; and it need not be liberal or democratic for its members to constitute themselves as a body politic with corporate moral personality. Of course, the development of stage three morality of principle capacities as rational and reasonable free equals will almost certainly stimulate demands for their more fully adequate exercise and so the liberalization and democratization of many domains of shared activity, including political and law-making activity. Developed moral capacities almost always seek conditions adequate to their full exercise. But this is compatible with recognizing that a polity meeting the basic needs of its members and reliably securing for them Articles 3–18 (along with the conventions on genocide and Apartheid) crosses a significant threshold that liberal democratic peoples should acknowledge. It would be hard to defend the claim that its domestic order is a *fully* unreasonable means to the reasonable end of realizing its members' moral capacities or realizing its own corporate moral personality.

Accepting this is consistent with acknowledging that its political and law-making activity (as well as activity within the family and civil society associations) would be more reasonable if more liberal and/or democratic. And it is consistent with acknowledging that at least for those members who seek to exercise in their political and law-making activities their developed moral capacities as free equals, the authority to coerce claimed by their political and legal order is illegitimate. These are important grounds for liberal democratic criticism. But the fact remains that "Kazanistan" represents a significant, and morally transformative, achievement. It resources and permits the full development of its members' moral capacities. It secures for them in different domains of shared activity various degrees of meaningful opportunity to exercise their developed moral capacities. And its members have endogenously constituted themselves as a body politic with corporate moral personality.

Within "Kazanistan," the moral force attaching to outcomes of political and law-making activity will fall short of that which attaches to the outcomes of political and law-making activity that is liberal and democratic. But some *prima facie* moral force will attach to outcomes simply because they are the result of political and law-making activity that is inclusive, deliberative, public, reason-giving, and sincerely aimed at a common good. Rulers do not unilaterally, even if benevolently, manage a subject population. The people of Kazanistan do not constitute or govern themselves as a liberal democracy, rather as a rule of law constitutional republic. Their political institutions and enacted laws have for them, and them alone, some *prima facie* moral force simply because they are their institutions and it is *their* law. This moral force may seem modest, but it is nevertheless significant, and the fact that it reaches only members of "Kazanistan" merits recognition.

The circumstance here is not unfamiliar. Consider any of the aforementioned common good civil society associations: churches, universities, teams, even families. Persons with fully developed moral capacities often seek, as rational and reasonable free equals, to exercise those capacities in such associations. If denied, they may reasonably insist that decisions made by such associations, even if benevolent or just, lack the moral force of legitimacy. But it would be a stretch for church members or university faculty to insist that decisions arrived at through inclusive, deliberative, public, reason-giving aimed sincerely at the common good of the association's members have for them *no prima facie* moral force. Indeed, even in the family, fully developed adult children typically recognize that parental decisions for the family that satisfy these conditions still have some *prima facie* moral force for them, even if it may be outweighed in their judgment by other considerations. This is why we typically feel some regret when we do not comply with decisions otherwise competently taken by associations of which we are a part simply because in their being made we were not recognized, or able to exercise our moral capacities, as rational and reasonable free equals. And it is why in such cases we typically insist that outsiders leave us free to decide for ourselves whether and how to dissent or resist. Outsiders are not subject to the same moral claims upon them.

Now, one might still insist that none of this shows that the domestic order of "Kazanistan" is even a minimally reasonable means to the reasonable end of securing the development and exercise of its members moral capacities and constituting its corporate moral personality. So, what else might one say in favor of Rawls's conjecture?

Here one might note the distinction between "Kazanistan" and the "benevolent absolutism." Both will secure conditions adequate to their members developing their moral capacities as rational and reasonable free equals able to engage one another within a morality of principle. And neither will secure conditions adequate to their members exercising these capacities in political and law-making activity. But the "benevolent absolutism" secures no meaningful opportunities for members to exercise any of their moral capacities in shared political and law-making activity. Its political and law-making activity is organized around what Rawls in *Theory* described as largely affective capacities to respond to love and care with loyalty and obedience within a "morality of authority." When developed and exercised, these proto-moral capacities can sustain forms of coordination important to the development of persons, to their acquiring and eventually exercising the genuinely moral capacities of later stages of development. But they cannot by themselves sustain any forms of well-ordered cooperation or institutionally realized corporate moral personality. And they are best thought of as liminal capacities, an anticipatory stage to the emergence of individual and corporate moral personality. One way to appreciate the moral significance of what a "Kazanistan" achieves is to focus not on how it falls short of the achievement of liberal democratic peoples, but on how it exceeds that of "benevolent absolutisms."

Finally, two countervailing points bear emphasis. First, in contrast to his appeal to the democratic peace thesis as a general reason for thinking that liberal democratic peoples committed to foreign policies and conceptions of international justice in accord with his eight principles would sustain peaceful relations with one another, Rawls makes no effort to show that there is a similar reason for thinking that "Kazanistan" and "benevolent absolutisms" similarly committed to his eight principles would do the same. He simply stipulates that liberal democratic peoples should tolerate both (each in its own way) so long as they remain internationally peaceful. Second, in contrast to his claim that it is reasonable and realistic to believe that a legitimate liberal democratic people could be stable in the right way, Rawls makes no claims about the stability of "Kazanistan" or "benevolent absolutisms." Indeed, he implies that neither is capable of being stable for the right reasons, since within neither is institutionally embodied right or justice sufficiently congruent with the rational nature and good of individual members as human beings capable of moral development.

## V. Welfare State Capitalism

In *Theory*, Rawls rejected welfare state capitalism as unjust. Indeed, around the time of *Theory*'s publication, he was publicly wondering whether justice might require public ownership of at least the "commanding heights" of the means of production, as a condition of securing for all fair value for their political liberties.[6] In *Justice as Fairness: A Restatement*, he reaffirmed his belief that welfare state capitalism was unjust.[7] Furthermore, correspondence and notes confirm that while he recognized throughout his life the value of markets and the price system, he was also throughout his life fundamentally opposed to capitalism. He thought that it encouraged a moral psychology of pride and humiliation; carried plutocratic oligarchy in its wake; led to corporate control of the military and an unreasonable foreign policy; ignored the fact that capitalism made people want what they got rather than giving them what they wanted; and tended more generally to deracinate persons, whether natural human persons or bodies politic as corporate persons, within shared political and law-making activity.

In *Theory*, Rawls characterized his two principles of justice as an expression of "democratic equality." He drew a staged contrast between systems of democratic equality and systems of what he dubbed "natural liberty." Systems of natural liberty formally secured familiar basic liberties and maintained a Pareto-efficient division of labor within which positions were open to talents under conditions of legal nondiscrimination. Systems of natural liberty were not precisely libertarian, which Rawls always rejected as fully unreasonable. For example, they required positions open to talents under conditions of legal nondiscrimination. Systems of natural liberty more closely approximated laissez-faire or classical liberalism. Though distinct from and more reasonable than libertarianisms, they nevertheless still unreasonably allow morally arbitrary social and natural lotteries, the accident of being born into a particular social circumstance or with a certain genetic endowment, to determine lifetime expectations of wealth and income within the division of labor. This unreasonableness reflected a failure to extend reciprocity between unavoidably interdependent free equals to the division of labor and the cooperative surplus it yields.

In contrast to systems of "natural liberty," systems of "liberal equality" aimed, through public education, public health, and similar measures, to check the impact of the morally arbitrary social lottery (the family and social group into which one is born) on lifetime expected earnings within the division of labor. They expressed something like "meritocracy." Systems of "natural aristocracy," on the other hand, aimed to check the impact of the morally arbitrary natural lottery (the genetic endowments with which one is born). They aimed at improving the condition of the naturally disadvantaged through wealth or income transfers from the naturally advantaged. They expressed a ethic of *noblesse oblige*. Though systems of liberal equality and natural aristocracy were each superior to systems of natural liberty (since both did a better job than any system of natural liberty at extending reciprocity between unavoidably interdependent free equals to the division of labor, and to the cooperative surplus it yields), systems of "democratic equality" were better still. Essentially, systems of "democratic equality" aimed to ensure that the division of labor and its cooperative surplus made Pareto-efficient use, with as little inequality as possible, of the morally arbitrary social *and* natural lotteries. Because it more fully extended reciprocity between unavoidably interdependent free equals to the division of labor and the cooperative surplus it yields, it was more reasonable than "liberal equality" or "natural aristocracy."

Now, welfare state capitalism does not map neatly onto this four-part schematic framework. In some respects, it looks like a system of natural liberty. But it aims to secure a social minimum and so would appear to be more reasonable than any system of natural liberty. However, the social minimum in a welfare capitalist state need not be specified to address the moral arbitrariness of either the social or the natural lottery, or even to ensure that all citizens have adequate resources to make meaningful use of their basic liberties, including their political liberties. It may be, perhaps typically will be, specified to win the passive peaceful acquiescence of the poor and working classes to the dramatic inequalities and persistent uncertainties of an "efficient" capitalist system. Welfare capitalist states are thus unlikely to be any better than systems of natural liberty at avoiding a politics of oligarchy or corporate plutocracy and a social psychology of pride and shame, exclusion and alienation. Whether and to what extent they might embody and express a degree of reciprocity or reasonableness between free and equal persons or citizens sufficient to legitimacy and stability as conceived in *Political Liberalism* is an open question.

Rawls does not carry the foregoing four-part taxonomy over into his later discussions in *Political Liberalism*, *Justice as Fairness: A Restatement*, or *The Law of Peoples*. It seems clear from *Political Liberalism* that he excludes from the class of generically liberal polities those organized as systems of "natural liberty," and that he includes some not organized as systems of "democratic equality." But he does not address welfare state capitalism. *Justice as Fairness: A Restatement* explicitly marks welfare capitalist states as neither just nor stable for the right reasons. But he does not explicitly discuss them in terms of legitimacy or the family of generically liberal political conceptions of justice as contemplated by *Political Liberalism*. With respect to the taxonomy Rawls deploys in *The Law of Peoples*, welfare capitalist states at their best look perhaps most like a secular, class-based version of "Kazanistan." Within the rule of law, a ruling class makes use of inclusive, group- and role-mediated consultation to sincerely aim in its political and law-making activity at a common good (e.g, efficiency conjoined with a social minimum). But at less than their best, welfare capitalist states can look more like "benevolent absolutisms." Ruling by law, an external force benevolently coordinates a subject population. At their worst, of course, welfare capitalist states can look like little more than some effectively advancing their own interests by purchasing the peaceful acquiescence of others. All this is to say that within the various taxonomies Rawls has provided it is unclear how to assess the relative degree of reasonableness or reciprocity realized by welfare capitalist states.

What about moral personality, corporate and individual? With respect to individuals, there seems to be little reason to doubt that welfare capitalist states can and do reliably secure conditions (secure families, diverse associations in civil society, etc.) adequate to their developing their moral capacities as rational and reasonable free equals within a morality of principle. They may not secure for individuals conditions adequate to their fully exercising those capacities in all domains of shared activity. But on this front legitimate liberal democratic peoples will themselves have, and tolerate, their different degrees of success. But it may be that welfare capitalist states do a worse job than all legitimate liberal democratic peoples do when it comes to both the development and opportunities for the meaningful exercise of its members' moral capacities. Whether Rawls thinks welfare capitalist states will secure for individuals conditions adequate to their fully developing and meaningfully exercising in enough domains of shared activity their moral capacities is unclear.

With respect to corporate moral personality, "Kazanistan" stands for the proposition that a people need not secure its members conditions adequate to their exercising stage three morality of principle capacities in political life for it to have and exercise corporate moral personality. And so nothing in the previous paragraph entails that a welfare capitalist state might not have corporate moral personality. But here Rawls's language is noteworthy. He distinguishes carefully between "states" and "peoples," and assigns corporate moral personality only to the latter. Nowhere does he ever use the language of "peoples" when discussing welfare state capitalism. This may reflect his sense that the natural tendency of welfare capitalist states is away from the sort of inclusive, consultative, deliberative, rule of law, reason-giving politics of a "Kazanistan" or a "liberal democratic" people, and toward the exclusive, managerial, edict-giving, rule by law, coordinative politics of the "benevolent absolutism."

Of course, as emphasized throughout above, Rawls recognizes that corporate moral personality is perfected, by liberalization and democratization, only through citizens in shared political and law-making activity expressing and exercising their individual moral capacities as rational and reasonable free equals. But the dispiriting and deracinating effects of welfare state capitalism on those subject to it may obstruct this process. It may do more to disable than to enable citizens through their own agency to realize and sustain together a body politic the corporate moral personality of which is oriented toward its own perfection, as a just liberal democratic people. Indeed, it may erode the capacities and obstruct the tendencies of individuals to perfect corporate moral personality in other areas of social life as well, such as churches, universities, teams, even families.

As previously noted, Rawls does not attempt in *The Law of Peoples* to extend the so-called democratic peace thesis to "decent" well-ordered peoples like Kazanistan or to "benevolent absolutisms." Whether there may be reasons to do so is an open question.[8] But Rawls clearly intimates that the thesis does not extend to welfare capitalist states. Indeed, he notes at various points in his work that in welfare capitalist states, control of the military and foreign policy all too often falls into the hands of corporations and the wealthy and that this leads welfare capitalist states to engage, often secretly, in impermissible international coercion, including war.[9] One might add that these corporations and wealthy individuals increasingly experience and understand themselves primarily in terms of international and global markets. When the national and international contexts of political and law-making activity prove to be an obstacle to their interests, they are naturally drawn to organizing and exercising political and law-making power as nonnational or supranational alliances. Rawls worried that European unification was being driven by precisely this dynamic; it was likely to serve the only or mainly the interests, and primarily as an instrument, of the international banking class.[10]

Rawls makes no claims regarding the stability of welfare state capitalist polities. And there are good reasons to think that they are incapable of being stable for the right reasons. But by contrast to "Kazanistan" and the "benevolent absolutism," neither of which would seem capable of being stable for the right reasons, welfare capitalist states seem ill-positioned for their instability to resolve itself in favor of moral progress or development. The materialist consumerist individualism they encourage is deracinating in ways absent from "Kazanistan" or the "benevolent absolutism."

The United States is welfare capitalist state. So too are several European and Latin American states. To be sure, they participate, at least formally, in liberal democracy to some degree. And to that extent they are more reasonable than many alternatives. But it is not clear how they fit into the vision that Rawls sets out in *Political Liberalism* and completes in *The Law of Peoples*. Are they, at least in an ideal form, simply the least reasonable members of the family of generically liberal democracies? Or are they, even in an ideal form, not members of that family but still, like "Kazanistan" and "benevolent absolutisms," polities the merits of which warrant, on the assumption that they are internationally peaceful, one or another form of toleration from liberal democratic peoples? Or are they, even in an ideal form, more like the obvious cases of fully unreasonable and "outlaw states," simply a cancer to be contained and eventually excised by liberal democratic peoples? I have not answered this question. But I hope to have contributed toward constructing a framework within which it might be profitably discussed.

NOTES

1. John Rawls, *The Law of Peoples* (Cambridge, MA: Harvard University Press, 1999). Rawls sets out the eight principles on page 37.

2. John Rawls, *Political Liberalism* (New York: Columbia University Press, 1993; rpt., 1996).

3. John Rawls, *A Theory of Justice* (Cambridge, MA: Harvard University Press, 1971; rpt., 1999).

4. Here it is worth noting that Rawls argues that liberal democratic peoples must include in their foreign policies and conceptions of international justice a commitment to securing one another reliable access to resources necessary only to sustaining their corporate moral personality, not to sustain their nature as liberal democratic peoples. The idea is that with reliable access to resources adequate sustaining corporate moral personality, a people's liberalization and democratization is its own responsibility.

5. This does not mean that every human being needs every other human being to realize and sustain itself as a person. If it did, Rawls would be driven to a more cosmopolitan position.

6. William Edmundson, *John Rawls: Reticent Socialist* (New York: Cambridge University Press, 2017).

7. John Rawls, *Justice as Fairness: A Restatement* (Cambridge, MA: Harvard University Press, 2001).

8. See, for example, Walter Riker, "The Democratic Peace Is Not Democratic: On Behalf of Rawls' Decent Societies," *Political Studies* 57, no. 3 (2009): 617–38.

9. Leif Wenar and B. Milanovic, "Are Liberal Peoples Peaceful?" *Journal of Political Philosophy* 17, no. 4 (2009): 462–86.

10. Philippe von Parij and J. Rawls, "Three Letters on *The Law of Peoples* and the European Union," *Revue de Philosophie Economique* 7 (2003): 7–20.

CHAPTER 10

# Equality and the Distributive Argument for Paternalism

Steven Wall

This chapter considers the distributive ideal of equality and its relation to legal paternalism.[1] By legal paternalism I have in mind the kind of paternalism that liberal writers on both the left and the right regard with suspicion. This has come to be called "hard paternalism" to distinguish it from the soft version that is present when, for example, you stop someone from crossing a bridge because you don't have time to warn him and you are confident that he would not want to cross it if he knew that it had rotten planks. Hard paternalism interferes with people's self-regarding—or, better put, what purport to be self-regarding—choices. It is often claimed to be objectionable because it treats adults as if they were children, usurps their sovereign right to lead their own lives on their own terms, or expresses an insulting message.

These are important concerns, and I will come back to them. But my focus in this chapter is circumscribed. I do not try to address every kind of worry that people have had about legal paternalism. My aim is to discuss the relationship between egalitarian distributive justice and legal paternalism. More specifically, I want to critically examine what I will call the egalitarian distributive argument for paternalism, or the *distributive argument* for short. This argument has not received much attention in the literature on legal paternalism. There is no discussion of it, for example, in Joel Feinberg's comprehensive study and critique of legal paternalism in his book

*Harm to Self*.[2] Nor is it discussed in Gerald Dworkin's important book on paternalism.[3] However, the distributive argument has found favor among a few writers. As far as I know, it was introduced by Richard Arneson in a paper on Mill entitled "Paternalism, Utility and Fairness."[4] As Arneson noted in this paper, anti-paternalism could be described as "the ideology of the good choosers." We will see that, with some additional plausible assumptions, it can also be characterized as the ideology of the well-off insofar as it serves their interests at the expense of those who fare less well.

My plan in this chapter to take a closer look at the distributive argument in the context of egalitarian distributive justice. I want to clarify its structure and scope, bring out its appeal, and consider how it might be resisted. One more stage-setting point is in order. I will follow Ronald Dworkin, who was perhaps our most imaginative contemporary thinker on egalitarian justice, in viewing it as comprising two basic parts—equality of concern and equality of respect. Since I will be engaging with Dworkin's arguments throughout this chapter, it will be useful to start with a passage from him.

> No government is legitimate unless it subscribes to two reigning principles. First, it must show equal concern for the fate of every person over whom it claims dominion. Second, it must respect fully the responsibility and right of each person to decide for himself how to make something valuable of his life. These guiding principles place boundaries around acceptable theories of distributive justice—theories that stipulate the resources and opportunities a government should make available to people it governs.[5]

The animating idea in this passage is that an adequate account of distributive justice must keep both equality of concern and equality of respect before the mind. Each component part of egalitarian justice must be interpreted in line with and tested against the other. To illustrate: any view about egalitarian justice must answer the currency question. Does distributive equality demand equality of resources, equality of welfare, or something else, such as equality of sets of capabilities and functionings? Dworkin was a powerful champion of the equality-of-resources view. He had multiple reasons for preferring this currency to the alternatives. But his most fundamental reason was that equality of welfare as well as Sen's view about capabilities and functionings, which he thought collapsed into the equality of welfare view, would favor policies that do not respect people's responsibility for their own lives. Thus, it was the second reigning principle about the responsibility and rights of individuals that impelled Dworkin to characterize the demands of his first principle—the principle of equal concern—in terms of resources rather than welfare.

In analyzing the distributive argument for paternalism, I take a different tack. I start by assuming that equal concern is best understood in terms of welfare. If governments care equally about the fate of those they govern, then they must care equally about how they fare. This yields a provisional result about the desirability of legal paternalism from the standpoint of egalitarian justice. With this provisional result in hand, I then consider several key concerns pressed by Dworkin that emanate from equality of respect, asking whether they force a retreat, and if so how much of a retreat, from the provisional result. In this way, the conclusions reached here about the distributive argument for paternalism make contact with, and are sensitive to, both of Dworkin's reigning principles.

## I. Equal Concern

Equality of welfare invites many questions. Among them is the obviously central question of whether equality of welfare requires strictly equal levels of welfare or whether it requires only that some substantial priority be given to those who are worse off.[6] I understand the view inclusively to encompass both of these more determinate positions, distinguishing between them only when it is necessary to do so.

Another central question I leave open is how welfare should be characterized for purposes of distributive justice—whether, for instance, it should be taken to be a matter of pleasure or pain or the achievement of objectively valuable goals. Since how we understand welfare can affect the plausibility of some of the claims advanced by the distributive argument, we need to bear this in mind at certain points in the discussion.

Notwithstanding this point, it seems clear that paternalistic policies will engage equal concern, however welfare is characterized. There is something close to an analytic connection between legal paternalism and the welfare of those subject to it. Legal paternalism is legal interference in people's purportedly self-regarding decisions for the sake of protecting or promoting their welfare. Sometimes, of course, legal paternalism fails in its aims. Mill stressed that governments are prone to pursuing foolish policies—hence his assertion that the "strongest of all the arguments against the interference of the public with purely personal conduct is that, when it does interfere, the odds are that it interferes wrongly and in the wrong place."[7] Whether this is indeed the strongest argument against paternalism, it is certainly a consideration that policymakers should keep in mind. But I put it aside here. The kind of paternalism that Mill targets is more aptly described as false paternalism, and few will be in favor of it under that description. My interest, accordingly, is with paternalism that succeeds, or can be expected to succeed, in its aims, and for this kind of paternalism the analytic connection obtains. (Well, I should say, to be precise, that the analytic connection comes close to obtaining, since an important wrinkle is introduced by the distributive argument. I will be positioned to comment on that wrinkle after I have reviewed the argument.)

Discussions of distributive justice and public policy tend to center on the tax and transfer system and property ownership.[8] This narrow focus is understandable. Taxes and property rights play the major role in determining the distribution of wealth in a society. But in this chapter I highlight a point often overlooked by writers on distributive justice. The distribution of welfare in a society is a product not only of the economic resources and power that its members possess, but also, and potentially more significantly, of the social and cultural environment in which they live, and the types and range of options that it makes available to them.[9]

We can refer to this environment as the *ethical environment* of the society. No member of the society can escape its influence, and it profoundly affects their ability to lead successful lives. The character of the ethical environment is determined by a bewilderingly large number of factors. Simplifying greatly, we can distinguish the effects the legal framework of the society makes on the character of the ethical environment from the effects of the decisions that people make within this framework. Call the former *framework effects* and the latter *decision effects*. We can assess different possible legal arrangements by considering their framework effects on the ethical environment, asking whether these effects are salutary and whether they confer benefits and impose costs on people that, when compared to other eligible alternative frameworks, are fair or just. Such an assessment will be complex, for alterations in the legal framework condition the decisions that people make within the framework. Proposals with good intentions are ripe for frustration, given the ever-present possibility of counterproductive and unforeseen decision effects. But let us assume here that we know what will happen if different legal frameworks are put in place.

Adopting a Dworkinian conceit, let us imagine that we are Herculean characters who are committed to equality of welfare and who have access to all the best social science.[10] What kind of legal framework should we favor?

Let's simplify even further. Imagine that we are choosing between two frameworks. Framework 1 is ideal with respect to anti-paternalist ideology. It is the framework that sophisticated and informed critics of paternalism would adopt, if given a free hand to do so. Framework 2 is ideal with respect to pro-paternalist ideology. It is the framework that sophisticated and informed proponents of paternalism would adopt, if given a free hand to do so. Both frameworks are otherwise identical to each other and both are otherwise ideal with respect to egalitarian justice. The distributive argument now invites us to assess the two frameworks at the bar of egalitarian justice.

Imagine further that Framework 2 is the established framework in the society in question and we are contemplating a switch to Framework 1, as the anti-paternalist writers would urge us to do. The choice between the frameworks almost certainly would influence the decisions different people would make about how to lead their lives, and these decisions, to varying degrees, almost certainly would have an impact on their welfare. The choice to move from Framework 2 to Framework 1 would engender winners and losers. Some would benefit from the shift, others would not.

Envisaging this scenario, you might think that the thing to do is to adopt the framework that would produce the greater sum of welfare aggregated across individuals. If Framework 2 would lead to more aggregate welfare than Framework 1, then we should stay put. If Framework 1 would yield more aggregate welfare, we should make the switch, assuming the transition costs would not be too great. This view is not obviously mistaken. But egalitarians, and distributive-sensitive theorists of distributive justice more generally, will hold that our choice presents an issue of distributive fairness, one that is not settled by aggregating gains and losses across affected parties.

Now consider the people who live under Framework 2—the pro-paternalism framework. Who would benefit and who would lose from the shift to the anti-paternalism framework? To think about this question, consider what I will term the "welfare-prudence link."[11] This is the claim that there is a positive correlation between people's welfare and their skill at making decisions about their own good. Given this link, it is plausible to hold that better-off people will, with necessary caveats and qualifications, tend to do better than worse-off people in avoiding engagement with bad options made available to them by their ethical environment. For this reason, and again assuming the welfare-prudence link, well-off people would benefit less from the pro-paternalism framework, and would incur lower costs from the switch to the anti-paternalism framework, than those who would be more likely to take up the bad options that the framework effectively targets.

These observations are especially compelling, given the case that we are now imagining. The welfare-prudence link is generally plausible, but even more so in our scenario. By stipulation, the two legal frameworks, bracketing the paternalism variable that distinguishes them, are ideal with respect to egalitarian justice. This means that both frameworks limit the impact of luck on people's welfare in ways required by egalitarian justice. The inequalities in welfare that can be expected under both frameworks will be both smaller and less attributable to brute luck than we find in actual, non-egalitarian societies. The biggest losers, then, from the shift from Framework 2 to Framework 1 will almost certainly be those who are less prudent, and hence expectably less well-off under both frameworks. The shift to the anti-paternalism framework would increase the inequality that obtains between the prudent and imprudent by opening up new opportunities for poor welfare-reducing choice.

The benefits in prospect from the shift also need to be considered, of course. Might they counterbalance the welfare costs engendered by the shift? Some people think that more liberty is always a benefit for people, even if having the liberty is not on balance beneficial to them. I doubt that that is true. But there are considerations of autonomy in play here, and these seem to me to be compelling. (I am thinking of autonomy here as an aspect of our welfare, much as Mill understood individuality to be a component of our well-being.) So, the thought is that paternalistic restriction sets back our autonomy, and hence our welfare, other things being equal. To appreciate the thought, consider the situation of two people, Jack and Jill, who would be affected by the shift to the anti-paternalism framework in our example, and let us consider one option—heroin for recreational use—that would be made available, or more readily available, by the shift. Being prudent, Jack would probably not take up the heroin option, but he might benefit nonetheless from its availability. For in not choosing it, and choosing instead to engage in other options, his choices may be more autonomous than they would have been had he not had access to the heroin option.[12] The autonomy welfare boost is likely to be small for someone like Jack, but if it registers on the scale at all, then Jack will be able to say correctly that his interests are advanced in this way by the shift to the anti-paternalism framework. Furthermore, Jack may be able to press a further complaint. He may know that he can use heroin for recreational purposes in a prudent way. Unlike most people, Jack may be able to use the drug without succumbing to its destructive effects. If so, Jack might benefit in a more direct way from the shift to the anti-paternalism framework, for the shift would open up an option that gives him enjoyment without self-injury.[13]

Turn now to Jill. She is the kind of person who when given access to bad options, tends to take them up. Presented with the heroin option, she would probably go for it, and she would probably suffer the kind of welfare-diminishing effects from the use of the drug that most heroin abusers suffer. I trust that we need not dwell on whatever possible benefits Jill may get from the shift to the anti-paternalist framework. These benefits will be swamped by the costs in welfare that Jill will experience as a result of the shift.

Jack and Jill represent classes of people. The Jacks in our imagined example could join ranks and press for the shift, pointing to the benefits that they would receive from it. The Jills could join ranks and oppose the shift. (If they were too imprudent to do so, we could press their case for them.) What then should our Herculean judge, with his mind fixed on egalitarian justice, advise us to do? If he is the kind of egalitarian who goes under the label "prioritarian," he will need to consider the numbers of people involved and the size of the relevant costs and benefits. But if we assume that his commitment to equality of welfare is strong (either because he is a strict egalitarian or because his prioritarianism strongly tilts to the worse-off), and if we bracket for the moment any concerns that he might have about equality of respect, then we should not be in real doubt about the call he will make. The shift to the anti-paternalism framework would benefit prudent and well-off folks like Jack at the expense of the imprudent and less-well-off folks like Jill. It is exactly the kind of shift that equality of concern condemns.

To be sure, in actual practice, matters will not be anywhere near this clear-cut. Complications abound, one of which is worth mentioning here. I have been speaking of good choosers and bad choosers as if these were uniform groups, but different members within each group will manifest different levels of imprudence. This means that paternalistic policies that benefit the poor choosers in general might set back the interests of some in this group. To illustrate: suppose the heroin targeting policy mentioned above succeeds in dissuading most poor choosers from taking up the drug, but fails to dissuade a significant minority from doing so. This unfortunate minority will take up the drug, acquiring it precariously from black market sources, for instance, and bear the extra risks and costs imposed on them by acquiring it in this way. As a consequence, they will be made worse off as a result of the policy. If this subset of the poor-choosing group were on average less well off than others in the group, the egalitarian character of the distributive argument could turn against the policy. Here everything would depend on the numbers involved and the degree to which members of the unfortunate subset of the poor-choosing group were worse off than others.

Before turning to discuss the appeal of the distributive argument that I have been outlining, it will be helpful to mention briefly a line of argument that might be thought to undercut it. Real, as opposed to false, paternalism succeeds in its aims. But some writers think that legal paternalism is self-defeating.[14] Suppose it is. Then the paternalism established in Framework 2 would set back the welfare of both Jack and Jill. Equality of concern, assuming that it did not take a leveling-down form, now would not speak in favor of the pro-paternalist framework.

Dworkin presented a conception of welfare that explains how this could work.[15] Living a good life, he claimed, is a performance. To succeed in living well, one must respond well to the challenges that one's circumstances present. The details of this challenge conception of welfare are not important here. The relevant point for present purposes is that if Dworkin is right, then political and legal interventions that foreclose bad options may harm their intended beneficiaries. They will harm them by spoiling the performance value of their lives. And this is exactly what happens, he thinks, when we use legal force to screen out bad options out of paternalistic concern. "[A] challenge cannot be more interesting, or in any other way a more valuable challenge to face, when it has been narrowed, simplified, and bowdlerized by others in advance."[16]

Dworkin's idea of the challenge value of a life finds expression in much popular thinking. We often hear people say that their lives are better because of the challenges they have overcome. They would not have wanted someone to protect them from making the mistakes they made. Life is full of pitfalls, but we lead better lives if we overcome the dangers ourselves rather than have others shield us from them. These ideas, I think, have genuine appeal, but they can mislead. We might know that there is a very high probability that Jill will ruin her life if exposed to heroin. In the face of this, to point out that she would lead a better life if she were exposed to heroin and overcame this challenge herself than if she were protected from it is to miss the crucial point. Jill needs protection from this drug. If you care about her, that is what you will be attending to. (By contrast, the challenge theorist seems to be maxi-maxing. He is focusing on what ethical environment gives Jill the best chance to lead the best life she could lead. But sensible concern for Jill should focus on the expected consequences for her of the different ethical environments being considered.)

There is a second point to make about the challenge conception of welfare.[17] Dworkin tells us that the challenge value of our lives is compromised when our options are narrowed, simplified, or bowdlerized by others in advance. But options in our environment can atrophy in a more organic way as well. Suppose that our ethical environment becomes flatter and less challenge-worthy as a result of spontaneous economic and cultural forces. Would this development deprive our lives of the value that challenge confers? Not according to Dworkin. He thinks that options narrowed by others is challenge-destroying, but options narrowed organically are not.

To explain: Dworkin relies on a distinction between parameters and limitations. The former define the challenge we confront, the latter make it impossible or difficult to succeed in the challenge so defined. The constraints and opportunities we confront can be either parameters or limitations. They are limitations only if they are unjustly imposed. Applied to paternalism, the lesson is plain. If paternalism is unjust, then it is a limitation, and if it is a limitation, then it diminishes or destroys the challenge value of our lives. But if this is the line that we take, we need independent reasons for thinking paternalism is unjust. The objection to paternalism from the challenge conception of welfare must advert to those reasons to get its grip.

This result nicely illustrates Dworkin's holistic method. You cannot, he says, understand what it means to live well without understanding unjust limitation. He may be right. For now, we can conclude only that without supplementation, the challenge conception of welfare does not show that paternalism is by its nature self-defeating.

## II. Reasonable Sacrifice

There is a difference between having a good life and living well. Further, living well is not simply a matter of living in a way that maximizes one's well-being. Dworkin's challenge conception is presented as an account of well-being, but it might be better conceived as an account of living well.[18]

Those who live well may do so in part because they make reasonable sacrifices to their well-being that benefit others or further valuable causes.

This matters for our discussion insofar as paternalistic measures, while successfully and fairly advancing the welfare of their beneficiaries, impede their efforts to live well. To take an example: consider the decision to enroll in a human challenge trial designed to further the development of a safe and effective vaccine for a dangerous infectious disease that has no known cure.[19] This decision, let us assume, is imprudent. The trial presents a substantial risk of harm to its healthy participants. Yet we should not classify the decision to enroll in the trial as a poor choice, since enrolling in it may be rational and admirable. Reasonable sacrifices of this kind can make a life better, even if they reduce the welfare of those who make them.

Equality of concern, it might now be said, encompasses more than equal concern for welfare. Concern should extend to people's efforts to live well, and Dworkin's challenge model neatly captures this idea. Taking this point on board, the scope of the distributive argument would need to be limited. It applies, let us say, only to paternalistic measures and policies that do not unduly frustrate efforts to live well, which are reflected in admirable acts of reasonable sacrifice.[20]

## III. Impersonal Value

The legal paternalism purportedly justified by the distributive argument is grounded in equality of concern. Equality of concern is, in a sense that I will now explain, an impersonal value. This fact about the nature of the value that grounds the distributive argument has implications for how the paternalism it justifies should be viewed.

Those who accept equality of concern can hold that a state of affairs in which the relevant individuals are equal in their welfare has impersonal value. This is a value over and above the personal value the state of affairs has for the people in it. To see point this more clearly, consider a version of equality of welfare that countenances leveling down. This view could favor a legal framework with restrictions on behavior that make everyone, the prudent and the imprudent alike, worse off relative to the eligible alternative. Such a framework might reduce the gap in welfare between the relevant parties. Here, in this kind of case, it is transparent that the distributive argument for the restrictions must be grounded in a concern for impersonal value. The argument must hold that it is impersonally good that equality of concern obtains, since its obtaining is not good for anyone.

Equality of concern that permits or requires leveling down is not an attractive view.[21] And we should not, at any rate, tie the distributive argument to it. Suppose then that the restrictions that are justified by equality of concern do make the imprudent better off, thereby reducing the gap in welfare between them and the prudent. One can still hold that the restrictions contribute to a state of affairs that has impersonal value. One can maintain that the restrictions are both good for some people—those who benefit from them—and impersonally good insofar as they contribute to a more egalitarian state of affairs.

This point, I believe, is important. The force of an objection to a paternalistic restriction can depend on the kind of consideration that has been offered in its support. Suppose, for example, that Jill protests the legal restriction that forecloses her access to heroin. She complains that this restriction treats her, an adult woman, as if she were a child. This complaint has force if the argument for the restriction is grounded in beneficent concern for Jill. But the distributive argument for the restriction, when it comes from the lips of the welfare egalitarian, need not evince any such concern. (Indeed, in the leveling down scenario, the argument could not be grounded in such a concern, since the restriction would make her worse off!) Suppose now that Jill tries a different tack. The restriction, she says, expresses an insulting message to her. The restriction expresses the view that she, Jill, cannot make responsible decisions about her life. Once again, the distributive argument for the restriction can sidestep this charge. The point of the restriction, in this argument, is to establish a just distribution of welfare among the affected parties. It has nothing to do with Jill per se. To be sure, if everyone were always prudent, there would be no need for the restriction. So, the argument may be taken to express the message that not everyone is always prudent. The argument may also be taken to express the message that people generally are not equally prudent. These messages are not insulting to Jill, however. In fact, they are messages that scarcely anyone would think were false.

Some familiar objections to paternalism, then, do not get traction, or get less traction, if the distributive argument is the argument doing the justifying work. The appeal to the impersonal value of a just distribution of welfare across persons, and not to any type of busybody mentality, can stand behind the paternalistic restrictions. Here is another way to express the point. Some critics of legal paternalism invoke the Rawlsian notion of a moral power that is associated with the formation, pursuit, and revision of a conception of the good. They then claim that legal paternalism is objectionable by virtue of the fact that it does not show proper respect for this aspect of people's personality. These writers, however, do not think that if a conception of justice were imposed on a person against his will, this would evince improper respect for his moral power to develop and act on a conception of justice. But the distributive argument for paternalism follows from a commitment to a background conception of justice. The proponent of such an argument is seeking to engage the first, and not the second, Rawlsian moral power. He is seeking to convince his opponents that distributive fairness reaches further than they have assumed.[22]

Having now explained the impersonal value of just distributions, and having noted the connection between the distributive argument for paternalism and this value, I can comment on the wrinkle about paternalism that I hinted at above. If sound, the distributive argument justifies a range of restrictions on the conduct of individuals that is widely perceived to be self-regarding. But I have just claimed that these restrictions can be justified by appeal to the impersonal value of a just distribution of welfare. For that reason, it could be said, the restrictions are not strictly speaking paternalistic. They are not imposed on people for their own sake. The analytic connection between paternalism and welfare does not obtain, and as a consequence, the restrictions, whether justified or not, are not aptly described as paternalism.

Semantic disputes over the meaning of the term "paternalism" are of limited value. The philosophical literature includes a variety of definitions of paternalism. Disputes over classification are often resolved by stipulation. Still, no one would think that restrictions on economic liberty for the purpose of securing a just distribution of wealth would qualify as paternalistic. Restrictions grounded in the impersonal value of a just distribution of welfare form a set that is larger than the set of restrictions justified by the distributive argument. Accordingly, something should be said to distinguish the smaller set from the larger. To do so, I introduce the idea of a *prudence deficit*. This can be defined as follows. Take the aggregate welfare of a society, given its legal framework, that would obtain if all persons in the society were maximally prudent in their decision-making, and then subtract the aggregate welfare that actually obtains in that society. This yields the prudence deficit for the society. We can now characterize paternalistic restrictions as restrictions that address and seek to reduce the size of the prudence deficit. As such, they encompass both restrictions imposed by individuals on others within the legal framework (e.g., parents imposing restrictions on their children) and restrictions established by the legal framework itself. It is the latter that is the focus of the distributive argument.

The distributive argument, accordingly, preserves the analytic connection between the paternalistic restrictions that it purports to justify and the welfare of those who are subject to them. And it establishes that connection in a distinctive way. The restrictions serve the value of equality of concern. This fact is their justifying ground. But they serve this value by reducing the prudence deficit of the society to which they apply, reducing it by legal/institutional means.[23]

## IV. Equal Respect

Egalitarian justice, I am allowing, is not exhausted by equality of concern. It also comprises equality of respect. Further, if Dworkin is right, then the content of equal concern cannot be understood independently of equal respect. Equal respect itself is complex, adverting to a range of different ideas. These different ideas are subsumed under Dworkin's second reigning principle—the idea, roughly, that an egalitarian society "must respect fully the responsibility and right of each person to decide for himself how to make something valuable of his life."

### *a. Responsibility*

Let us postpone the discussion of rights for the moment and consider the appeal to responsibility on its own terms. A popular response to the distributive argument is that, in focusing single-mindedly on equality of welfare, it ignores the contribution that personal responsibility makes to distributive fairness. This single-minded focus yields implausible results. For example, if we can save only one of two swimmers in distress, and one swimmer is in peril through no fault of her own, and the other is in peril because she ignored warnings and freely assumed the risk, then other things equal, we ought to save the first swimmer. Further, it would be unfair to give both an equal chance of rescue, since that would make the first swimmer bear the costs of the second swimmer's imprudence.[24]

This simple example naturally extends to the inequalities in welfare that the distributive argument highlights. The transition from the pro-paternalism to the anti-paternalism legal framework introduces inequalities, but the inequalities may be traceable to responsible choice. If so, it can be said that they are not unjust or unfair.[25] To be sure, one can resist this line of argument by denying that people are ever responsible in the sense that is required. Responsibility skepticism is a live option.[26] But I want to grant the reality of the requisite responsibility, not simply because I believe in it, but because doing so allows us to take seriously the objection that the distributive argument overlooks it.

So, assuming the reality of responsibility, we can ask what kind of responses are available to the proponent of the distributive argument. I want to press two responses. The first grants that responsibility assessments condition judgments of distributive fairness, but then denies that they eliminate the unfairness targeted by the distributive argument. To illustrate: suppose that Jill is fully responsible for the bad decision-making that makes her worse off than Jack. From a robust view of responsibility for bad choice, Jill should bear the full consequences of her bad choices. But another, less austere view is available. On a moderate view of responsibility for bad choice, it is appropriate for Jill to bear some, but not all, of the consequences of her imprudent choices.

The robust view of responsibility rebuts the distributive argument, canceling the unfairness of the inequalities engendered by the switch to the anti-paternalism framework. But the moderate view leaves room for the argument to get its grip. In effect, in the moderate view, inequalities engendered by the switch remain unfair, but their degree of unfairness is discounted by the responsibility assessments in play.[27] The moderate view is not sharply formulated. To gauge its threat to the distributive argument we would need to know the discounting rate it imposes on the unfairness of the inegalitarian consequences that result from responsible choice. A very high discounting rate would bring it close to the robust view, eliminating much of the purported unfairness, whereas a very low discounting rate would leave the distributive argument largely unscathed.

Figuring out the magnitude of the discounting rate is a challenging task, one that probably does not permit precision. Further, we should not assume that the discounting rate is a constant function. It may vary along different dimensions. For example, with increases in the size of the inequality in welfare between the relevant groups—good choosers, bad choosers—the discounting rate may decrease. Small inequalities that result from responsible choice may be discounted highly, leaving little to no unfairness in the distribution. But large inequalities could trigger a lower discounting rate, leaving much of the presumed unfairness unchanged. Another possibility is that the discounting rate is sensitive to the absolute levels of welfare of the responsible individuals. The imprudence of very-well-off people may be subject to little or no discounting, whereas the imprudence of those at low absolute levels of welfare may call for significant discounting.

This second possibility fits well with prioritarian versions of egalitarian justice. In these views, the moral value of benefiting people, or of preventing them from suffering a loss of welfare, is greater the less well-off they are in absolute terms. This feature of such views holds independently of responsibility considerations, but when responsibility assessments are incorporated into the view,[28] we should expect these assessments to have a greater impact on the overall assessment of the fairness of the inequality when the parties in question are at high levels of welfare than when they are at low levels of welfare. The reason for this is that the prioritarian tilt offsets the unfairness discounting from responsibility at low levels of welfare, but does not do so, or does so less significantly, at high levels of welfare.[29]

The upshot for the distributive argument is as follows. The paternalistic restrictions justified by the argument, given the welfare-prudence link, primarily benefit the less well-off. Assuming that we are not in the happy circumstance where all, including the less well-off, are very well-off in absolute terms, the discounting introduced by responsibility assessments, accordingly, should not be thought to cancel, even if it mitigates somewhat, the unfairness of the inequalities engendered by the switch in legal framework.

This first response to the responsibility objection to the distributive argument rests on a plausible, but admittedly particular and controversial, version of egalitarian justice, one that is both prioritarian and responsibility-sensitive. The second reply does not rest on such a narrow foundation. To introduce it, recall the distinction between framework effects and decision effects on the shape of an ethical environment, introduced above. Imagine now that the framework effects for a given society were constant by virtue of the fact that it had an unalterable legal framework. The only factor that would shape the ethical environment for this society would be the decisions that its members make within it. In this imagined society, the prudence deficit would be a simple function of the imprudent decisions that its members make. If Jill is worse off than Jack in this society, then she may have only herself to blame. Perhaps they both had equal opportunities for welfare, but Jill imprudently squandered her opportunities while Jack took full advantage of them. Now drop the assumption about the unalterable legal framework and assume that the society has made a transition from a pro-paternalism to an anti-paternalism legal framework, thereby making available new options. Under the anti-paternalism framework, Jill may be held responsible for the consequences of her bad decisions. But Jill, or those who care about her, can raise a different responsibility question. Who is responsible for the character of the ethical environment that has been brought into being by the shift in frameworks?

The answer to this question is not "Jill," or if Jill is responsible here, then she is no more responsible than other citizens who supported the change. (And, for all that has been said here, Jill may have opposed the change.) In short, Jill is responsible for the choice she makes, but she is not responsible for the menu of options from which she chooses. The distributive argument targets inequalities in welfare that are engendered by framework shifts. The responsibility for these inequalities rests both on those who make or support the shifts and on those who make imprudent decisions once the shift has been made. The unfairness of the resulting inequalities is perhaps mitigated by the fact that they are the consequence of imprudent choice, but they are not eliminated by this fact, since it can be unfair to people to place them in choice environments where they are likely to fare poorly.[30]

Unfair inequalities in welfare are a function of both framework effects and decision effects. For this reason, it is an error to focus on the latter to the exclusion of the former. An analogy from the economic realm may be helpful here. Suppose that Jack has a very idiosyncratic set of talents. Under his current legal framework, the talents command little return. But, fortunately for Jack, his society switches to a legal framework that handsomely rewards those who have talents like his. To get the rewards, he will need to make responsible choices to exercise his talents. Suppose he does. Then should we say that he is entitled to the full increase in welfare that accrues to him by virtue of his responsible choices? If we believe in economic desert, then we should say that he deserves some reward for his responsible choices, but we should not conclude that there is no unfairness in him having as much as he does under the new framework. To know that, we would need to address the fairness of the shift in framework that so greatly improved Jack's choice environment.

This analogy is helpful in a second respect. In comparing frameworks, we need some baseline or criterion for unfair shifts. Shifts from a just framework to different, and less just, frameworks will be shifts toward injustice. If Jack's talents command a high return by virtue of the fact that the new framework unjustly subsidizes the output of his talents, then even though he made responsible choices to exercise his talents in ways that garnered him that high return, it would be false to say that he deserved the full amount of that return because of his responsible choices. Likewise, shifts from an unjust framework to a just framework will be shifts toward justice. Thus, if it is assumed that the anti-paternalism framework is the just framework, then a shift to the anti-paternalism framework, while it might engender inequalities in welfare that result from responsible choice, it would not introduce unjust inequality.

Assuming that the anti-paternalism framework is the just framework is not an option in the present context, since that assumption is the very claim that is being interrogated. Dworkin, however, has another arrow in his quiver, one that brings us back to the idea of "organic" changes to an ethical environment. He claims that an ethical environment is just if it emerges "organically" from a legal framework that honors "ethical independence." This legal framework is incompatible with the kind of paternalism, or at least some instances of it, that the distributive argument purports to justify. Accordingly, in Dworkin's employment of it, the responsibility objection to paternalism does not stand alone. It presupposes ethical independence—the "right of each person to decide for himself how to make something valuable of his life."

### *b. Rights*

Responsibility now chases rights. The idea that an ethical environment that emerges organically, and therefore in a just way, and therefore in a way that takes proper account of responsibility considerations, is an elliptical way to say that it emerges from a situation in which everyone's rights have been respected. If Jill is worse off than Jack by virtue of the responsible decisions that they both made, and if Jill and Jack made their decisions within a legal framework that fully safeguarded their rights, then Jill cannot object that the framework under which she made her poor decisions was unfair to her. The sole responsibility for her fate lies with her. But plainly, for this to amount to an objection to the distributive argument, the rights-respecting privileged legal framework must indeed be the anti-paternalist framework.

What supports that last crucial claim? Someone might claim that people have a basic right to form and carry out self-destructive plans of action, so long as these plans do not injure others without their consent. Given this, it follows that the anti-paternalism legal framework would do better in respecting the rights of people than the pro-paternalism framework. But this maneuver defeats the distributive argument by fiat. Dworkin's appeal to the value of ethical independence strives to mount a more satisfying justification.

Ethical independence is achieved when people make their own judgments and decisions about the values and goals their lives should display. It is compromised when they are denied options, or penalized for pursuing options, because others "deem those options unworthy."[31] The compromise occurs irrespective of whether people are right to deem the options unworthy. At first pass, this appears to be an unpromising articulation of the value. A pedophile might object that he is being forced to accept the judgments of others about the values his life should display, but his complaint should not move us. His claim to ethical independence does not cover the option to pursue the kind of lifestyle he values. The formulation of ethical independence thus needs sharpening. Ethical independence does not include moral independence, where this latter idea includes the freedom to pursue options that harm or wrong others.

The distinction between ethical and moral independence is illustrated by the following metaphor provided by Dworkin.

> Morality, broadly understood, defines the lanes that separate swimmers. It stipulates when one must cross lanes to help and what constitutes forbidden lane-crossing harm. Ethics governs how one must swim in one's own lane to have swum well.[32]

Ethical independence is a moral value that defines the lanes in which people can lead lives that express their values and concerns. But for these rights to be adequately respected, paternalism must be rejected. The kinds of paternalistic measures justified by the distributive argument constitute forbidden lane-crossings.

This conclusion is too strong. Dworkin rightly allows that some kinds of paternalistic interference do not compromise ethical independence. This issue is discussed below. For now, let us assume that the argument from ethical independence, as we can call it, does target the kinds of measures that the distributive argument supports. Is it a compelling argument? On inspection, the notion of ethical independence seems too close in content to the anti-paternalism in question to provide a satisfying justification for it. Ethical independence is not the same value as autonomy. It is not a function of the options available to us or the limits we confront in taking up the options available to us.[33] Instead, it is a relational concept. And its relational content is defined in terms of the rights of noninterference that it demands. These rights just are rights against paternalistic restrictions and other kinds of moralistic restrictions. Anyone who thought the paternalistic restrictions supported by the distributive argument were justified would probably not be impressed by an argument that crafts a new notion largely defined by its anti-paternalist content.

The relationship between ethical independence and anti-paternalism is better viewed as one of specification rather than justification.[34] Anti-paternalism is too integral to ethical independence for the latter to provide a justification for the former. But if anti-paternalism is viewed as a specification of the more abstract value of ethical independence, it may gain some purchase. Some people may find that this notion allows them to express more articulately their concerns about paternalism.

The argument from ethical independence is unlikely to impress the friend of the distributive argument for a second, and more telling, reason. The distributive argument targets the fairness or justice of the anti-paternalistic framework. Employing Dworkin's metaphor, it addresses the definition of the lanes that separate the swimmers. To be sure, the paternalism that the argument recommends will have effects on how the swimmers swim in their lanes, but its justification centers on the fairness of how the lanes are defined. Once the lanes are fairly defined, the distributive argument has done its work. No further direction about how to swim need follow.

Continuing with the metaphor, a new point might be pressed at this point. The pro-paternalistic framework establishes inequality between the swimmer's lanes. Different people have different liberty rights. That is why it would be condemned by egalitarian justice. For equality of respect requires equal liberties.[35] To address this concern, it is necessary to say a little more about the character of the pro-paternalism framework. Such a framework might be designed to restrict only the liberties of those who were likely to make imprudent choices. If such a framework were feasible, it would have the advantage of minimizing the restriction of liberty consistent with achieving the goals of paternalism. This advantage, however, would bring a cost. The argument now would indeed justify unequal liberties. In effect, it would parcel out wider swimming lanes for the prudent than for the imprudent.

From the standpoint of egalitarian justice, this cost might be worth paying. Prioritarians might conclude that the gains in welfare from the selective restriction of liberty justify the inequality in liberties. But we need not settle this issue here. For if one thought that equality of respect requires equal liberties, and if one thought equality of respect informs equality of concern, then one would have reason to favor a pro-paternalism framework that restricts the liberty of all—prudent and imprudent alike—equally over a framework that imposes selective, and therefore unequal, paternalistic restrictions. The appeal to equal liberties, then, does not militate against the distributive argument, even if it speaks to the form that the paternalistic restrictions justified by the argument must take.

Equal respect, it now might be said, demands that each person have an equal maximally wide set of liberties. To be sure, there are difficult issues in defining a maximally wide set of liberties; but intuitively, if one set of liberties is otherwise equal to another, but does not contain paternalistic restrictions, then it is wider. Here we have an argument that, if sound, rebuts the distributive argument. If equal respect requires that persons have access to an equal, maximally wide set of liberties, and if equal respect either takes priority over equal concern or informs its content, then egalitarian justice speaks against paternalistic restrictions.

However, on reflection, it is hard to credit the thought that equal respect requires that people have access to an equal, maximally wide set of liberties. Some types of paternalistic restriction seem fully consistent with equal respect. Dworkin notes that most people think that mandatory seat belt requirements are permissible instances of paternalism, since they help "people achieve what they actually want in spite of moments of acknowledged weakness."[36] It is clear from the context that he does not think that such people are making a mistake. He agrees with them. So, the set of liberties consistent with equal respect is not in Dworkin's view the maximally wide set.

The seat belt restriction example shows that one cannot explain why paternalistic restrictions flout the demands of equal respect by appealing simply to an ideal of maximal equal liberty. Discriminations between kinds of paternalism need to be made. So called "soft paternalism" is consistent with equal respect, whereas other types of paternalism may not be. This is not surprising. As noted at the beginning of this chapter, the distributive argument seeks to justify hard paternalism, the type of paternalism generally rejected by those who describe themselves as liberals. But hard paternalism can be understood in different ways. Some writers have held that if an action is sufficiently voluntary, then even if it is unreasonable and contrary to the acknowledged aims of the person in question, interference with it for the sake of the person's good would qualify as hard paternalism. Akratic actions can be sufficiently voluntary, and so interference with them could count as hard paternalism.[37] Dworkin's discussion suggests a different contrast with soft paternalism. For Dworkin, objectionable paternalism is ethically laden. It reflects judgments about the worth or value of various forms of acting that are not accepted by those, or at least some of those, whose liberty is restricted. Seat belt restrictions do not compromise ethical independence insofar as they do not rest on contested judgments that some ways of living are better than others.

The argument from ethical independence now can be understood to be effective only against one form of paternalism—ethically laden paternalism. With respect to legal paternalism that is not ethically laden, considerations of fairness could support paternalistic restrictions without compromising ethical independence. I have suggested that anti-paternalism, and now we can say more precisely (anti) ethically laden paternalism, follows analytically from ethical independence, as defined by Dworkin. But this specification of the demands of ethical independence also receives support from Dworkin's challenge conception of welfare. For if Dworkin were right that you cannot make a person better off by imposing a restriction on him that runs counter to his ethical convictions, then his distinction between unobjectionable and ethically laden paternalism would have independent support. Here, once again, equal respect and equal welfare would fuse, providing interlocking support for the anti-paternalistic stance that Dworkin champions.

Mutual support, in this case, looks damagingly circular. To defend the claim that paternalistic restriction of options would not help people because it would diminish the challenges they face, Dworkin appeals to the thought that such restrictions would unjustly limit their liberty. But to vindicate this thought, he appeals to the value of ethical independence, which is, by stipulation, compromised by the restrictions.

## V. Mistake and Contempt

The previous section found no dialectically effective argument from equal respect to the rejection of legal paternalism that is presumptively justified by the distributive argument. It certainly does not follow that no such argument exists. For one thing, this chapter has mainly wrestled with Dworkin's ideas of equal respect, not attempting to address ideas from others that might be grouped under that abstract value. Further, the circularity in the Dworkinian case against paternalism might not be as damaging as I have suggested. His method of argument embraces a holism of value, self-consciously seeking coherence across domains of evaluative thought. Where I see vicious circularity others may find satisfying coherence.

So, by way of concluding, let me suppose for argument's sake that the kind of paternalism I have been discussing does indeed offend equal respect. Would this establish that these measures, if undertaken by governments, would be illegitimate? Not necessarily. In the passage I quoted at the beginning of this chapter, Dworkin proclaimed that no government could be legitimate if it did not show equal concern and respect for every person over whom it claimed dominion. But this was not his considered view. Governments, he thought, could be unjust, but still legitimate, requiring obedience from those subject to them.

They can be legitimate if their laws and policies can nevertheless reasonably be interpreted as recognizing that the fate of each citizen is of equal importance and that each has a responsibility to create his own life. A government can be legitimate, that is, if it strives for its citizens' full dignity even if it follows a defective conception of what that requires.

In this picture, legitimate governments can make mistakes about what must be done and not done to show equal concern and respect for their members. These mistakes will not manifest contempt for their victims if they can reasonably be interpreted as sincere efforts to show them equal concern and respect.

Legitimate unjust governments err. Illegitimate governments, by contrast, manifest contempt or disregard for those over whom they rule. These are matters of degree, of course. A government that nearly perfectly achieved equality of concern and equality of respect, while imposing a few misguided paternalistic policies, would remain largely just and legitimate. But still we can ask how we ought to think about the misguided policies. The distributive argument for paternalism, even if it failed to persuade committed egalitarian opponents of paternalism that the policies were sound, could persuade them that they were well motivated. Given its grounding in egalitarian justice, the distributive argument for paternalism is particularly well placed to discharge that burden.

Since the argumentative bar for legitimacy is lower than the bar for justice, the distributive argument can succeed even when it fails to persuade. Studying the argument teaches us that the kinds of paternalism and the degree of paternalism that is called for by equal concern and equal respect is a debate internal to egalitarian justice. It is hard to maintain that different resolutions of that debate could not be reasonably interpreted as sincere efforts to satisfy Dworkin's two reigning principles.

NOTES

1. Portions of this chapter draw on material from chapters 6 and 7 of my *Enforcing Morality* (Cambridge: Cambridge University Press, 2023).

2. J. Feinberg, *The Moral Limits to the Criminal Law*. Vol. 3: *Harm to Self* (New York: Oxford University Press, 1986).

3. G. Dworkin, *The Theory and Practice of Autonomy* (Cambridge: Cambridge University Press, 1988). Nor does Dworkin discuss the distributive argument in his SEP entry on paternalism.

4. R. Arneson, "Paternalism, Utility and Fairness," *Revue Internationale de Philosophie* 43 (1989): 409–37. See also R. Arneson, "Joel Feinberg and the Justification of Hard Paternalism," *Legal Theory* 11 (2005): 259–84, and "Egalitarian Perspectives on Paternalism," in *The Routledge Handbook of the Philosophy of Paternalism*, ed. K. Grill and J. Hanna (New York: Routledge, 2018), 194–205.

5. R. Dworkin, *Justice for Hedgehogs* (Cambridge, MA: Harvard University Press, 2011), 2.

6. D. Parfit, "Equality or Priority?," reprinted in *The Ideal of Equality*, ed. M. Clayton and A. Williams (New York: Palgrave, 2002), 81–125.

7. J. S. Mill, *On Liberty* (Indianapolis: Hackett, 1978), 81.

8. John Rawls's hugely influential account of distributive justice highlights both tax and transfer schemes and regimes of property ownership. See J. Rawls, *Justice as Fairness: A Restatement* (Cambridge, MA: Harvard University Press, 2001).

9. For more on this idea see my "The Good Society" in *The Oxford Handbook on Distributive Justice*, ed. S. Olsaretti (Oxford: Oxford University Press, 2018).

10. Dworkin introduces the Herculean Judge in his *Law's Empire* (Cambridge, MA: Harvard University Press, 1986).

11. The welfare-prudence link is best conceived as a tendency claim. See Arneson, "Egalitarian Perspectives on Paternalism."

12. T. Hurka, "Why Value Autonomy?" *Social Theory and Practice* 13 (1987): 361–82.

13. I am assuming here, plausibly but not uncontroversially, that pleasure of this kind contributes to one's well-being to at least some degree.

14. The claim here is not that some instances of legal paternalism are self-defeating, but that legal paternalism as such is self-defeating.

15. The challenge conception was first advanced in his Tanner Lectures, "Equality and the Good Life," a revised version of which appeared in *Sovereign Virtue* (Cambridge, MA: Harvard University Press, 2000). Dworkin speaks of good lives as opposed to lives high in welfare. But it is clear that he thinks the concept of a good life and that of welfare are substantially the same (see *Justice for Hedgehogs*, 273).

16. R. Dworkin, *Sovereign Virtue*, 273.

17. See my *Liberalism, Perfectionism and Restraint* (Cambridge: Cambridge University Press, 1998).

18. R. Arneson, "Cracked Foundations of Liberal Equality," in *Dworkin and His Critics*, ed. J. Burely (Oxford: Blackwell, 2004), 79–98, at 80–88 (distinguishing an "admirable life" from a desirable life).

19. For discussion of trials of this kind see A. Rohrig and N. Eyal, "A New

Day for Human Challenge Trials?," *Trends in Molecular Medicine* 28, no. 7 (2022): 531–32.

20. Not all sacrifices are reasonable. Participation in high-risk challenge trials that targeted relatively minor diseases would not be reasonable, and the decision to enroll in them would not reflect well on those who decided to do so. Such decisions would be neither admirable nor prudent.

21. But see L. Temkin, "Equality, Priority and the Leveling Down Objection," in *The Ideal of Equality*, 126–61.

22. Rawls briefly discusses paternalism in *A Theory of Justice* (Cambridge, MA: Harvard University Press, 1971), 249. He claims that the parties in the original position would want to "protect themselves against the weakness and infirmities of their reason and will." This might imply that when a basic structure does not include paternalistic restrictions of the sort here envisioned, it is open to the charge of injustice. So, perhaps the distributive argument for paternalism in some form or another would be amenable to Rawls.

23. Imagine a set of restrictions that increase the prudence deficit of a society by inducing the better-off to choose less wisely than they currently do, thereby reducing the welfare gap between them and the less well-off. Such restrictions might be justified on a leveling-down conception of equality of welfare, but they would not qualify as paternalistic under the proposal here.

24. Proponents of responsibility-sensitive accounts of distributive justice often focus on comparative cases of this kind. For if one could save both swimmers, then the appeal to responsibility as a justification for letting one swimmer drown would indeed seem unduly callous.

25. One might deny that they are even "inequalities" at all, since one might hold that the relevant currency is equal opportunity for welfare, and not simply welfare. See K. Lippert-Rasmussen, *Relational Egalitarianism* (Oxford: Oxford University Press, 2018).

26. For a defense of such skepticism see D. Pereboom, *Free Will, Agency and Meaning in Life* (Oxford: Oxford University Press, 2014).

27. For such a moderate view see K. Laspert-Rasmussen, "Egalitarianism, Option Luck and Responsibility," *Ethics* 111 (2001): 548–79.

28. That is, when prioritarianism becomes "responsibility-catering" in Arneson's terms.

29. I assume that the prioritarian tilt toward those who are less well off in absolute terms diminishes as their level of welfare increases.

30. It would be odd to say "Yes, we treated Jill unfairly by placing her in that environment, knowing full well how she would likely fare in it, but since Jill made responsible choices in that environment, the resulting loss in welfare that she suffered is not at all unfair."

31. Ethical independence is a component of a more general value that Dworkin refers to as the principle of authenticity (see *Justice for Hedgehogs*, 209–13). Since ethical independence is the component of that principle that bears on the justification of paternalism, I focus on it rather than on the more general value.

32. Dworkin, *Justice for Hedgehogs*, 371.

33. Dworkin grants that autonomy cannot block the type of paternalism in

question, the paternalism that removes some options while leaving a wide range of other options open for pursuit. The distributive argument for paternalism discussed in this chapter would need to be qualified to take account of the value of autonomy. For some discussion, see my "Moral Environmentalism" in *Paternalism: Theory and Practice*, ed. C. Coons and M. Weber (New York: Cambridge University Press, 2013).

34. See G. A. Cohen, "Luck and Equality: A Reply to Hurley," *Philosophy and Phenomenological Research* 72 (2006); 439–46, at 119 (describing this distinction, albeit in a different context).

35. Arneson, "Egalitarian Perspectives on Paternalism," 204–5: "In a society of equals, we all extend the same basic rights of self-regarding freedom to all regardless of their choice-making and choice-executing talents."

36. Dworkin, *Justice for Hedgehogs*, 336.

37. Feinberg, *Harm to Self*, 109.

# Contributors

**Richard Arneson** is Distinguished Professor of Philosophy, Emeritus, at the University of California, San Diego

**Jon Garthoff** is Professor of Philosophy at the University of Tennessee

**Mollie Gerver** is Lecturer in International Ethics at King's College London

**Anca Gheaus** is Assistant Professor of Political Science at Central European University

**Alexander Kaufman** is Professor of Political Science at the University of Georgia

**Ortrud Leßmann** is an independent scholar and Senior Researcher at the German Youth Institute in Munich

**David Reidy** is Professor of Philosophy at the University of Tennessee

**Shlomi Segall** is Professor of Political Philosophy at the Hebrew University of Jerusalem and the Institute for Futures Studies, Stockholm

**Nicholas Vrousalis** is Associate Professor in Practical Philosophy at Erasmus University Rotterdam

**Steven Wall** is Professor of Philosophy at the University of Arizona

# Index